Campaigns against
Corporal Punishment

SUNY Series in American Social History
Charles Stephenson and Elizabeth Pleck, Editors

Campaigns against Corporal Punishment

PRISONERS, SAILORS, WOMEN, AND CHILDREN
IN ANTEBELLUM AMERICA

Myra C. Glenn

State University of New York Press   Albany

Published by
State University of New York Press, Albany

©1984 State University of New York

all rights reserved

Printed in the United States of America

No part of this book may be used or reproduced
in any manner whatsoever without written permission
except in the case of brief quotations embodied
in critical articles and reviews.

For information, address State University of New York
Press, State University Plaza, Albany, N.Y. 12246

Library of Congress Cataloging in Publication Data

Glenn, Myra C.
  Campaigns against corporal punishment.

  (SUNY series in American social history)
  Bibliography: p. 199
  Includes index.
  1. Corporal punishment—New England—Prevention—
History—19th century. 2. Corporal punishment—New
England—History—1775-1865. 4. New York (State)—
History—1775-1865. 5. Prison discipline—United States—
History—19th century—Case studies. 6. Naval discipline
—United States—History—19th century—Case studies.
7. Discipline of children—United States—History—
19th century—Case studies. 8. Wife abuse—United
States—Prevention—History—19th century—Case studies.
I. Title. II. Series.
HV8621.U5G55 1984   364.6'7'0973   84-8476
ISBN 0-87395-812-8
ISBN 0-87395-813-6 (pbk.)

Contents

Para mis padres, Ramón y Nanci Gomila

Acknowledgments

I N THE COURSE of writing this book I have benefited from the advice and encouragement of numerous friends and colleagues. Lewis Perry provided the right mixture of support and criticism when he directed my doctoral dissertation. Michael Frisch and David Gerber patiently read several drafts of this book and offered needed advice as well as collegiality. Another reader of the manuscript, Elizabeth Pleck, helped me to clarify my thoughts on a number of issues, especially the relationship between gender and punishment. I have also benefited from discussing my work with Maxine Seller, Roger Burton, Mary Hill, Ellen Du Bois, Scott Eberle, and Martin Pernick.

I am indebted to the numerous librarians who provided me with invaluable assistance. In particular I wish to thank the staffs of the New York Public Library, Boston Public Library, Massachusetts Historical Society, Library of Congress, Houghton Library of Harvard University, Schlesinger Library of Radcliffe College, Lockwood Library of the State University of New York at Buffalo, and the National Archives in Washington, D.C.

During the past decade I enjoyed financial support from several institutions and organizations. The State University of New York at Buffalo generously provided me with graduate assistantships and fellowships. A 1981 summer grant from Bucknell University and a 1982 Albert J. Beveridge Grant helped to defray the cost of research trips to Boston and New York.

Portions of my manuscript first appeared in article form. "The Naval Reform Campaign Against Flogging: A Case Study in Changing Attitudes Toward Corporal Punishment, 1830–50" appeared in *American Quarterly* 35 (Fall 1983) and "School Discipline and Punishment in Early Antebellum America" appeared in *Journal of the Early American Republic* 1 (Winter 1981):395–408. Chapter 4 appears in a slightly different form as "Wife Beating: The Darker Side of Victorian Domesticity" in *Canadian Review of American Studies* 15 (Spring 1984). My thanks to the editors of these journals for permission to reprint these articles.

Finally, I wish to thank my husband David for his steadfast love, support, and friendship. Thanks to him I manage to retain a sense of humor about myself and the world.

Introduction

I N RECENT YEARS the use of physical punishment in homes, schools, prisons, asylums, and the armed forces has provoked widespread concern and publicity. The current controversy over corporal punishment has an important, if complex, history. This history merits investigation for several reasons. First, changes in either the practice or ideology of punishment can illuminate what a society defines as "deviant" behavior, liable to punishment; and what it regards as "normal" and therefore acceptable behavior. Studying the history of punishment can also reveal how attitudes toward violence, pain, discipline, and ultimately human nature change over time. In short, the history of punishment can serve as a lens to illuminate major cultural changes in a society.

American historians have begun to explore the punishment of seamen, children, and convicts, with particular emphasis on the late eighteenth and first half of the nineteenth centuries. This scholarship, however, has generally examined the issue of punishment in the context of discussing the development of either a particular reform movement or institution. Carl Kaestle, for example, has argued that the antebellum controversy over schoolroom corporal punishment reflected parental resentment of teachers' growing authority over children.[1] David Rothman's brief discussion of corporal punishment in antebellum prisons and asylums illustrated the shift from a reformatory to a custodial function in these institutions.[2] Harold Langley discussed the mid-nineteenth-century campaign against naval flogging in the context of exploring reform efforts to improve the United States Navy.[3]

Although historians have discussed the immediate reform contexts in which criticisms of corporal punishment occurred, they have yet to analyze the underlying concerns which cut across the seemingly disparate reform campaigns against corporal punishment. The need for such analysis becomes apparent when one recalls that these campaigns were part of a broad spectrum of transatlantic reform designed to limit, if not abolish, a range of violent, punitive practices. During the late eighteenth and first half of the nineteenth centuries British as well as American reformers criticized the use of sanguinary punishments in homes, schools, prisons, and the armed forces.[4] These efforts occurred concurrently with Anglo-American campaigns against capital punishment, war, duelling, cruelty to animals, and of course slavery.[5]

Why did Anglo-American reformers criticize a variety of violent, punitive practices during the first half of the nineteenth century? Michel Foucault has recently explored this question in *Discipline and Punish.* Foucault contends that the disappearance of public torture from European penal codes during the approximate period 1760 to 1840 indicated the emergence of a therapeutic, repressive state, one which sought to control people by disciplining their minds, not punishing their bodies.[6]

Foucault's provocative thesis underscores the need to examine the underlying concerns which girded various reform campaigns against physical chastisement. This book will explore these concerns through a comparative analysis of the naval, prison, domestic, and educational reform campaigns against corporal punishment in New England and New York during the period from the late 1820s to the late 1850s.

The book will primarily discuss the common forms of *physical* punishment inflicted on antebellum seamen, prisoners, and children. The standard form of punishment for the first two groups was flogging with the cat-o'-nine tails or colt.* Parents and teachers frequently used the birch, rod, and whip, as well as the open hand, to chastise children.

Like many present day psychologists,[7] antebellum reformers often distinguished between moderate and abusive corporal punishment. This was especially the case with educational and domestic reformers, most of whom upheld a teacher's or a parent's *right* to inflict *moderate* chastisement but condemned its frequent and especially abusive use.

"Abusive" corporal chastisement usually referred to the infliction of physical punishment which caused *serious* or *permanent* bodily or mental injury. Most reformers stressed that abusive punishments often exceeded the legal or prescribed amount of punishment. Inflictors of abusive punishment allegedly did so with "great passion" and sought to cause pain and humiliation in the victim. Given this view of abusive corporal punishment, parents or teachers who frequently and passionately whipped children were allegedly abusive. By contrast, those who calmly and only occasionally chastized a child by spanking him were not.

Several reasons have prompted the chronological, geographic, and institutional boundaries of my study. I focused primarily on the period from the late 1820s to the late 1850s because it was during these four decades, especially during the 1830s and 1840s, that corporal punishment generated widespread public controversy. Public concern over the issue of corporal punishment declined in the mid-1850s because of political and cultural reasons, which I will discuss in chapter seven.

Since I am particularly concerned with the antebellum reformers who led the *organized* opposition to corporal punishment, I have focused my attention on the urban Northeast, the hub of mid-nineteenth-century reform activity. As various scholars have noted, far-reaching economic, political, and cultural

---

*The cat-o'-nine tails consisted of nine small hard twisted cords, each about eighteen inches long, fastened to a wooden handle. The colt was a piece of eighteen-inch thread ratline or one-inch rope with two hard twine whippings on each end. Sometimes to intensify pain the colt or cat was dipped in brine.

changes began occurring in this area during the early national period (1780s to the 1820s). How significant were these changes in shaping antebellum attitudes toward punishment and discipline?

In exploring this question, I examine the relationship between the crusade against corporal punishment and various other reform movements. What kinds of comparisons can we draw between reform efforts against this punishment and those against other perceived social ills such as intemperance and slavery? How did sectional and political divisions over reform in general and abolitionism in particular shape antebellum discussions of punishment and discipline?

To raise such questions is to.underscore the book's primary purpose, namely, to explore the issue of corporal punishment from a broad, comparative perspective. With this goal in mind, I divided the book into seven chapters. Chapter 1 will review post-Revolutionary statutes and regulations on corporal chastisement, trace the emergence of widespread public opposition against this punishment, and identify the leading reformers who orchestrated this opposition. This chapter will also explore how reformers' personal experiences with corporal chastisement shaped their public response toward punishment.

Chapter 2 will discuss how a desire for institutional efficiency, uniformity, and specialization promoted reformers' opposition to frequent and particularly abusive punishment. It will also explore how particular institutional concerns—the "feminization" of middle-class homes and schools, rivalry between the congregate and separate systems of prison discipline, and the navy's manpower shortage—shaped the antebellum crusade against corporal punishment.

Chapter 3 will view the different reform campaigns against corporal punishment in the context of broad cultural concerns. I am particularly interested in exploring how a Victorian concern with moral character development, revised views of human nature, and heightened sensibility to physical pain shaped public discussions of punishment and discipline. In the context of discussing these themes, I will discuss how the dimensions of class, ethnicity, and gender shaped reformers' perspective on punishment.

Chapter 4 will examine how Victorian attitudes toward marriage, domesticity, and sexuality thwarted widespread public discussion of the problem of wife beating. Discussion of this issue suggests the limits of the antebellum reform campaigns against corporal punishment.

Having examined different aspects of these campaigns, I will next discuss extant seamen and convict writings on punishment in Chapter 5. These writings illuminate important questions: How did ordinary sailors and prisoners regard corporal punishment? How did they regard the officers who inflicted and the reformers who condemned this punishment? Exploration of these questions enables us to view the issue of corporal chastisement from the perspective of the victim.

Chapter 6 will discuss the views of those who publicly defended corporal punishment during the antebellum period. It will compare the disciplinary views of two seemingly disparate groups—an Association of Boston Schoolmasters who became embroiled in an 1843–45 controversy over school discipline, and Southern legislators who defended flogging during a series of 1848–52 Congressional debates over naval discipline.

I am particularly concerned with exploring how attitudes toward human nature, God, and authority shaped these two groups' defense of corporal punishment. Such a discussion will serve as a counterpoint to my earlier analysis of antebellum reforms. Exploring the highly publicized debates over corporal chastisement will also reveal the amount of public support which critics of this punishment enjoyed during the antebellum period. Finally, a comparative analysis of two specific controversies over corporal punishment—one involving a group of Bostonians and the other involving Southern political leaders—can illustrate how political and especially sectional concerns shaped public attitudes toward punishment and discipline.

The last chapter will explore changes in the actual disciplinary practices of American institutions by examining available records and regulations on punishment in prisons, schools, and the navy. Various kinds of impressionistic evidence, including the personal correspondence, diaries, and reminiscences of former children and parents, provide insight into the actual use of parental corporal punishment. Chapter 7 will also discuss reformers' experimentation with a range of proposed substitutes for corporal punishment. Many of these were psychologically, if not physically, punitive.

Chapter 1
The Antebellum Crusade against Corporal Punishment: Origins and Leaders

I N 1839 VETERAN SEAMAN and ex-convict Horace Lane published an autobiographical narrative aptly titled *The Wandering Boy*. Lane, who was born in 1788 and grew up in upstate New York, experienced corporal punishment as a young boy. Lane's father occasionally whipped him when he played truant from school and floated down the Hudson River on a makeshift raft. After his mother died in 1795, Lane was apprenticed to several different men, including a "sturdy, athletic, avaricious farmer and cobbler" who regularly beat the young boy.[1]

Restless and bored, Lane ran away to sea at the age of ten. While aboard British and American men-of-war he frequently suffered severe corporal punishment, especially in the form of flogging. At the age of twelve, for example, Lane was sentenced to three dozen lashes for attempting to desert from a British man-of-war. He reacted to the sentence with a mixture of dread, shock, guilt, and anger:

Three dozen! What a sound! It fell with the force of thunder upon my already depressed mind and heart, while trembling and reluctant I got into the barge; and while we were gliding toward my horrid home, at each stroke of the oars, the sound reverberated *three dozen!* and again, when climbing the ship's side, *three dozen* was sounding to my soul. . . . I know not how to describe my feelings, other than by saying that I had a true falsified impression on my mind. I felt guilty, but I was not guilty, for I had no more business there, than Queen Victoria has to come here and become my servant.[2]

Although the wife of the sailing master intervened on Lane's behalf and reduced his sentence to six lashes, he did not always escape harsh naval punishment. Somewhat bitterly Lane recalled that he suffered "many severe floggings" for a variety of offenses, including fighting, omission or neglect of duty, and stealing the ship's grog ration.[3]

Corporal punishment was a regular feature of Lane's life in another institution—prison. Lane served a total of five years in Auburn and Sing Sing State Prisons for theft. He noted that Sing Sing prison guards were particularly cruel. They severely whipped and beat convicts who worked slowly due to illness. Worn out from nineteen years of naval service, alcoholism, and rheumatism, Lane was unfortunately one of their victims. At one point he received a severe blow to the head which caused blood to run down his pant legs and into his shoes.[4]

Lane's autobiography suggests that physical chastisement was a common practice in the late eighteenth and first half of the nineteenth centuries. At the same time Lane's exposé of abusive treatment suggests that corporal punishment, especially its frequent or harsh use, provoked controversy in the antebellum period. The purpose of this chapter is to explore the issues raised by Lane's memoir. When and why did corporal punishment become controversial? Who were the leading antebellum critics of this punishment?

During the colonial period corporal chastisement was a legitimate way to punish deviant behavior. According to Benjamin Wadsworth's popular eighteenth-century work on domesticity, *The Well Ordered Family*, parents should punish disobedient children through a judicious use of the rod.[5] In a similar vein, laws and statutes upheld the right of teachers and masters to chastise their respective wards. A local school regulation in seventeenth-century Dorchester, Massachusetts, for example, declared that the "rod of correction" was an "ordinance of God" and a necessary means of classroom discipline.[6] Similarly, the first code of laws in Massachusetts, printed in 1648, allowed masters to chastise their servants and apprentices for various offenses, such as stealing or neglect of duty.[7] Corporal punishment was also an accepted form of military and penal discipline. All of the American colonies prescribed public flogging, branding, and other forms of mutilation for various crimes, ranging from Sabbath breaking and petty larceny to sedition and rape.[8] At the same time, colonial military statutes made flogging the standard punishment for drunkenness, swearing, insubordination, and other offenses.[9]

During the post Revolutionary period a series of regulations and statutes legitimized the practice of corporal punishment in the new republic. The United States Congress, for example, authorized flogging aboard American men-of-war. The first of these regulations was drawn up by John Adams in 1775 when he served on the Continental Congress's Naval Committee. Recognizing the need for discipline in a newly established colonial navy, Adams' "Rules for the Regulation of the Navy" permitted colonial navy commanders to inflict up to twelve lashes on any enlisted man. In 1797 the United States Congress endorsed these "Rules" for the newly founded Republic. Two years later the Congress in its "Articles for the Government of the Navy" authorized flogging for *specific* offenses such as profane swearing or drunkenness. Although this act further perpetuated the use of the lash in the navy, it also sought to regulate both the manner and extent of flogging. The "Articles" forbade commanders to inflict punishment beyond the already permitted twelve lashes for non-court martial offenses. To abolish the widespread use of the particularly painful "colt" this regulation also permitted only the cat-o'-nine tails in naval floggings.[10]

Another legal milestone in naval discipline regulations was "An Act for the better government of the navy of the United States," which governed the navy from 1800 to 1850.* This act

---

*Congress abolished naval flogging on September 28, 1850. For more details see Chapter 6.

not only confirmed the regulations established the preceding year but also explicitly extended to a naval court martial the use of the lash as punishment. A sailor convicted of an offense by this court could receive up to one hundred lashes for any one infraction. The Act of 1800 also broadened the number of offenses punishable by the whip. A sailor could be flogged for "oppression, cruelty, fraud, profane swearing, drunkenness, or any other scandalous conduct tending to the destruction of good morals."[11]

Children were also subject to corporal punishment during the late eighteenth and first half of the nineteenth centuries. As long as parents did not administer clearly abusive punishment, they retained the legal right to chastise their children. Meanwhile local school boards and judicial rulings invoked loco parentis arguments to justify teachers' correction of schoolchildren. In other words, teachers had the right to inflict moderate correction on their students since they allegedly acted as substitute parents.[12]

In discussing the punishment of criminals it is important to recall that the period 1780 to 1820 was one of prison reform and experimentation. During the 1780's and '90's various state legislatures revised their criminal codes and established penitentiaries. In 1786, for example, the Pennsylvania legislature established a system of solitary confinement at hard labor for most major offenses. Criminals who formerly had been punished through corporal or capital punishment were now incarcerated. In 1796 New York State followed Pennsylvania's lead. The New York legislature reduced the number of offenses punishable by death and authorized the erection of Newgate State Prison. Significantly, the legislature also prohibited the whipping of convicts.[13]

These successes in prison reform, however, were shortlived. During the first two decades of the nineteenth century there was a discernible trend toward the corporal punishment of criminals. Shifts in the disciplinary practices of the New York State prison system illustrated this trend. Despite the opening of Auburn and Sing Sing (also known as Mount Pleasant) Prisons in 1817 and 1829 respectively, New York prisons became increasingly overcrowded. This led to serious disciplinary problems which in turn precipitated the reimposition of corporal punishment. A serious mutiny in Newgate Prison, for example, prompted the New York legislature in 1819 to repeal their earlier prohibition on prison whippings. Head keepers could now whip convicts who refused to work, destroyed property, or resisted an officer. The legislature also authorized the use of prison irons and stocks. A subsequent act passed in 1835 gave subordinate officers the power to whip convicts when and where they pleased.[14]

Plagued by overcrowding, escapes, and riots, other state prison systems followed New York's lead and increasingly relied on corporal punishment to control unruly inmates. Shortly after its opening in 1805, the Massachusetts State Prison at Charlestown, for example, earned a reputation for inflicting harsh corporal punishments, especially flogging.[15] Although Pennsylvania prisons did not use the whip, they inflicted other forms of corporal punishment, including the strait jacket and the gag, an iron mouthpiece which pried open a convict's jaws.[16]

In the early 1840s various state prisons also experimented with another type of corporal punishment—the shower bath. Victims of this punishment were placed in a small closet, their legs, arms, and neck confined in wooden stocks. They were then drenched with streams of water for hours at a time.[17]

During the late eighteenth and first half of the nineteenth centuries, convicts, seamen, and children were subject to various forms of corporal punishment. This punishment, however, became increasingly controversial in the North, especially urban Northeast. A minority of reform-minded Americans began to question the widespread use of corporal punishment during the period 1780 to 1820. Noted Quaker philanthropists, including Benjamin Rush, Caleb Lownes, and Thomas Eddy, condemned the sanguinary public punishments inflicted on criminals,[18] while leading educators such as Noah Webster urged teachers to use suasion as well as punishment in school discipline.[19] In a similar vein, naval surgeon Dr. Edward Cutbush urged the military to use less punitive forms of discipline than the whip.[20]

These comments notwithstanding, public criticism of corporal punishment did not become widespread until the mid 1820s. As noted earlier, this criticism gained momentum in the 1830s and especially the 1840s. It declined in the early 1850s.

During these four decades leading Northern newspapers and periodicals condemned the corporal punishment of seamen and prisoners. A May 11, 1850 editorial in the *New York Tribune*, for example, denounced naval flogging as a cruel, degrading punishment and urged its immediate aboliton.[21] Similarly, an 1846 article in the *United States Magazine and Democratic Review* condemned the lash as the worst and most degrading atrocity ever inflicted on convicts.[22]

The corporal chastisement of children also generated widespread public criticism. One 1847 editorial in the Brooklyn *Daily Advertiser* condemned the use of the school rod and whip and urged the New York Board of Education to prohibit all schoolroom corporal punishment.[23] Articles in the *Boston Post*, the *New York Daily Globe*, and the *North American Review* also criticized teachers who whipped and caned their students.[24] In a similar vein, popular antebellum writers on childrearing criticized punitive parents and urged the substitution of moral suasion for corporal punishment in domestic discipline.[25]

Opposition to corporal punishment was also evident in public petitions which urged the abolition of this punishment. In 1826 the citizens of Auburn, New York petitioned their state legislature to prohibit the flogging of prisoners.[26] The public also petitioned the United States Congress to abolish flogging aboard American men-of-war. In 1850, for example, the Senate received 271 such petitions.[27]

In the midst of these public protests, organized campaigns against corporal punishment emerged. As recent scholarship has shown, these campaigns occurred in the context of antebellum reform movements. The American Seaman's Friend Society and its periodical, the *Sailor's Magazine*, for example, provided a central clearing house for organized opposition to naval flogging. This Society condemned flogging in the context of demanding other reforms: abolition of the navy's grog ration;

and the establishment of a network of seamen's saving banks, Sunday schools, and temperance houses.[28] Similarly, prison reformers campaigned against the corporal punishment of convicts while demanding extensive reorganization of prisons. Organizations such as the Prison Association of New York and the Prison Discipline Society of Boston, established in 1844 and 1825 respectively, provided the institutional framework for their efforts.[29]

Organized opposition to the chastisement of children occurred in the context of educational and domestic reform. Horace Mann, of course, was America's leading educational reformer in the antebellum period as well as one of the foremost opponents of schoolroom corporal punishment. While serving as Massachusetts' first Secretary of the Board of Education from 1838 to 1849, Mann successfully campaigned for reform in school discipline.[30] Similarly, domestic reformers urged the disuse of parental corporal punishment in the context of offering advice on various aspects of childrearing and homemaking.[31]

Antebellum reformers, including leading critics of corporal punishment, shared common backgrounds, interests, and beliefs. Most of them were born in the late eighteenth and early nineteenth centuries in rural or small town Northeastern communities.[32] They therefore matured in an area and in a period of rapid social transformation. During the early national period the development of an intensive, specialized economy promoted the commercialization of agriculture as well as the rise of industry in the Middle Atlantic and New England states. Linked to the East and South by railroads and canals, the antebellum Northeast catered to the rapidly expanding national market for goods and services. By 1850 the Northeast accounted for three-fourths of the nation's manufacturing employment.[33]

Social and economic mobility as well as industrialization characterized the antebellum Northeast. As the center of economic activity shifted away from the farm to the factory and other new economic centers, thousands of rural New Englanders and newly arrived immigrants flocked to rapidly growing cities in search of work. At the same time, the settling and cultivation of the frontier encouraged westward immigration. By 1850 approximately one-quarter of New England's native-born population had emigrated to western states.[34]

The increasing complexity of American life and economy had a tremendous impact on basic social institutions. The emergence of commercial capitalism in the Northeast, for example, undermined established religious beliefs. The determinist framework of orthodox Calvinism, especially the doctrines of predestination and innate human depravity, gradually gave way to a more activist and anthropocentric Christianity which stressed man's benevolence and capacity for moral regeneration.[35] The development of industrialization also undermined the preindustrial productive function of the middle-class family. Increasingly the family became a specialized institution, catering to the emotional needs of its immediate members.[36] The growth of voluntary organizations, such as benevolent fraternities, professional associations, and political parties, also reflected this process of institutional specialization. Based along "horizontal" lines of economic class, social status, political allegiance, and occupational interests, these organizations fulfilled particular economic, social, and political functions.[37]

The various changes which transformed the Northeastern United States during the late eighteenth and first half of the nineteenth centuries had a crucial impact on reformers. Horace Mann's early life particularly illustrates this point. Born in 1796 on his family's ancestral farm outside the town of Franklin, Massachusetts, Mann spent his early childhood in a tightly knit, self-sustaining farming community. For the past three generations the Mann family had personified the "Age of Homespun," producing all of its own food and clothing through a hierarchical division of authority and labor.[38]

Shortly after the turn of the century, however, this traditional way of life was undermined. The rise of a local hat manufactory and of several neighboring textile mills in the early 1800s steadily turned Franklin into an industrial community. By 1812 the town was producing various manufactured goods, especially bonnets, for a market economy rather than for household consumption. In his memoirs Mann recalled how his own family increasingly concentrated its energies on the "sedentary occupation" of braiding straw into plaits for the town's hat manufactory.[39]

This shift in Franklin's economy precipitated other changes. Increasingly dependent on distant market forces in Boston, Providence, and New York, Franklin residents lost their economic self-sufficiency and began to use their newly acquired money to buy many of the goods they had formerly made. Franklin's burgeoning industrial development also encouraged a greater mobility among its young. Hoping to take advantage of the new opportunities in manufacturing, many Franklin farm boys migrated to surrounding textile centers while others used their family's recent prosperity to attend college. Horance Mann's elder brother and heir to the family farm, Stanley, for example, left Franklin to manage a nearby textile mill; while Horace himself sought a needed "escape" from the monotonous, hard work of braiding and farming by attending Brown University in Providence, Rhode Island.[40]

During Mann's youth, Franklin also experienced a significant religious reorientation. Like other Americans, Franklin residents began to reject the tenets of orthodox Calvinism. Mann's own religious life illustrates this development. He had bitter memories of his boyhood pastor, the staunch Calvinist Nathaniel Emmons. Mann recalled that the latter's sermons made

> physical hell . . . a living reality as much so as though I could have heard the shrieks of the tormented, or stretched out my hand to grasp their burning souls, in a vain endeavor for their rescue.[41]

Not surprisingly, such morbid visions often caused Mann to cry himself to sleep as a young boy.

By the age of twelve, however, Mann was skeptical of Calvinist theology, especially the doctrines of predestination and innate depravity. During an "agony of despair" he rejected Calvinism. As an adult Mann became a Unitarian. A mixture of eighteenth-century rationalism and Christian humanism, Unitarianism culminated a trend toward an anthropocentric Protestantism.[42]

Mann's religious beliefs were typical of other leading critics of corporal punishment. Most of them espoused a liberal Protestantism which stressed God's benevolence and man's capacity for goodness.[43] Like Mann most of these critics increasingly channelled their religious fervor into secular reform activities. This shift was evident in the case of naval chaplain and reformer Reverend Walter Colton. A graduate of Yale College and Andover Seminary, Colton began his professional career as a Congregational minister. Colton, however, embraced a benevolent Christianity which stressed moral improvement, not sectarian piety.

In his efforts to improve society, Colton participated in various reform and political activities. In 1837, for example, he edited the *Colonization Herald*, a newspaper which advocated the gradual emancipation of slaves and their subsequent emigration. In his career as naval chaplain, Colton was active in various naval reform activities, including campaigns against grog and flogging. Colton was also prominent in California politics. In 1846 he became chief judge of Monterey, California and helped to establish the state's first schools and newspapers.[44]

Colton's numerous activities illustrate another common characteristic among reform critics of corporal punishment. They enjoyed multiple career patterns. The majority of them were lawyers, academicians, physicians, and ministers who combined their professions with wide ranging interests in politics and reform.[45]

The career of Samuel Read Hall was representative of this pattern. Born in Croyden, New Hampshire in 1795 and raised in several Vermont towns, Hall enjoyed several careers. At various times he was a minister, a lecturer and writer on geography and astronomy, and the principal of a private academy in New Hampshire. In addition, he was an indefatigable worker on behalf of common school reform. In 1830 he helped to establish the American Institute of Instruction, the first national association of teachers. Hall also headed the first teacher training institute in the United States at Phillips Andover Academy in Massachusetts.[46] Hall used this influential position to promote disciplinary reform in public schools. In both his lectures to students and in his popular teaching manuals, Hall urged the substitution of reason and moral suasion for corporal punishment in school discipline.[47]

It was significant that both Hall and Colton had been in the ministry. Liberal Protestant ministers were active in the domestic, educational, prison, and naval reform campaigns against corporal punishment. Naval chaplains were particularly prominent in the antebellum campaign against flogging on the high seas. In fact these chaplains were the most outspoken critics of the lash *within* the navy.[48]

As Ann Douglas has suggested, clerical participation in moral reform reflected far reaching changes in both the social position and economic status of the ministry between 1820 and 1875. "Clerical disestablishment," coupled with the "general democratization and industrialization" of American culture, eroded a minister's traditional prestige and authority, while promoting his economic insecurity, political irrelevance, and intellectual sterility. These worsening conditions for the liberal clergy often produced a sense of "cultural isolation" and "self-depreciation." In a revealing comment to a friend, Unitarian clergyman Orville Dewey confessed, for example, that as a minister he was "not fairly thrown into the field of life . . . [but rather] hedged around with artificial barriers . . . a sort of moral eunuch." Displaced from the centers of tangible power in an increasingly secular world, the American ministry sought to influence their society through the empire of benevolent reform which flourished in the antebellum period. Through their leadership in reform, ministers sought to transcend their shrinking social role by exerting a pervasive moral influence on the nation.[49]

Middle-class women also sought to influence their society through participation in antebellum reform. A significant minority of these women reformers emerged as outspoken critics of corporal punishment. These included author and domestic reformer Catherine Sedgwick; controversial prison reformer Eliza Wood Farnham, who headed the women's division of Sing Sing prison from 1844 to 1848; and Dorothea Lynde Dix, who campaigned against the cruel treatment of convicts as well as the insane.[50]

The men and women who criticized corporal punishment did not necessarily seek its immediate or complete prohibition. Indeed most reformers sought the limitation or gradual disuse of this punishment. Chapter 3 will explore why outspoken critics of corporal chastisement advocated this moderate approach to disciplinary reform. First, however, let us discuss why antebellum reformers criticized corporal punishment.

In exploring this latter question, it is important to examine reformers' own personal experiences with corporal punishment. Did reform critics of this punishment ever receive or administer punishment themselves? If they did, what were their reactions? How did reformers' personal encounters with corporal chastisement shape their attitudes toward punishment and discipline?

Unfortunately a lack of evidence makes it impossible to fully answer these questions. This fact notwithstanding, some critics of corporal punishment left vivid and detailed recollections of parental and school chastisement. Although necessarily speculative, analysis of these recollections offers insight into the personal motivations of those who campaigned against corporal punishment.

Horace Mann's childhood experiences with corporal chastisement, for example, shed light on his adult attitudes toward this punishment. Mann had bitter memories of the harsh punishments which he suffered as a young schoolboy in Franklin. While recollecting his unhappy childhood, Mann stressed how his schoolmasters repressed his youthful exuberance and curiosity:

> I well remember that when the impulse to express in pictures what I could not express in words was so strong, that . . . it tingled down to my fingers, then my knuckles were rapped with the heavy ruler of the teacher, or cut with his rod, so that an artifical tingling soon drove away the natural.[51]

These painful childhood memories influenced Mann's later approach to schoolroom discipline. As first Secretary of Massachusetts' Board of Education, Mann angrily denounced the rod as a barbaric punishment because it repressed children's natural exuberance. To make small children sit "dumb and motionless, for three successive hours," out of an "overwhelming, stupefying sense of fear," contended Mann, was both cruel and unnatural.[52]

Author and critic of naval flogging Richard Henry Dana also experienced harsh schoolroom punishment as a child. Dana bitterly described his boyhood schoolmasters as cruel men who frequently whipped and caned their students. When Dana was eight years old, a "thoroughly enraged" teacher seized him by the ear and "dragged him over the bench on which he was sitting and back again." This punishment tore the skin connecting Dana's ear to his head. As a result of Dana's father's protests, the school subsequently prohibited the practice of ear pulling. Teachers, however, could still whip students with the ferule, a practice which "sickened" young Dana.[53]

Dana was again subject to abusive corporal punishment when he was ten years old. He wrote a graphic and detailed description of this incident, one which resulted in the dismissal of his teacher:

He [the schoolmaster] had placed me in the middle of the floor for some offense or other, and my station being near the stove, and the room very hot, I became faint and asked to be allowed to go out and gave my reason, but to no purpose. In a few minutes we had our usual recess of a quarter of an hour, and I went out. Here I came very near fainting again, looked very pale, and asked leave to go home. This was refused. As I was really sick, at the suggestion of the boys, I went home, which was but a few minutes' walk, to get a written excuse. My father saw that I was ill and kept me at home, and sent me the next morning with a written excuse for my non-appearance, alleging faintness and sickness. Mr. W. was mortified and angry at this and said that the excuse only covered my not returning, while the chief offense was my going home without leave, which he could not excuse, and calling me out, took his ferule and ordered me to put out my left hand. (He also intimated that my sickness was all a sham.) Upon this hand he inflicted six blows with all his strength, and then six upon the right hand. I was in such a frenzy of indignation at his injustice and his insulting insinuations that I could not have uttered a word for my life. I was too small and slender to resist, and could show my spirit only by fortitude. He called for my right hand again, and gave six more blows in the same manner and then six more upon the left. My hands were swollen and in acute pain, but I did not flinch nor show a sign of suffering. He was determined to conquer me and gave six more blows upon each hand, with full force. Still there was no sign from me of pain or submission. I could have gone to the stake for what I considered my honor. The school was in an uproar of hissing and scraping and groaning, and the master turned his attention to the other boys and left me alone. He said not another word to me through the day. If he had I could not have answered, for my whole soul was in my throat and not a word could get out.[54]

Many years after this incident Dana still felt "the deepest in-dignation at the degrading treatment" which he endured.[55] Un-fortunately Dana's experiences with corporal punishment were by no means over. When he was fifteen years old Dana attended a private school where teachers frequently and severely flogged their students. Somewhat bitterly Dana recalled that "there was never a half-day without a good deal of flogging."[56]

Dana's personal experiences with school punishment do not "explain" why he later criticized the practice of naval flogging. These experiences, however, do illuminate one aspect of Dana's complex response to naval punishment. Having experienced harsh, even abusive punishment himself, Dana had good reason to feel "disgusted, sick, and horror-struck" when he witnessed flogging during the 1834-36 voyage of the *Pilgrim*.[57] Dana's own bitter experience undoubtedly helped him to sympathize with flogged sailors and to poignantly describe their suffering and degradation in *Two Years Before the Mast*.

Similarly, Eliza Wood Farnham's early life must have made her particularly sensitive to the plight of abused convicts. Farnham's slightly fictionalized autobiography offered a poignant and de-tailed account of an abused childhood. Born in Rensselaerville, New York in 1815, Farnham went to live with foster parents after her mother died in 1820 (her father allegedly deserted the family for another woman before the mother's death). Farnham's foster mother frequently beat, cursed, and humiliated her. Although kind, her foster father was a weak-willed man, afraid of his own wife, and therefore unable to intervene on Farnham's behalf.[58]

Not all reformers who recollected their personal experiences with corporal punishment did so from the perspective of victim. Some reformers, especially those who had taught in their youth, inflicted harsh corporal punishment themselves. As a young schoolmaster in early nineteenth-century Nantucket, educational reformer Cyrus Peirce, for example, relied on the rod and birch to discipline his students. Peirce, however, gradually substituted moral suasion for corporal punishment in his classroom and subsequently emerged as a particularly outspoken critic of school chastisement.

Although various concerns fostered this change, one contributing factor was Peirce's fear that corporal punishment aroused sadistic impulses in himself. Privately he admitted that he "could not . . . administer corporal punishment, without awakening or yielding to emotions of a doubtful character." Upset by this disturbing realization, Peirce began to reevaluate his punitive approach to school discipline.[59]

Personal recollections of physical chastisement illuminated the motivation of individuals who publicly criticized this punishment. These recollections, however, do not adequately explain why the infliction of corporal punishment became problematic in the antebellum period. Why were reformers able to channel their personal hostility against the rod, birch, and whip into a popular campaign against corporal chastisement? Why did this punishment, an accepted form of discipline in colonial times, provoke public opprobrium in the antebellum period? To explore these questions it is important to discuss the institutional and cultural concerns which fueled the different reform campaigns against corporal punishment.

Chapter 2
Reform Campaigns against Corporal Punishment: Institutional Concerns

A NTEBELLUM REFORMERS campaigned against corporal punishment while advocating a series of extensive reforms in their respective institutions. What major institutional concerns promoted these seemingly disparate reform efforts? How did these concerns shape reformers' attitudes toward punishment and discipline? Exploration of these questions illuminates an important dimension of the antebellum reform campaigns against corporal punishment.

Antebellum reformers who criticized corporal punishment did so in the context of developing increasingly specialized institutions characterized by efficiency, uniformity, and professionalism. Domestic reformers, for example, advocated the development of a private, mother-centered family which specialized in childrearing and nurturing. By idealizing the family as a haven of piety, morality, and affection, didactic writers on domesticity promoted this development.

Reverend A. B. Muzzey's *The Fireside* offered representative views on domesticity. According to Muzzey the family was a private sanctuary where "Christianity erect[ed] her throne." Sheltered from the cares of the world, the private, consecrated sphere of domesticity enabled Americans to "unveil" their inner "true selves" and to cultivate a "spirit of unaffected kindness."

Muzzey's tract articulated another important aspect of the cult of domesticity—the belief that women were the natural custodians of the home and of children because of their allegedly pure, gentle, and pious natures. "Woman always" declared Muzzey,

> exhibits [piety] in a more engaging view than the man. It seems in her innate and less earthly; some of the sweetest Gospel graces are hers almost by inheritance. Angelic meekness, faithful affection, enduring patience, uncomplaining resignation . . . grow up in her to most enviable ripeness.

Women, therefore, were "naturally" suited to the "moral" sphere of domesticity.[1]

Despite this belief, domestic reformers believed that women needed to increase their efficiency within the home. To promote this goal, popular didactic writers like Catherine Beecher offered detailed advice on a range of household and childrearing tasks. In her influential and popular *Treatise on Domestic Economy* Beecher stressed that homemakers were professionals and therefore must perform their duties as rationally and efficiently as possible.[2]

Naval, educational, and prison reformers also advocated the development of greater specialization, professionalism, and efficiency in their respective institutions. After the War of 1812 the United States' expansion into the Carribbean and Pacific areas highlighted the need for a larger and more efficient navy. Spearheading the call for reform were an influential minority of officers and secretaries. They included disgruntled young career men such as Lieutenant Matthew F. Maury, author of a series of anonymous and influential articles on naval reform; naval chaplains; politically influential commodores such as Robert Stockton and Matthew C. Perry; and several Secretaries of the Navy, especially former Virginia planter Abel Parker Upshur (1841–43).[3] Despite their different positions and ranks, these men sought to effect far-reaching changes in bureaucracy and personnel.

The structural reorganization of the navy was an important goal for these reform-minded officers. They repeatedly descried the inefficiency and ineffectiveness of the Board of Navy Commissioners, which was created in 1815 to oversee the "construction, armament, equipment and employment" of naval vessels under the civilian supervision of the Secretary of the Navy, and was increasingly characterized by waste and ineptitude throughout the 1820s and 1830s. Lieutenant Maury criticized the Board's wastefulness in repairing, equipping, and docking ships, while naval Secretary Upshur, in his 1841 *Annual Report* to Congress, argued that the Board's "multitude of duties" precluded an efficient and economical organization. To remedy these defects, reform-minded officers urged Congress to abolish the Board and to establish five specialized bureaus, each responsible for particular duties such as the construction and repair of ships.[4]

Although bureaucratic reorganization was an important aspect of naval reform, changes in personnel regulations received greater emphasis in reform proposals. It was "an easy thing to build a ship of war," asserted Secretary of the Navy Upshur in one of his *Annual Reports* to Congress, but it was "a difficult thing to qualify an officer to command her." To achieve the latter goal Upshur repeatedly urged Congress to institute various reforms in the recruitment, preparation, and promotion of naval officers. His proposals summarized most of the major goals of reform-minded officers. Upshur urged, for example, the addition of several graded ranks among junior officers. Noting the need for "greater respect and deference" among subordinate officers towards their commodores, Upshur also urged Congress to create the rank of admiral. He particularly recommended the abolition of the system of nepotism and patronage in recruiting and promoting officers. Merit, not family or political influence, was the only fair criterion for promotions. To ferret out incompetent officers, Upshur proposed a system of compulsory furloughs. Criticizing midshipmen's lack of professional preparation and moral supervision, Upshur also urged the establishment of naval schools and compulsory service at sea for incoming recruits.[5]

While Upshur sought congressional legislation to effect needed naval reforms, Commodore Matthew C. Perry spearheaded the formation of several organizations and periodicals dedicated to officers' moral and professional improvement. The *Army and Navy Chronicle*, the *United States Naval Magazine*, and the Naval

Magazine repeatedly urged officers to be temperate, gentlemanly, and well-informed professionals. They also published various articles dealing with navigation, naval architecture, and other technical concerns.[6]

Paralleling these reforms in the Navy was the establishment of a uniform and centralized system of free, public education. Starting in the mid 1820's educational reformers promoted this development by demanding the use of standardized textbooks and curricula; graded classrooms; and compulsory school attendance.[7]

Leading educational reformers in Massachusetts also spearheaded a successful movement to centralize their state's school system. In 1826 the Massachusetts state legislature undermined districts' traditional power over local schools by providing that every town should annually choose a school committee which would superintend all of the schools and also select textbooks. Although local school districts quickly checkmated this erosion of their power, the movement towards centralization continued. These latter efforts culminated in 1837 with the establishment of Massachusetts' first Board of Education. Officially limited to collecting data and offering recommendations, the Board quickly became a powerful force for school centralization under its first secretary, Horace Mann.[8]

Another major goal of educational reformers was to professionalize the vocation of teaching. Traditionally satirized as bumbling, ignorant, and cruel itinerants, teachers were not held in high public esteem. During the antebellum period educational reformers sought to improve the status and competency of teachers through various means. These reformers advocated the formal training of teachers in normal schools. They also established a network of organizations and publications which offered advice on various aspects of teaching and encouraged a professional esprit de corps. Perhaps most importantly of all, educational reformers popularized a crucial moral role for teachers. The latter were allegedly moral guardians of Christian piety and republican virtue.[9]

These reforms in public education occurred concurrently with the development of the state prison system. Prison reformers experimented with two rival systems of penal discipline during the antebellum period. The Pennsylvania or separate system advocated the complete solitary confinement of criminals, while the Auburn or congregate plan, which characterized most state prisons, permitted convicts to labor together in absolute silence during the day.[10]

Despite their rivalry both prison systems shared common goals: to check crime by reforming convicts and to promote the efficiency and orderliness of penitentiaries. To accomplish these ends, both systems imposed a uniform and regimented code of conduct on convicts, one characterized by silence, hard labor, prison uniforms, and the lock step. Like schools and the navy, antebellum prisons also developed an administrative hierarchy of institutional officials which included wardens, assistant keepers, and guards.[11]

Antebellum reformers sought to make their respective institutions more efficient, uniform, and professional during the antebellum period. Corporal punishment, especially its frequent or arbitrary use, was at odds with these developments. Reformers declared that spectators as well as recipients of punishment became less efficient workers. Seaman-author and naval reformer Richard Henry Dana, for example, noted that sailors performed their tasks in a sluggish and despondent manner after witnessing punishment.[12]

Slack performance of one's duties was not necessarily intentional. Some individuals were so upset by the spectacle or even the threat of punishment that they were simply unable to function in an efficient and productive manner. Domestic reformer William Alcott provided a graphic example of such a case when he described his former neighbor, Mr. L———, a man who beat his children and verbally abused and physically threatened his wife. Upset by her husband's behavior, Mrs. L——— became inefficient in her household duties and sometimes inadvertently did the opposite of what her husband commanded, for which she received a "much severer reprimand than before."[13]

Individuals who actually experienced corporal punishment were particularly unlikely to function productively, let alone efficiently. This fact was of special concern to prison reformers and officials. In an effort to defray the public expense of prisons and to inculcate the habit of industry in inmates, penitentiaries contracted out convict labor. Convicts, the majority of whom had been common laborers prior to their imprisonment, worked at various tasks from shoemaking to stone cutting. In 1844, for example, Sing Sing prison officials noted that "new contracts have been made for 50 shoemakers, at 41 cents per day; for 40 coopers, at 35 cents per day; for 30 men cutting fur, at 32 cents per day; and for 54 convicts at saddlery and harness hardware, at 35 cents per day."[14]

Harsh corporal punishment jeopardized such experiments with convict labor in several ways. First, such punishments deprived the state of the victim's labor. Penitentiaries might also incur medical expenses for individuals who required hospitalization as a result of severe punishment. The 1847 annual report of the agent of Clinton State Prison articulated these intertwined concerns. The report criticized those who argued that less punishment as well as adequate provisions were "coddling" criminals at the expense of the tax payer. The "pecuniary interests of the community," noted the report, "required that convicts should labor instead of occupying the hospital." To enable them to labor with "vigor and profitable effect," convicts must not only be adequately nourished, clothed, and lodged, but also be governed with firmness, not harshness.[15]

Even if the lash and other forms of corporal punishment did not incapacitate a man for labor, he was still unlikely to work with alacrity or efficiency. Reformers believed that the most effective way to ensure maximum productivity was through the use of positive incentives, not punishment. Horace Mann illustrated this belief when he discussed how the use of rewards increased the productivity and therefore profitability of Southern slaves. Southern slave drivers who appealed to a slave's desire for personal profit, declared Mann, got significantly more work out of their slaves than did drivers who relied on the lash. Mann stressed that the former slave drivers substituted rewards for the scourge "not from compassion, but from cupidity."[16] In other words, it was simply good business to govern slaves through the systematic use of rewards, rather than through the lash.

Although most educational reformers, including Mann, were ambivalent about the systematic use of rewards in governing children (see Chapter 7), they did urge teachers to substitute kindness and suasion for corporal punishment. Children governed through these former techniques allegedly became model students, quickly and eagerly learning their assigned lessons. Veteran educator and prolific author of children's textbooks Lyman Cobb illustrated this point in his 1847 diatribe against school and parental punishment. Cobb described how a boy who had been unable to remember his lessons in a punitive classroom quickly became the leading scholar of his class under the guidance of a kind teacher.[17]

Naval reformers also viewed moral suasion as the key to productivity and efficiency. Walter Colton, for example, noted that sailors governed by "virtue ... [and] ... moral rectitude ... spared no pains to please their superior officers." Indeed ships governed by moral suasion allegedly ran like "well contrived machinery," efficiently functioning through a self-regulating mechanism of regimented discipline.[18]

In their efforts to promote efficiency reformers advocated the development of greater uniformity in their respective institutions. This latter reform goal also promoted opposition to corporal punishment. Available institutional records on punishment revealed a gross lack of uniformity in the infliction of corporal chastisement. An 1847 report on punishment in the New York State Prison at Auburn, for example, showed that assistant keeper James M. Servis whipped 19 of the 45 convicts under his charge during a twelve month period. Altogether Servis administered 96 blows with the cat-o'-nine tails.[19] By contrast, assistant keeper Samuel Odell whipped 33 of his 52 convicts during a six month period. Although he had served only half the time that Servis had, Odell administered almost twice as many blows—174.[20]

A similar lack of uniformity characterized naval discipline. During a four month period in 1846 the *Vincennes* reported only 17 cases of corporal punishment while the *Columbus* reported

60 cases.[21] Although the commander of the *Princeton* reported only three floggings for a four-month period in 1846, thirty cases of corporal punishment occurred on board the *Plymouth* between May 1 and June 30, 1848.[22]

Although most antebellum teachers and certainly most parents did not record their use of corporal chastisement, educational and domestic reformers declared that a lack of uniformity also characterized the punishment of children. While some teachers and parents rarely, if ever, chastized their children, others relied on corporal punishment.[23]

Although distressed by the lack of uniformity in domestic discipline, family reformers did not advocate *legally* restricting a parent's traditional right to punish children. Various factors, particularly parents' allegedly God-given authority to discipline children and the increasingly private nature of middle-class domesticity, precluded efforts to regulate parental punishment within the home.[24]

Unlike their attitudes toward the family, most middle-class antebellum Americans viewed schools, prisons, and the navy as man-made and public institutions. This latter view prompted reform efforts to insure a more uniform approach to discipline in these institutions by regulating and monitoring officials' use of corporal punishment. With this goal in mind, reformers demanded that teachers, naval officers, and prison guards record the number and kinds of punishment inflicted in their respective institutions. Such reports would then be subject to public scrutiny.[25] They would also form the basis for future regulations and restrictions on the institutional use of corporal chastisement.

The desire to check the broad disciplinary prerogatives of local school teachers, naval officers, and prison guards lay behind these reform efforts. This desire in turn underscored reformers' commitment to the development of centralized, bureaucratic institutions, headed by reform-minded professionals like themselves.

A common desire to increase the uniformity, efficiency, and productivity of their respective institutions fueled the seemingly disparate reform campaigns against corporal punishment. Antebellum reformers also objected to this punishment because of concerns which were specific to an individual institution. What were these latter concerns? How did they promote a particular reform group's opposition to corporal chastisement?

In exploring these questions it is important to recall that family reformers criticized parental corporal punishment in the context of portraying the home as a haven of piety, morality, tranquility, and affection. Corporal punishment, especially its frequent and harsh use, contradicted this idyllic image of domesticity. Punitive parents and their suffering children were a far cry from the loving, gentle, happy families depicted in popular didactic works such as Catherine Sedgwick's *Home.*

Harsh domestic discipline also suggested how an allegedly sacred, loving, peaceful bond—that between parent and child—could degenerate into a blatantly cruel power relationship. T.S. Arthur explored this theme in his didactic novella *The Iron Rule; or, Tyranny in the Household.* In this work Arthur described how a "rigid" moralist named Andrew Howland cruelly whipped and scolded his son for minor grievances.[26]

It was significant that Arthur discussed the punitive discipline of a father, not mother. Popular antebellum writers on domesticity associated kindness and gentleness with femininity. By contrast, coercive and severe punishments usually connoted a masculine or paternal form of discipline. Arthur's *Iron Rule* characteristically juxtaposed Howland's harsh paternal discipline with his wife's gentler, softer rule.

Domestic reformers associated corporal punishment with barbarism as well as patriarchy. An 1835 article in *Ladies Magazine,* for example, declared that the punitive domestic discipline of ancient Romans was characteristic of a pagan, barbaric era. Significantly, the author also associated severe domestic discipline with unlimited patriarchal authority. Entrusted with supreme authority over their families, many Roman patriarchs had cruelly misused their authority to tyrannize, abuse, and even murder their children. The author happily noted, however, that the Romans' bloody and despotic patriarchal rule gradually gave way to a more limited and gentle exercise of domestic authority in Christian civilization.[27] A gentle and kind domestic discipline, therefore, suggested the development of a more civilized as well as a more feminine approach to family government.

A crucial set of sexual characteristics, then, suffused family reformers' views on parental discipline. Associating gentleness with femininity and civilization, popular writers on the family such as T. S. Arthur urged the substitution of "feminine" gentleness for the "iron rule" of corporal punishment.

Such advice furthered as well as reflected the feminization of the middle-class home. The gradual shift in the Northeastern economy from a primarily agricultural and household production base into an increasingly commercial and industrial one served to give middle-class women greater control over the home. With male breadwinners increasingly working outside the home, the mother, not the father, gradually assumed primary responsibility for various domestic duties, including parental discipline.[28]

These developments paralleled another important change— the feminization of the teaching profession. Given their allegedly innate moral natures and their availability as a cheap labor force, women seemed ideally suited to teaching. By 1860 women constituted the majority of teachers in New England schools.[29] By the end of the century, teaching had become a distinctly feminine occupation throughout the United States.[30]

The influx of women into teaching promoted educational reformers' opposition to schoolroom punishment for several reasons. Like their counterparts in domestic reform, educational reformers believed that corporal chastisement was out of place in an increasingly feminine institution. Women's allegedly gentle natures predisposed them to substitute moral suasion for corporal punishment in the classroom as well as at home. Educational reformers also feared that the continued use of corporal punishment might provoke a physical confrontation between female teachers and their male students. Convinced that delicate young schoolmarms were no physical match for strong adolescent boys, these reformers declared that persuasion, not force, must govern the classroom.[31]

Criticism of schoolroom corporal punishment also indicated concern about the public reputation of teachers. Recall that educational reformers instituted various reforms to improve the traditionally poor public image of teachers. Corporal punishment jeopardized these reform efforts. Punitive teachers reinforced, rather than undermined, the traditional stereotype of incompetent and cruel pedagogues. For this reason Mann accused punitive Boston schoolmasters of making the word teacher, "that most intrinsically honorable of all appellations, a hissing and a by-word among men."[32]

Educational reformers had good reason to fear that corporal punishment hurt the public reputation of teachers. As noted earlier, public opinion increasingly condemned punitive teachers as cruel and tyrannical. In 1831, for example, Bostonian parent Moses Jaquith publicly accused his son's teacher, Mayhew Grammar Schoolmaster William Clough, of "inhumane" cruelty. Clough had severely whipped Jaquith's son when the latter had been unable to pronounce a word because of a speech impediment. Several other parents also charged Clough with cruelty. In a November 8, 1831 letter to the *Boston Gazette* another parent accused Clough of severely whipping his son for "a trifling cause." Angered by Clough's cruelty, four hundred Boston citizens unsuccessfully petitioned the local school committee to dismiss him.[33]

Such abusive cases of punishment, of course, tarnished the public reputation of schools as well as teachers. As Carl Kaestle has noted, harsh schoolroom punishment also provoked parental resentment against the emerging public school system. Seeking to shore up their traditional authority over children, parents frequently questioned and some opposed the school's right to inflict punishment.[34] Significantly, Moses Jaquith demanded not only Clough's dismissal but also urged an end to corporal punishment in Boston public schools.[35]

Seeking to expand, not restrict, the authority of public schools, most educational reformers did not support public efforts to prohibit corporal punishment. Like other reformers, they instead urged the *voluntary* disuse of this punishment.[36] Through such advice educational reformers hoped to placate public opinion, uphold a teacher's *authority* to chastize, and limit the *actual* use of corporal punishment. Punitive schoolmasters like Clough, however, thwarted all three goals. Little wonder, then, that Mann and other educational leaders angrily condemned teachers who refused to substitute moral suasion for the rod and birch.

Corporal punishment, especially its frequent or abusive use, also jeopardized prison reform efforts to enhance the authority and prestige of penitentiaries. The punitive practices of two New York prison wardens, Elam Lynds and Robert Wiltse, particularly outraged public opinion. They also helped to discredit the claim that penitentiaries primarily sought to reform, not punish, their inmates.

Elam Lynds, a former hatter and infantry captain, was principal keeper of both Auburn (1817–25; 1838–39) and Sing Sing (1825–29; 1843–44) prisons.[37] In both these institutions he quickly developed a reputation for cruelty. Convicts complained that Lynds underfed them and then flogged them when they complained. Lynds also allegedly beat insane and sick convicts. In 1839, for example, Lynds dragged out of a hospital bed an allegedly ailing and deranged Auburn convict named Louis von Eck. Accusing Eck of shamming sickness, Lynds beat and kicked him. After a series of severe beatings and floggings, Eck died.[38]

Similar cases of cruelty characterized Wiltse's administration as Sing Sing warden from 1830 to 1840. The testimony of Sing Sing guards, employees, and convicts showed that Wiltse severely beat and flogged men for minor offenses. He inflicted one hundred lashes, for example, on an insane convict named Little when the latter made a "considerable noise" at night. Wiltse then ordered guard Paul H. Lent to gag Little. Several days after this abusive treatment, Little committed suicide by drowning himself in the river.[39]

Such cases of abusive punishment precipitated widespread opprobrium, especially among the citizens of Sing Sing and Auburn. Angry citizens of Auburn, for example, threatened to burn down the prison after Eck's death in 1839. In response to public demands for his dismissal, Lynds resigned on April 19, 1839.

Similarly, Wiltse's administration angered the citizens of Sing Sing. The local newspaper, the *Hudson River Chronicle*, described Wiltse's regime as one of barbaric cruelty and demanded a state investigation of conditions at Sing Sing.[40]

The rivalry between the Auburn and Pennsylvania systems of prison discipline added an important dimension to the public controversy over abusive penal punishment. Advocates of the Pennsylvania plan sought to discredit their rival by arguing that flogging was an indispensable part of the congregate system of prison discipline. Dorothea Dix and Samuel Gridley Howe, for example, contended that the latter system gave convicts an opportunity to talk with one another and to plot insurrection. Only the frequent and harsh use of the lash, they concluded, checked this infraction against the rule of silence.[41]

This charge received important support from available statistics on prison punishment. Although convicts regularly suffered the lash for insolence, fighting, laziness, and other offenses, the most common cause of punishment was for talking. The inspectors of Sing Sing Prison, for example, reported that there were 776 violations in 1845: 362 were punished with the cats, and 414 with the shower bath, solitary confinement, and deprivation of food and bedding. Significantly, 329 of the 776 punishments administered were for talking. This offense was also a leading cause of punishment in Auburn Prison. Out of the 1,279 cases of corporal punishment administered in this prison in 1844 and 1845, 491 were inflicted for talking.[42]

Prison reformers who supported the congregate plan recognized that the widespread use of corporal punishment, especially the lash, discredited their prison system. Not surprisingly, these reformers became increasingly defensive about the continued use of flogging in penitentiaries modelled after the Auburn plan. Both the Boston Prison Discipline Society and the New York Prison Association, for example, pointedly denied that the lash was necessary to govern convicts under the congregate system of prison discipline.[43]

In an effort to vindicate the Auburn plan, both organizations also urged the disuse of flogging in penitentiaries. In 1841, for example, the Prison Discipline Society declared that "stripes ought to be, if they are not, either a very small part, or no part" of the Auburn system of prison discipline.[44] John W. Edmonds, one of the founders of the New York Prison Association and an inspector of New York State Prisons from 1843 to 1845, shared these views. In a February 6, 1846 letter to the New York State Committee on State Prisons, Edmonds warned that the use of the lash discredited the Auburn system abroad as well as at home. The Committee agreed with Edmonds. They declared that this system's harsh discipline had caused various European nations to pattern their penitentiaries after the Pennsylvania plan.[45]

The rivalry between the Auburn and Pennsylvania systems of penal discipline promoted prison reformers' criticism of flogging. Particular institutional concerns also shaped the naval reform campaign against this punishment. This latter campaign was part of a wider reform movement to increase the efficiency of the navy by attracting native-born Americans to the service. After the War of 1812, westward expansion and various economic opportunites siphoned off potential naval recruits into civilian life. The merchant service, by offering higher wages and better living conditions than the navy, further depleted the number of American-born seamen.[46]

To compensate for this manpower loss, the American navy increasingly relied on foreign-born seamen. This influx of "foreign" sailors into the navy, however, worried both naval officials and the public. Seaman-author William McNally expressed widely shared views when he criticized Dutch, Italian, Portuguese, and Spanish sailors. Motivated by money, rather than patriotism, these foreigners were cowardly "parvenus," well schooled in habits of sycophancy and treachery. They were therefore unable to uphold the honor of the American flag. In short, a serious shortage of American sailors thwarted the improvement of the United States Navy.[47]

Various proposals sought to alleviate the navy's shortage of native-born recruits. Secretary of the Navy James K. Paulding, for example, urged Congress to increase seamen's wages and benefits in order to attract men into the navy.[48] Commodore Matthew C. Perry sought to attract American born recruits into the service by establishing a naval apprentice program, designed to advance young enlisted men to the rank of "petty officer" through vocational training and moral supervision.[49]

Critics of naval flogging contended that this punishment counteracted any efforts to attract American "freemen" to the service. Like their counterparts in other reforms, these critics also declared that flogging tarnished the public reputation of the navy. Naval surgeon John Lockwood articulated these beliefs in a series of anonymous articles on flogging. After noting that the United States Navy was manned primarily by dissipated Americans and "the refuse of other nations," Lockwood declared: "Neither patriotism nor lucre can induce men of character to risk the humiliation of stripes." Lockwood also noted that the continued use of the lash provoked a "storm of popular indignation" against the navy. This "storm" might promote successful efforts to dismantle the navy and therefore "extinguish its cruelty and oppression."[50]

Harsh, punitive discipline had already helped to destroy the apprentice system. Public outcry against this system gained momentum after the notorious Somers Mutiny episode. The *Somers* was a training ship for apprentice seamen which set off on a mission to Africa in April 1842. Matthew C. Perry's brother-in-law, Commander Alexander Slidell Mackenzie, headed the 120 member crew, 99 of whom were apprentice sailors. The crew also included three particularly well connected midshipmen: Oliver Hazard and Matthew C. Perry Jrs, and Philip Spencer, son of President Tyler's Secretary of War.

During the *Somers'* return voyage, discipline deteriorated and there was a great deal of flogging administered aboard ship. Rumors of an imminent mutiny quickly provoked Mackenzie to take more extreme measures. He summarily hanged three suspected mutineers: gunner's mate Samuel Cromwell, able seaman Elijah Small, and the alleged ringleader, Midshipman Spencer. Mackenzie's actions, especially his summary execution of Spencer, led to his court-martial in 1843 on charges of murder, illegal punishment, and "cruelty and oppression."[51]

Although the navy exonerated Mackenzie of these charges, the tragedy aboard the *Somers* helped to discredit the naval apprentice program. Throughout 1843 and 1844 public criticism of naval apprenticeship grew. Significantly, critics of this program charged that young apprentices were cruelly treated. One anonymous writer to the *New York Tribune,* for example, charged that apprentices were neither educated nor promoted. Instead they endured an endless routine of "kicks," "cuffs," and "colts" from "aristocratic" officers.[52] Such charges of cruelty precipitated the failure of the apprentice system in 1845.[53] Harsh corporal punishment, therefore, hindered naval efforts to recruit young Americans into the service.

To sum up the argument so far, naval, prison, educational, and domestic reformers criticized corporal punishment for various institutional reasons. Family reformers worried that punitive parental discipline jeopardized the idyllic image of domesticity which they popularized. Educational reformers believed that the continued use of schoolroom punishment hindered their efforts to upgrade the public reputation of teachers. Both groups of reformers also believed that corporal punishment was an inappropriate means of discipline in allegedly feminine institutions such as the school and home. A desire to alleviate the navy's manpower shortage and to protect the congregate prison plan fueled respectively the naval and prison reform campaigns against corporal punishment. Underlying these specific institutional concerns was a common desire among reformers to enhance the prestige, authority, and efficiency of their respective institutions.

Institutional concerns, however, only partially explained why different groups of reformers campaigned against corporal punishment. Reformers' criticism of this punishment also indicated a significant shift in attitudes toward violence, pain, discipline, and authority. Exploration of this cultural change illuminates another important aspect of the antebellum reform campaigns against corporal punishment.

Chapter 3
Reform Campaigns against Corporal Punishment: Cultural Concerns

I N A FEBRUARY 9, 1849 Congressional speech against naval flogging, New Hampshire Senator John Parker Hale condemned this punishment as a "relic of feudalism and barbarity."[1] Numerous naval, prison, domestic, and educational reformers echoed Hale's condemnation of corporal punishment. An 1844 issue of the *District School Journal*, for example, declared that corporal punishment was "emphatically a relic of barbarism," out of place in the "enlightened civilization of the nineteenth century."[2] The *Prisoner's Friend* expressed similar sentiments when it declared that corporal punishment was "barbarous and wicked and is a gross blot upon the civilization of the Nineteenth Century."[3]

Denunciations of corporal chastisement in these terms indicated reformers' perceptions of this punishment as antiquated, cruel, and ineffective. What concerns lay behind these criticisms of corporal punishment? In exploring this question, it is important to note the cultural context in which the reform campaigns against corporal punishment occurred. Leading critics of this punishment condemned a range of violent, punitive practices, including slavery, war, duelling, capital punishment, and cruelty to animals. Significantly, they condemned these latter practices in the same way that they denounced corporal punishment, namely, as "relics of barbarism." As the first United States Senator to be elected on an antislavery ticket, Hale, for example, denounced slavery as well as flogging in these terms.[4] Similarly, the *Common School Journal* condemned not only the school rod and birch but also daggers, knives, pistols, and sword-canes as the "paraphernalia of barbarism." An 1843 article in this periodical also criticized military academies since they trained young men to kill. "Instead of badges of honor," declared the anonymous author, the armor of these academies should be "stamped with Death, Mourning, Widowhood, [and] Orphanage."[5]

Perhaps the *Moral Advocate*, a monthly magazine begun in 1821, best illustrated the widespread revulsion against violence which suffused antebellum reform campaigns against corporal punishment. In its opening editorial, the *Moral Advocate* pledged to work toward the abolition of not only sangunjary punishments but also war, duelling, and capital punishment. All of these practices, emphatically declared the *Moral Advocate*, were "barbarous" practices and obstacles to moral progress. Subsequent issues of the *Moral Advocate* condemned slavery and cruelty to animals in similar terms. A June 1822 editorial, for example, declared that slavery was a barbarous and violent institution, and poems in this journal condemned those who enjoyed the "barbarous" practice of cock fighting or the "savage sport" of killing birds.[6]

The *Moral Advocate* also articulated another important concern in the reform campaigns against corporal punishment—temperance. This periodical as well as the *Prisoner's Friend* declared that intemperance, like violence, was a crucial obstacle to civilized progress.[7] The writings of Horace Mann, John Parker Hale, and other leading critics of corporal punishment echoed these sentiments.[8]

The antebellum reform campaigns against corporal punishment were ultimately part of a broad spectrum of reform designed to establish a nonviolent, temperate society. Such a broad reform impetus suggests a profound change in attitudes toward discipline, pain, violence, and ultimately human nature. The purpose of this chapter is to explore antebellum prison, naval, educational, and domestic reform campaigns against corporal punishment in the context of these important cultural changes.

A major theme in all four of these campaigns was the belief that corporal punishment was an ineffective means of social discipline because it "merely" repressed an individual from wrongdoing. This punishment, however, allegedly failed to accomplish the "true" aim of discipline, namely, the reformation of individual moral character. Horace Mann expressed widely shared sentiments when he declared that the fear of corporal punishment might "make an offender cease to do ill," but it can never "make him love to do well."[9]

Mann's comments occurred in a context of concern about the development of moral character. Often described in vague and prescriptive terms, "character" ultimately referred to the moral potential within each individual to develop disinterested benevolence and especially internalized moral restraints. Countless reform writings articulated these crucial, often intertwined, aspects of character. A story recounted in an April 1844 issue of the *Common School Journal* was typical. After a great fire occurred in Hamburg, Germany, children in a nearby orphanage selflessly risked their lives to rescue town victims and to protect private property. Their heroic deed exemplified not only disinterested social service but also self-discipline. By resisting the temptation to loot stores and by readily sharing their meagre food supplies with fire victims, these orphans practiced perfect self-restraint.[10]

The development of internalized moral restraints in individuals assumed particular urgency during the antebellum period. The majority of middle-class Americans, including reformers, ultimately had misgivings about the various economic, political, cultural, and demographic changes transforming their society. Despite their professed optimism in the United States, many Americans worried that rapid and extensive social change might precipitate widespread disorder and moral decay.

These fears fueled reformers' concern about the rapid urbanization of the Northeast. Like so many of their middle-class contemporaries, antebellum reformers singled out cities as centers of corruption and instability. Cobb articulated these widely shared views when he quoted a Troy, New York newspaper's description of urban blight:

> Bad Boys ... congregate at corners of the streets, ragged, filthy, and saucy, insulting passers-by with their profane and often times obscene language. At night they assemble in herds, marching through the streets and disturbing quiet citizens with their unearthly yellings and boisterous demonstrations.[11]

Not surprisingly, Cobb predicted that most of these boys would become criminals.

The fact that cities attracted not only impoverished native Americans but also immigrants exacerbated reformers' concern about rapid urbanization. Reflecting their middle-class and nativist backgrounds, reformers viewed the urban, especially immigrant, poor as a serious threat to social stability. This perspective was especially pronounced in the writings of Horace Mann. Within the "recesses" of America's urban "moral jungles," declared Mann, "the poor, the ignorant [and] the vicious" allegedly formed an "increasing fund of pauperism and vice, ... a vital, self-enlarging, reproductive mass of ignorance and crime," which jeopardized basic American institutions.[12]

As part of their concern with social order, reformers also feared the rise of mob rule in a democratic society. Not surprisingly, this fear was almost an obsessive theme in Mann's writings. Convinced that the freedom of American institutions gave "full play" to human passions, Mann worried that republican liberty would degenerate into licensed anarchy. Unrestrained "natural passions" would become "ravenous and tyrannizing" appetites and precipitate "mobs, ... riots, ... burnings [and] ... lynchings...."[13]

Given their misgivings about society, reformers sought to strike a needed balance between individual liberty and social order, rapid change and moral stability. Like many of their middle-class contemporaries, these reformers wished to harness, rather than repress, the forces of social change. They therefore sought to socialize Americans to a more flexible, competitive society *and* to an allegedly historical tradition of republican virtue and order.

For countless American educators, employers, ministers, and especially reformers, the development of an internalized moral code in individuals offered both a secure and flexible basis for order in a changing society. The spate of popular books on child-rearing and domesticity which began appearing in the 1820s stressed the importance of a child's self-control over his physical and moral faculties. Muzzey expressed representative views when he declared that "self-restraint" and "self-government" was necessary in a changing American society. Adolescents who were thrust into the world at an early age must particularly develop these qualities. According to Muzzey, they must become "self-governed [and] both lovers and doers of right."[14]

Marital and health reformer Henry Clarke Wright shared Muzzey's commitment to internalized moral restraints. Wright sought to "civilize" man by subordinating his physical, especially sexual, impulses to rational self-control.[15] A similar goal promoted the antislavery crusade. Abolitionists condemned slavery because it allegedly cultivated man's "animal passions" while thwarting the development of inner moral restraints. According to Theodore Dwight Weld, these latter restraints were the "web of civilized society, warp and woof."[16]

A consensus on the importance of internalized moral restraints also promoted opposition to intemperance and corporal punishment. Antebellum reformers declared that both of these practices thwarted the development of self-discipline. The resonance between the temperance and anti-corporal punishment campaigns became particularly apparent in naval reform. Participants in this latter reform contended that the navy's daily grog ration thwarted a sailor's moral elevation because it allegedly "degraded" Jack Tar into an undisciplined, animal-like creature. In an 1832 article on temperance, the *Sailor's Magazine* described the grog as an "infernal poison" which excluded seamen from Christianity, the moral restraints of civilization, and "almost everything which gives value to character, and hedges up the road to ruin."[17] To emphasize how horrible the "road to ruin" was, countless stories vividly described the misery of drunken sailors. These men were a "lump of loathsomeness" who suffered from ulcers, sores, starvation, apoplexy and madness. Often "maltreated, beaten, cheated [and] robbed," these "poor creatures" frequently became "turbulent, obstreperous, pugnacious" and sometimes lawless.[18] Liquor not only destroyed the sailor's life but also jeopardized the social order.

The desire to transform seamen into "respectable" citizens generated naval reformers' opposition to the lash as well as to grog. Indeed most reformers intertwined their discussion of these two evils, viewing intemperance as the chief cause of corporal punishment on board ships. "Ardent spirits," the *Sailor's Magazine* repeatedly argued, made sailors disorderly, surly, negligent, and sometimes even mutinous.[19] The lash, therefore, frequently followed the cup of grog. Statistics made available after 1848 regarding the corporal punishment practices aboard individual ships supported these assertions. Drunkenness or offenses resulting from drunken behavior, such as "insolence," "insubordination," "noisiness," or "smuggling liquor on board" were the leading causes of punishment on all naval ships.[20]

Like grog, naval flogging allegedly blocked a seaman's moral elevation. Opponents of this punishment argued that flogging degraded seamen instead of elevating them to self-disciplined beings. Several articles in the *Sailor's Magazine*, for example, argued that the attempt to govern sailors by "brute force" instead of by the higher moral motives of reason and suasion invariably destroyed seamen's "last vestige of self-respect" and transformed them into "miserably degraded wretches."[21] The lash, therefore, thwarted Jack Tar's progress towards a higher, more enlightened moral development.

Prison, educational, and domestic reformers leveled similar criticisms against corporal punishment. Cobb expressed representative sentiments when he described how a school whipping degraded a "good boy" he had once known: "From a *noble, dignified,* and *manly* boy, he became DEGRADED AND DEBASED, and seemed to lose all self-respect."[22] Similarly, Massachusetts State Prison warden and reformer Gideon Haynes declared that "rash and cruel punishment" destroyed the "spark of manhood" and therefore the self-respect of prisoners.[23]

Individuals who lost their self-respect were allegedly beyond any hope of moral reformation. They were also beyond the pale of civilized society since the latter demanded the development of self-imposed moral restraints. Antebellum reformers stressed the savage or uncivilized state of chastised victims when they described the latter as "brutes." One 1850 article in the *Sailor's Magazine*, for example, declared that sailors who suffered the lash began to act like brutes instead of men.[24]

Such comments, of course, echoed temperance advocates' descriptions of drunkards. Shared fears as well as a common language highlighted the close parallel between the temperance and anti-corporal punishment reform campaigns. Reform efforts against the lash, like those against drunkenness, reflected an underlying fear about social order. Critics of the former worried that brutalized victims of corporal punishment might jeopardize this order by becoming angry and vengeful. Didactic writings on childrearing and education, for example, stressed that corporal punishment nurtured hatred, anger and a desire for revenge in children.[25] For this reason John Griscom, founder of the New York House of Refuge for juvenile delinquents, referred to this punishment as the "sting of a venomous insect."[26]

Fears that flogged men would become bitter, angry, and vengeful particularly worried naval and prison reformers. An 1835 article in the *Army and Navy Chronicle*, for example, warned that flogging transformed sailors into desperate and hardened men, "callous to all virtuous feeling [and] . . . an enemy . . . to law and government. . . ."[27]

Frederick Robinson, who criticized corporal punishment when he became warden of the Massachusetts State Prison in 1843, expressed similar sentiments: "Excessive severity always tends to harden the heart, and make the convicts look upon society as their enemies, and nourish a desire for vengeance and retaliation, which leads them to re-commit depredations, and wage war upon society. . . ."[28]

These comments articulated another fear of antebellum reformers, namely, that victims of punishment would revenge themselves on society by committing additional, more serious offenses. Significantly, Cobb noted that the "good boy" who had been debased by a school whipping subsequently became one of the "very worst" boys he knew. Cobb believed that this transformation in character was typical. Countless boys who had been harshly disciplined by parents as well as teachers allegedly revenged themselves for this treatment by becoming "reckless, dissolute, and abandoned young men."[29]

Victims of corporal chastisement could also exact their revenge against the institution which inflicted punishment. Naval and prison reformers particularly worried about this possibility. Naval surgeon and reformer John Lockwood, for example, blamed frequent and severe floggings for the notorious bloody mutiny on board the British ship *Hermione*. Convinced that "tyranny is the parent of rebellion," Lockwood feared that American as well as British sailors would mutiny from harsh, tyrannical officers.[30] Gideon Haynes had good reason to share these fears. Haynes recalled that a serious mutiny occurred in the Massachusetts State Prison in 1824 when convicts, armed with workshop tools, forcibly prevented the flogging of three fellow inmates.[31]

Even when it did not provoke open rebellion, corporal punishment allegedly posed subtle and insidious threats to a civilized, orderly society. Antebellum reformers worried that corporal chastisement bred a sadistic appetite for cruelty in the inflictors of punishment. Richard Henry Dana offered a particularly graphic description of sadism aboard the *Pilgrim*. While inflicting punishment, the captain danced about the deck, screaming, "If you want to know what I flog you for, I'll tell you. It's because I like to do it!—because I like to do it."[32]

By associating whipping with uncontrolled emotion and bestiality, reformers tacitly explored the connection between corporal punishment and illicit sexuality. An underlying fear of homosexuality probably heightened anxiety about this connection. The existence of homosexual behavior was particularly worrisome to prison and naval reformers. The segregation of men in crowded prisons for long periods of time, unhappily noted the Prison Discipline Society of Boston, encouraged the "crime of sodomy" to a "melancholy degree."[33]

Given the all-male and usually youthful composition of the crew, as well as the long voyages, infrequent furloughs, and close living quarters of most ships, homosexual behavior also occurred on board seafaring men-of-war. Despite the opprobrium attached to this behavior, the discipline records of various naval vessels indicate that sailors were occasionally punished for committing "unnatural" acts.[34]

Ironically the punishment usually meted out to homosexual offenders—whippings—may well have aroused the sexual emotions which institutional officers sought to repress. Whippings, declared reformers, aroused the sadistic impulses of spectators as well as inflictors of punishment. Although disgusted by his captain's cruelty, Dana conceded that he himself felt "excited" as well as "horror struck" by witnessing punishment. Altogether he experienced a powerful mixture of emotions which he could hardly control.[35] Fears that whipping aroused the sadism of spectators worried prison and educational reformers. An 1822 *Report* on the penitentiary system, for instance, expressed shock over the sight of adolescent boys "flocking to a whipping post, to enjoy in revelry and mirth, the tortures of fellow beings."[36]

Reformers also expressed concern over the pleasure which some victims seemed to derive from corporal punishment. An 1822 editorial in the *Moral Advocate*, for example, recounted the bizarre proposal which a school boy made to his teacher: "they would enter into a partnership, if the master would find switches, he would find back."[37]

This story suggests that corporal punishment, especially flogging, nurtured masochistic tendencies in some victims. Some reformers could draw upon their own personal experiences to discuss this issue. They themselves had experienced masochistic pleasure when chastised as children. In a March 24, 1847 letter to Lyman Cobb, John Griscom, for example, suggested that he derived masochistic pleasure from his father's whippings. Griscom recalled that "after a well-merited flagellation from my father, [I] felt a glow of regard for him, far beyond what I had enjoyed while in a state of rebellious feeling."[38]

It is significant that when reformers discussed the enjoyment of painful punishments they usually cited examples of masochistic or sadistic males, not females. As noted earlier, reformers thought of violence and cruelty in gender prescribed terms. Like other middle-class Americans, they viewed the female sex as the embodiment of gentleness and tranquility. Given this belief, it is not surprising that the *Moral Advocate* dismissed as useless and disgusting the notion of female soldiers, duellists, or boxers.[39] The obverse side of this Victorian view of women, of course, was the belief that males were naturally aggressive and therefore susceptible to violent impulses.

The *Moral Advocate* urged parents, especially mothers, to check these impulses in their male children by prohibiting them from playing with toy caps and guns. Parents were also to check the "fondness for killing insects [since this] has often been associated in the same character with the fondness for killing men, and perhaps was the first budding of the germ of cruelty and violence."[40]

A crucial assumption lay behind this advice to parents, namely, the belief that human beings, especially young children, were socialized into violent and cruel behavior. Antislavery tracts particularly stressed this point when they noted how the "peculiar institution" cultivated cruelty and violence in children, even young girls. In her *Key To Uncle Tom's Cabin* Harriet Beecher Stowe illustrated this point by describing the actions of a three-year-old white girl. A far cry from the angelic Little Eva portrayed in *Uncle Tom's Cabin*, this three-year-old harnessed six to eight young slave children to her carriage as if they were horses. An older slave then gave his young mistress a whip and urged her to flog the harnessed children: "There Misse, whip 'em well; make 'em go! They're all your niggers."[41]

The actions of this slave illustrated how the institution of slavery degraded adults, blacks as well as whites, into sadists. Stowe, of course, explored this theme in her classic novel *Uncle Tom's Cabin*. Her graphic depiction of the lash-wielding Simon Legree, who relished the sufferings of his slaves, symbolized for many antebellum Americans the effects of slavery on whites. At the same time Stowe's description of Legree's overseers, Quimbo and Sambo, highlighted how slavery cultivated sadistic brutality in blacks. Stowe noted that Legree had trained his overseers in "savageness and brutality as systematically as he had his bulldogs; and, by long practice in hardness and cruelty, brought their whole nature to about the same range of capacities."[42]

Stowe underscored the brutality of all three men by describing them in animal-like terms. Quimbo and Sambo had "coarse, dark, heavy features" and spoke in "barbarous, guttural, half-brute intonation[s]"; while Legree had a "round bullet-head, . . . [a] large, coarse mouth . . . [and] his hands were immensely large, hairy, sunburned, . . . and very dirty, and garnished with long nails, in a very foul condition."[43]

Participation in wars as well as slavery allegedly cultivated an appetite for brutality and cruelty, especially in males. The *Moral Advocate* stressed how fighting gradually "dulled" a soldier's initial horror of war. Once inured to violence, the soldier allegedly derived "enjoyment from the most horrid scenes of carnage."[44]

Intemperance allegedly went hand in hand with this sadism. Indeed the *Moral Advocate* asserted that war depended on the custom of drinking since alcohol aroused "malevolent passions," especially those of cruelty and injustice.[45]

These comments highlighted reformers' close association of violence and cruelty with intemperance. Indulgence in "spiritous liquors" as well as exposure to violence allegedly cultivated "malevolent passions," including an appetite for cruelty. Such passions, of course, destroyed moral character and degraded human beings, especially males, to the level of animals or savages. It was in this context that antebellum reformers described the victims of both corporal punishment and intemperance as "brutes."

Antebellum reformers condemned corporal punishment as well as alcohol out of a desire to socialize human beings toward a highly self-disciplined code of ethics, one which checked violent or sadistic impulses. Why, however, did these reformers believe that proper moral training could check, if not banish, "malevolent passions"? Why did reformers believe that they could "reform" not only disobedient young children but also debauched seamen and even criminals? Ultimately these beliefs suggested a profound reorientation in attitudes toward human nature and social deviancy.

Throughout the colonial period most Anglo-Americans believed that social deviancy, including criminal behavior, was a sign of man's innately depraved human nature. As David Rothman has noted, the association of deviancy with innate depravity had a profound impact on colonial attitudes toward social discipline. Most American colonists believed that harsh, even cruel punishments were necessary to restrain the alleged depravity of various social offenders. It was this belief which girded not only the colonial criminal codes but also the punitive code of military discipline.[46]

Even children were not exempt from pessimistic views regarding human nature and social discipline. Various religious and domestic works in the seventeenth and first half of the eighteenth centuries declared that a judicious use of corporal punishment was necessary to restrain children's "natural" propensity to evil. Seventeenth century Puritan leader John Robinson in a 1628 essay on education argued that children's "natural pride" must be "broken and beaten down" through a judicious use of the rod.[47] Similarly, Daniel Defoe in *The Family Instructor* (1720) argued that the "Rod of Correction" was sometimes necessary to "drive out" the "Folly that is bound up in the Heart of a Child ... [the] natural Propensity ... to Evil. ..."[48]

The Anglo-American belief in innate human depravity, however, waned during the latter half of the eighteenth century. Various factors, including the erosion of orthodox Calvinism, the legacies of the Enlightenment and Romanticism, and the republican ideology of the American Revolution, promoted a more optimistic view of human nature during the early national period. Post-Revolutionary Americans increasingly perceived human beings as malleable and rational, if not innocent, creatures.[49]

Revised views of human nature had a profound impact on antebellum reform attitudes toward deviancy and punishment. Unlike most colonial Americans, antebellum reformers declared that deviant behavior reflected bad environmental influences, not innate human depravity. Prison surveys articulated this belief when they discussed the causes of crime. According to an

1836 report of the Auburn State Prison Chaplain, 121 of the 228 convicts in his prison had either lost or left their parents before the age of seventeen. Many inmates had come from homes marred by intemperance and poverty. Deprived of "parental control" at an early age, young men often travelled to cities where they led dissipated lives and lacked both a stable home life and "steady work."[50] Personal instability and dissipation, therefore, were allegedly to blame for crime.

Antebellum reformers blamed impulsive behavior as well as a bad environment for an individual's deviant, if not criminal, acts. Educational and domestic reformers often declared that children disobeyed from impulse, not malice. Cobb, for example, declared that "very few children ever do wrong *for the sake of doing wrong* as such." Instead most children disobeyed from "mere thoughtlessness."[51] A similar view characterized naval reformers' descriptions of insubordinate seamen. Walter Colton, for instance, declared that "sailors are of all beings in the world the most thoughtless. The monitions of the future are lost in the impulses of the present." Although seamen were allegedly impulsive creatures, Colton also depicted them as generous and kind hearted men, in need of guidance and sympathy.[52]

Given reformers' revised views toward human nature and deviant behavior, it is not surprising that they criticized corporal punishment as an unnecessarily harsh means of discipline. In his lectures to teachers, Samuel Read Hall expressed representative views among educational reformers. Although the whip may be necessary to govern brutes, declared Hall, it was not needed to govern intelligent, rational beings who could distinguish between right and wrong.[53] Naval and prison reformers echoed Hall's sentiments. Lockwood, for example, pointedly denied that sailors were "gangs of desperadoes . . . only to be governed as . . . ferocious animals . . . by harsh words and severe chastisement." Instead most sailors were "reflecting men" who became "more attentive to their duties, the more humane and rational the treatment they receive."[54] In a similar vein, the annual reports of the Boston Prison Discipline Society declared that convicts were "creatures of the same glorious Creator" and therefore possessed "feelings susceptible to kindness and minds capable of improvement."[55]

To substantiate their view, reformers cited numerous examples of apparently incorrigible children, seamen, and convicts who were allegedly "reformed" when governed by reason and kindness. In the already cited story by Arthur, the harsh patriarchal discipline of Andrew Howland prompted his son's rebellion. The latter became a "hardened" and seemingly incorrigible young man who ran away to sea. Significantly, Andrew Howland Junior became a loving son, good husband, and model citizen under the loving and gentle influence of his widowed mother. Similarly, educational reformers noted how the kindness of female teachers transformed recalcitrant schoolboys into obedient, conscientious students.[56]

It was one thing, however, to argue that young children could be reformed under the guidance of a loving mother or school teacher, but what about the reformation of unruly seamen and convicts in all-male environments? Reform critics of corporal punishment contended that reason, kindness, and persuasion were effective in governing most men aboard seafaring vessels or in prisons. Once again, reformers cited examples of individuals allegedly reformed by kindness to support their views. New York prison inspector and reformer John Edmonds, for example, recalled how a "stout, athletic, turbulent" convict, a former pirate, emerged as the ringleader of mischief in Sing Sing's workshop. Frequent and severe whippings only made this convict more insubordinate and lazy. Edmonds recalled that he "reasoned with" this convict and treated him with kindness. The latter became a "pattern of good order." He was now industrious, obedient, respectful. After his discharge, he became an honest, hard-working citizen. While visiting Edmonds, the former convict credited kind treatment with his reformation: "I could bear any thing you could inflict, but your kindness, which I didn't deserve, and that overcame me."[57]

As with similar anecdotes involving children and seamen, these stories reveal more about the values and wishes of reformers than about those who were allegedly reformed. Antebellum reformers often mistakenly equated the inhibition of undesirable behavior with an individual's internalization of prescribed values. Although Edmonds' anecdote was intended to illustrate the efficacy of gentle suasion in reforming "hardened" convicts, the story actually had more ambiguous implications. The convict's subsequent industry and gratitude suggested that a process of moral reformation *did* occur. The latter's "reformation," however, might also have been motivated by fear of more punishment, as well as by the desire for an early pardon and for Edmonds' subsequent help. Several motives, therefore, may have precipitated this man's transformation into a model prisoner.

For our purposes, however, the essential point is that antebellum reformers perceived "moral suasion" as a more effective means of reformation than corporal punishment. They therefore viewed the former approach to discipline as the mainstay of social order. Samuel Read Hall expressed widely shared sentiments when he declared that only "firmness, discretion and kindness" established "perfect" classroom order. Elaborating on this point, Hall contrasted the classroom of a punitive disciplinarian with that of one who relied on suasion to govern students. In the former case, the children became unruly the moment the teacher left the room. "Perfect order," however, continued to reign in the classroom governed by a kind, yet firm teacher.[58]

The desire to achieve "perfect order" through individual reformation was not the only concern of those who criticized corporal punishment. These critics also acted out of compassion and sympathy for chastised victims. Compassion for the sufferings of one anonymous Sing Sing convict identified only as T—— was apparent in the memoirs of prison chaplain John Luckey. Luckey bitterly recalled how T—— received twenty to sixty lashes when he inquired about undelivered letters from his mother. The repeated floggings as well as the regimental discipline destroyed the mind and body of T——. By the time he left prison, T—— was allegedly "used up as a man."[59]

Occasionally reformers' sympathies with the victims of corporal punishment threatened to overwhelm their own self-control. While watching a teacher punish a ten-year-old boy, Cobb became so emotionally distraught by the child's cries that he had to leave the room.[60] Similarly, naval chaplain Charles Stewart recalled: "The *keenest emotions* I have known on board the Guerriere, have come suddenly upon me in the sound of the lash and the cry of some wretch suffering at my side.... I felt every stroke almost as if across my own shoulders...."[61]

These expressions of empathy suggested not only a concern with chastised victims but also a revulsion against the infliction of painful punishment. As Martin Pernick and James Turner have recently observed, this revulsion precipitated the widespread use of anesthesia by British and American physicians in the nineteenth century.[62] Revulsion against inflicting pain also prompted a range of transatlantic reforms in Victorian culture. These included not only societies to abolish cruelty to animals, slavery, and war, but also efforts to improve the treatment of the insane and poor.[63]

Leading critics of corporal punishment viewed all of these reform developments as part of a broad humanitarian movement designed to alleviate pain and suffering. Cobb characteristically declared that the abolition of the public whipping post, public executions, military flogging, and imprisonment for debt; as well as the establishment of hospitals and asylums reflected significant progress in "the cause of humanity and philanthropy." Cobb added that the complete abolition of corporal punishment would not only further this progress but also encourage abolition of another revolting practice—cruelty to animals.[64]

The desire to alleviate pain and suffering was an important theme in the antebellum reform campaigns against corporal punishment. Concern for the innate human rights, if not civil liberties, of chastised victims was another. Cobb, for example, stressed that children had an innate right to "kind treatment."[65] Meanwhile Frederick Robinson noted that flogging violated a convict's inalienable right to "human sympathy, kindness, and respect."[66]

Concern for the civil liberties as well as innate human rights of free white citizens fueled criticisms of naval flogging. Herman Melville articulated these intertwined concerns in his 1850 novel *White Jacket*. Melville declared that:

... flogging in the navy is opposed to the essential dignity of man, which no legislator has a right to violate; ... it is utterly repugnant to the spirit of our democratic institutions; indeed ... it involves a lingering trait of ... a barbarous feudal aristocracy.[67]

Flogging, therefore, was a despotic punishment, out of place in a democratic society.

Denunciations of corporal punishment as a despotic punishment which violated the innate human rights, if not civil liberties, of its victims reflected a fundamental shift in attitudes towards institutional patterns of authority. A series of essentially hierarchical relationships between superiors and inferiors bounded individuals together in the colonial period. Wives were subordinate to husbands, servants and apprentices to masters, church congregations to ministers and elders, and subjects of state to rulers. By contrast, a growing equality among group members characterized institutions in the late eighteenth and nineteenth centuries. The changes in political structure and ideology inaugurated by the American Revolution perhaps best illustrated this shift in the nature of authority. No longer subjects of an absolute ruler, Americans were now "citizens," governed only by their formal consent and constitutionally guaranteed "inalienable rights" and equality before the law. The electoral system created by the American Revolution, coupled with its republican ideology of egalitarianism, also dealt a death blow to the traditional pattern of deferential politics. Post-Revolutionary elections of "ordinary" citizens to state and local offices, for example, destroyed the monopoly of elite rule by the well-born, wealthy, and educated. The rise of Jacksonianism in antebellum America furthered the Revolutionary legacy of political democracy in various ways, most notably by broadening the franchise to include virtually all free, white male citizens.[68]

The emergence of a democratic society with its stress on civil liberties and inalienable human rights shaped antebellum attitudes towards social discipline. Different groups of reformers argued that discipline in their respective institutions should reflect the democratic principles of the nation. Not surprisingly, this theme was particularly apparent when reformers discussed how to discipline the free white men who manned the United States Navy. An anonymous 1842 pamphlet on naval reorganization characteristically declared that the American navy must not exact a "blind and crawling servility" from its recruits but rather promote a rational subordination which recognized, rather than violated, the basic civil liberties of Jack Tar.[69]

Although convicts were certainly not free men, prison reformers believed that the latter's discipline should reflect the republican principles of the nation as much as possible. It was in this context that the 1841 *Report* of the Boston Prison Discipline Society declared that "absolute . . . unlimited . . . despotic power are entirely inadmissible in the American Penitentiary System."[70]

Educational and domestic reformers believed that school and parental discipline should reflect the future citizenship status of American children. "Children of a republic," declared Mann in his *Ninth Annual Report*, should not be governed by "arbitrary power" but by means that are consistent with democratic principles. Teachers and parents, therefore, should substitute reason and moral suasion for corporal punishment.[71]

Antebellum reformers believed that the disciplining of individuals should be consistent with the democratic principles of the nation. Why, however, did reformers assume that corporal punishment violated these principles? Why did they perceive this punishment as despotic? Underlying this perception was a particular view of individual freedom.

Like many of their middle-class contemporaries, antebellum reformers believed that liberty from external constraints was the essence of freedom in a republic.[72] This view of freedom shaped reform attitudes toward a wide range of issues. The desire to liberate individuals by emancipating them from tight and cumbersome clothing, for example, prompted dress reform. One anonymous writer in the *Common School Journal*, hoped to be the "Wilberforce or Clarkson" that freed the child from the "slavery" of bounded waists and tight shoes and caps.[73] The analogy between dress reform and abolitionism suggested the resonance between these two seemingly disparate reform efforts. Like dress reformers, abolitionists sought to liberate individuals from physical restraints.

The equation of liberty with freedom from external restraints, however, limited reformers' awareness of other forms of oppression. As the recent historiography on abolitionism has pointed out, this view of freedom simultaneously prompted opposition to slavery while obscuring the oppression of another group— factory workers. Since the latter were not *physically* coerced into working, their oppression became less visible than that of slaves.[74]

Although the desire to liberate individuals from external constraints obscured certain kinds of oppression, it did highlight others, most notably slavery. This desire also prompted condemnation of corporal punishment. Significantly, critics of corporal chastisement often described this punishment as "slavish." Articles in major educational journals, for example, condemned corporal punishment as a "slavish" form of discipline, more befitting the "negro plantation," than the republican schoolhouse.[75]

The "slavish" and hence the oppressed condition of chastised victims became particularly apparent in Dana's description of his captain's despotism. Whip in hand, the latter screamed to his men:

> You see your condition! . . . I'll make you toe the mark, every soul of you, or I'll flog you all. . . . You've got a driver over you! Yes, a *slave-driver—a negro-driver!* I'll see who'll tell me he isn't a negro slave.

Dana noted that such punishment was particularly degrading for a white Southerner named Sam. Flogging "seemed completely to break down" Sam. He became quiet and withdrawn and significantly ceased one of his favorite pastimes—telling "Negro stories."[76]

Several concerns clearly motivated the naval, prison, domestic, and educational reformers who condemned corporal punishment during the antebellum period. These included the desire to alleviate pain and suffering and to safeguard the rights and liberties of chastised victims. The desire to insure social order by reforming the character of deviant individuals was another concern of these reformers. Seeking to develop a highly self-disciplined and nonviolent code of ethics in Americans, antebellum reformers urged the substitution of moral suasion for corporal punishment in disciplining children, seamen, and convicts.

Although antebellum reformers meshed together these various concerns, the last one— the desire to safeguard order by developing the moral character of deviant individuals—ultimately outweighed humanitarian objections to corporal punishment. Horace Mann perhaps best summarized the priorities of the reform campaigns against corporal punishment when he declared that:

> The primary question is not, whether we shall have punishment, or whether we shall not have it, ... but by what means we can best secure good order; and that punishment is useful or admissable only as a means to this end.[77]

It was this overriding commitment to insure "good order" which prompted most reform critics of corporal chastisement to demand the retention of this punishment as a "last resort." An 1834 article in the *American Annals of Education* offered representative advice. Although the author vehemently condemned teachers who relied on the whip and birch to discipline their students, he did not favor the immediate or total abolition of corporal punishment. "We are not ready to concede," he stressed, "that because corporal punishment is not useful to *drive in learning*; or because it may be wrongly administered, that it is not sometimes important (we believe very rarely) in subduing violent passion. . . ."[78]

These comments suggest that reformers ultimately took a utilitarian approach to corporal punishment. As Martin Pernick has recently observed, this reform approach toward punishment paralleled physicians' attitudes toward surgery in the mid-nineteenth century. Generally most reformers and physicians did not invoke absolute standards when they discussed the necessity for either painful punishments or surgery. Instead both groups sought to devise methods which minimized pain but did not jeopardize their chief objectives; the achievement respectively of moral discipline and physical well-being. A fundamental challenge for both groups, therefore, was to calculate the least amount of pain that was necessary in order to accomplish their respective objectives.[79]

The parallels between reformers' and physicians' cost-benefit approach to pain became particularly apparent when Mann compared corporal punishment to the poison which a physician administered to a sick patient. Although both corporal punishment and poison were usually bad, they were occasionally needed to "arrest a fatal malady" in a "diseased system." Corporal punishment, therefore, should be retained as a "last resort."[80]

Individuals from impoverished or immigrant backgrounds, believed reformers, were particularly likely to require punitive discipline. According to Mann, corporal punishment was occasionally necessary in schools which "scooped up" children from diverse backgrounds. "Contaminated" by "vicious parental example and the corrupting influences of vile associations," lower class urchins needed strict, sometimes punitive, discipline in the classroom.[81] Similarly, Dorothea Dix declared that the prison lash could not be abolished altogether since convicts were drawn from the lowest stratum of society.[82] Richard Henry Dana stated that naval captains must retain the *right* to inflict corporal punishment in order to discipline "ignorant foreigners" who were as familiar with the "knife" as with the "marline-spike."[83]

Another consideration which shaped reformers' responses to the abolition of corporal punishment was the gender of those chastised. A growing perception of females as the embodiment of gentleness, virtue, and tranquility made the chastisement of girls and women a particularly repugnant practice. Both Mann and Cobb, for example, denounced the whipping of schoolgirls as a particularly heinous and shocking practice.[84]

These comments notwithstanding, reformers believed that a minority of girls and women had allegedly unsexed themselves by engaging in violent and depraved behavior. Prostitutes and female criminals provided the most blatant example of such females. The fact that a significant number of these women were either black or impoverished immigrants made it easier to classify them as "fallen" and "unnatural" women.[85] Racial sentiments, for example, were particularly apparent when the inspectors of Sing Sing penitentiary described the prison's allegedly "depraved and abandoned" women convicts: "Many of them are blacks from the stews and brothels of our large cities, lost to all sense of shame and impervious to all good impressions."[86]

A similar view of women convicts prompted prison reformers to tolerate corporal punishment as a "last resort" in female penitentiaries. After an extended tour of the Ohio State Penitentiary in 1843–44, Gerrish Barrett, representative of the Prison Discipline Society of Boston, concluded that the horsewhip was occasionally needed to punish nine female convicts, three of whom were black, since they "fight, scratch, pull hair, curse, swear, and yell."[87]

Although New York prison inspector John Edmonds did not condone the whipping of female convicts, he did defend the use of the gag and strait jacket on Sing Sing female convicts. Like his friend Sing Sing prison matron Eliza W. Farnham, Edmonds believed that a minority of female convicts, especially immigrant and black women, were incorrigibly depraved and therefore required some form of corporal punishment. This belief became particularly evident when Edmonds defended the use of the strait jacket and gag on a "colored" female inmate who persistently resisted Farnham's system of kindness and who escaped from solitary confinement. Significantly, Edmonds described this woman as an aggressive and violent person whose first act after her escape was to viciously beat a white female inmate.[88]

Edmonds' comments suggest that most antebellum critics of corporal punishment harbored doubts about the efficacy of reforming *all* human beings. Ultimately they believed that a minority of individuals, especially impoverished, black, or immigrant offenders, would remain incorrigible. Corporal punishment, therefore, must allegedly repress such individuals from wrongdoing.

The antebellum reform campaigns against corporal punishment illustrate both the underlying anxiety as well as dominant optimism which characterized different reform experiments during the first half of the nineteenth century. On the one hand, antebellum reformers looked forward to an enlightened, progressive, and orderly society which dispensed with such "relics of barbarism" as the birch, whip, and rod. Continued anxiety about social order, however, prompted reformers to tolerate corporal punishment as a painful yet occasionally necessary way to maintain discipline.

Reformers' reluctance to abolish corporal punishment altogether suggests the need for a more detailed examination of the limits of the antebellum crusade against this punishment. Chapter 4 will explore these limits by examining antebellum middle-class attitudes toward the problem of wife beating.

Chapter 4
Wife Beating and the Limits of the Anti-Corporal Punishment Crusade

W HILE RECALLING her life in the slave state of Kentucky nineteenth-century abolitionist and suffragist Jane Swisshelm
described the pervasive cruelty of Southern slave dealers and
owners. Deceptively dressed as "gentlemen" in their "satin vests"
and "stove pipes," these men frequently whipped slave women.
In graphic detail Swisshelm recounted several particularly heinous examples of this common crime. After bearing her master
five children, one old slave woman was "flogged almost to death"
because she wept and protested when two of her sons were
sold. Slaveholders severely punished not only maternal love but
also female chastity. Several young beautiful quadroons, recalled
Swisshelm, were repeatedly lashed at the public whipping post
for refusing the amorous advances of their master. Not content
with this punishment, one jealous master also severely whipped
the slave suitor of his prospective concubine. Outraged by the
sufferings of female slaves, Swisshelm became an ardent abolitionist and moved to free soil where Christian men, not "women
whippers," lived.[1]

The physical cruelties endured by slave women provided
Northern abolitionists with a powerful indictment against the
"peculiar" institution of slavery. Abolitionist John Rankin in his
anti-slavery book, for example, described how a female slave was

"stripped shamelessly and wrongly flogged" for allegedly break-ing a piece of furniture.[2] Angelina Grimké also narrated cases of female slave whippings in Weld's *American Slavery As It Is*. She recalled, for example, how one Charlestown slave mistress had her young female servant "stripped naked" and publicly flogged at the local workhouse. The whipping was so severe, empha-sized Grimké, that large pieces of flesh were cut out by the "tor-turous lash."[3]

While Northern abolitionists denounced slaveholders' cruelty to black women, Southerners pointed out that "woman whip-pers" existed above the Mason-Dixon line. Northern white men, contended several Southern apologists for slavery, often beat not only their children but also their wives. One Southern clergy-man, for example, asserted that a "horrid examination" of New York City alone would reveal "more cruelty from husband to wife, parent to child, than in all the South from master to slave in the same time."[4]

Although Southerners levelled these charges in an effort to discredit mounting abolitionist attacks against slavery, wife beat-ing did occur in the Northern United States. Various sources, including divorce court records, newspaper articles, and per-sonal reminiscences, documented the existence of this problem in the nineteenth century.

Newspapers regularly reported violent family quarrels which resulted in the serious injury or death of the wife. Many of these cases involved drunken husbands. One article in the February 15, 1863 issue of the *New York Times*, for example, noted that an alcoholic husband had beaten his wife to death in New York by stomping and kicking her.[5] Several months later in July, the *Times* reported that another husband, a penniless drunkard, had shot his common law wife to death when she refused to get him a drink.[6]

Although these cases involved the "lower classes," the *Times* also reported cases of wife beating among "respectable," well-to-do people. On November 25, 1866, for example, the *Times* reported that the Second United Presbyterian Church of Pitts-burgh, Pennsylvania had excommunicated its minister, Dr. Pries-tley, because he had committed adultery and had behaved in an "unkind, cruel, and violent" manner towards his family. Dr. Priestley regularly kicked, choked, and spat at his wife, while calling her an "infernal bitch."[7]

Personal reminiscences of the friends and relatives of abused wives also suggested that wife beating occurred in all kinds of families. In her memoirs suffragist Susan B. Anthony recalled her efforts to aid the abused wife of a prominent and wealthy Massachusetts politician, a leader in the state senate. When confronted with evidence of his chronic philandering, this husband pushed his wife down the stairs. To avoid any further recriminations, he quickly committed his wife to an insane asylum.[8]

Although it is impossible to estimate what percentage of American wives in the nineteenth century suffered physical abuse from their husbands, available statistics on divorce for cruelty suggest that wife beating was a serious social problem. In the early 1880s, the Chief of the Bureau of Statistics on Labor provided divorce statistics for various states during the 1860–78 period. These statistics show that a significant percentage of divorces were for intolerable or extreme cruelty. Out of the 7,233 divorces granted during this period for a variety of reasons such as adultery, impotency, drunkenness and desertion, 2,949 were for cruelty, 375 for extreme cruelty, and 223 for cruel and abusive treatment.[9]

In an era when corporal chastisement was increasingly denounced as a "relic of barbarism," wife beating seemed a likely target for critics of the former punishment. Did antebellum Northerners, especially reformers, publicly condemn the beating of wives as they did the beating of other groups? Discussion of this question enables us to explore reform attitudes toward violence, punishment, and discipline in the most basic social institution—marriage. It also provides a comparative perspective on reformers' opposition to the corporal punishment of children, seamen, convicts, and slaves.

With these themes in mind, chapter 4 will explore the following issues: (1) the lack of consensus regarding what constituted marital cruelty and abuse in the antebellum period; (2) the relationship between the issue of marital violence and the Victorian cult of domesticity. In examining this latter issue, chapter 4 will discuss how prescribed views of women, marriage, and domesticity shaped Northern, middle-class attitudes toward wife beating from 1820 to 1861.

Any discussion of antebellum attitudes toward women must stress a crucial fact: Anglo-American religion, custom, and law historically promoted a wife's subordination and deference to her husband. Popular religious homilies on marriage in the seventeenth and eighteenth centuries repeatedly enjoined wives to obey the following Biblical injunctions: "Wives be subject to your husbands;" "The man shall rule over thee;" "Ye wives be in subjection to obey your husbands . . . for the husband is the head of the woman, as Christ is head of the church. . . ."[10] In a similar vein, popular tracts on domesticity such as Benjamin Wadsworth's *The Well Ordered Family* stressed husbands' superiority and authority within the home. Since the husband was the "head" of the family, wives were to "reverence and honour" their spouses and to esteem the latter as their "Superior."[11]

While sermons and marriage tracts prescribed wifely submission to patriarchal authority, Anglo-American laws legitimized women's subordinate status within marriage. According to William Blackstone's *Commentaries on the Laws of England* women became legally dead when they married: "By marriage the husband and wife are one person in law, that is, the very being or legal existence of women is suspended during marriage."[12] This common law precedent gave husbands tremendous power and control over their wives. Under common law husbands had a legal right to their wives' inheritance, property, earnings, and to any children born within the marriage.* Husbands also had ex-

---

*Throughout the 1840s and '50s wives did gain greater control over their property, especially inherited property. This development, however, did not necessarily reflect a growing advocacy of married women's legal rights. The passage of New York State's Married Women's Property Act in 1848, for example, reflected state legislators' desires to codify and modernize feudal property laws and to protect family wealth inherited by married daughters. For a fuller explication of these ideas, see: Peggy A. Rabkin, "The Silent Feminist Revolution: Women and the Law in New York State from Blackstone to the Beginnings of the American Women's Rights Movement." Ph.D. dissertation, State University of New York at Buffalo, 1975.

tensive control over their wives' persons. American jurist James Kent in his *Commentaries* perhaps best articulated this established legal view when he declared:

> But as the husband is the guardian of the wife, and bound to protect and maintain her, the law has given him a reasonable superiority and control over her person, and he may even put gentle restraints upon her liberty, if her conduct be such as to require it.... The husband is the best judge of the wants of the family, and the means of supplying them; and if he shifts his domicile, the wife is bound to follow him wherever he chooses to go.[13]

A husband's legal authority and responsibility for his wife, therefore, gave him extensive control over her person.

Indeed a husband's legal authority over his wife was so extensive that he even had the right to chastise her. Under the common law a husband could administer a "moderate correction" to his wife, in much the same way that he could "correct his servants or children." It is important to note, however, that British jurists began rejecting this conjugal right of husbands as early as the reign of Charles II.[14]

In the case of the United States, American courts generally did not recognize a husband's common law right to chastise his wife.[15] This was true even in colonial times. Significantly, the Massachusetts Bay Colony in a 1650 statute declared that "no man shall strike his wife, nor any woman her husband, on penalty of such fine not exceeding ten pounds for one offense, or such corporal punishment as the county shall determine."[16]

This early prohibition against wife beating should not obscure an important fact: the American judicial system did not offer much legal protection to abused wives in the colonial period. As Lyle Koehler has recently noted, New England colonies, including Massachusetts, did not deal severely with abusive husbands. In the few cases where such men were actually prosecuted and convicted, they usually paid a small fine or were admonished to reform.[17]

The liberalization of divorce laws in the Northern United States, which began in the late eighteenth century and continued throughout the nineteenth, suggests that courts became more responsive to the plight of abused wives. In response to the growing number of wives who petitioned their state legislatures for divorces from abusive husbands, various states, including Connecticut, Pennsylvania, Ohio, Indiana, and Illinois, made "extreme" or "intolerable" cruelty grounds for divorce by the 1850s.[18]

Ironically, however, these liberalized divorce laws illustrated the continued lack of adequate legal protection for abused wives. The wording of these divorce statutes demonstrates that American courts were reluctant to interfere in the conjugal relationship, even if it was to aid battered wives. The latter could get a divorce only if their husbands inflicted "intolerable" or "extreme" cruelty.

Ambiguity about what constituted legal cruelty also worked to the disadvantage of wives physically abused by their husbands. Joel Prentiss Bishop, one of the foremost nineteenth-century legal scholars on American marriage and divorce, noted that cruelty was not a term one could define in an "exact, comprehensive, and neat" fashion.[19] This fact notwithstanding, Bishop and other legal scholars sought to define cruelty by citing a landmark 1790 British decision, Evans versus Evans. Since this decision established the foundations for a legal definition of cruelty, it merits detailed examination.

Presiding Justice Lord Stowell began by noting that the causes for a divorce based on cruelty must be "grave and weighty." Indeed these causes must

> show an absolute impossibility that the duties of married life can be discharged. In a state of personal danger no duties can be discharged; for the duty of self-preservation must take place before the duties of marriage, ... but what falls short of this is with great caution to be admitted.

To underscore the need for a cautious interpretation of cruelty, Stowell offered the following caveat:

> Mere austerity of temper, petulance of manners, rudeness of language, a want of civil attention and accomodation, even occasional

sallies of passion, if they do not threaten bodily harm, do not amount ot legal cruelty.

For cruelty to occur, concluded Stowell, there must be actual violence committed with "danger of life, limb, or health" or a *"reasonable apprehension* of bodily hurt."[20]

As various scholars have noted, this milestone decision broadened the definition of cruelty in some cases while restricting it in others. Stowell's ruling that a "reasonable apprehension of bodily harm" could constitute cruelty enabled jurists to view abusive language which threatened violence as cruel.[21] At the same time Stowell's decision left unresolved a crucial question: when did corporal chastisement endanger life, limb, or health, and therefore constitute cruelty?

Significantly, several widely cited decisions in the antebellum period pointedly declared that not all acts of marital violence were necessarily cruel. Perhaps the most important of these decisions occurred in the 1819 New York case, Barrere versus Barrere. While discussing what constituted adequate grounds for divorce based on cruelty, Chancellor Kent made the following statement:

> Though a personal assault and battery, or a just apprehension of bodily hurt, may be ground for this species of divorce, yet it must be obvious to every man of reflection, that much caution and discrimination ought to be used on this subject. The slightest assault or touch in anger, would not, surely, in ordinary cases, justify such a grave and momentous decision. Pothier says (*Traite du Contrat de Marriage*, s.509) that a blow or stroke of the hand would not be a cause of separation, under all circumstances, unless it was often repeated. The judge, he says, ought to consider if it was for no cause, or for a trivial one, that the husband was led to this excess, or if it was the result of provoking language on the part of the wife, pushing his patience to extremity. He ought, also to consider whether the violence was a solitary instance, and the parties had previously lived in harmony.[22]

Kent's remarks suggest that various factors determined whether or not an act of violence constituted legal cruelty. Was the violence habitual? Was it severe enough to endanger a wife's life or cause her serious bodily injury? Was the husband provoked to violence by his wife's misbehavior? In elaborating on the latter question, Bishop declared that a wife who provoked her husband's violence through her own "ill conduct" could not "ordinarily complain with effect" unless the violence reached an "extreme point."[23]

To sum up the argument so far, antebellum jurisprudence was ultimately ambivalent in its response to marital violence. On the one hand, most states did not uphold the common law tradition which gave husbands the right to inflict a "moderate correction" on their wives. On the other hand, American jurists did not view all marital corporal punishment as cruel. Various factors, including the wife's own conduct, determined whether or not a husband's marital violence constituted legal cruelty.

Ambiguity in the legal definition of marital cruelty suggests that antebellum Americans did not always characterize a husband who chastised his wife as "abusive." An incident related by suffragist Emily Collins particularly illustrated this point. Collins noted that in her rural, "secluded" community of South Bristol, New York, wife beating was a common and accepted form of punishment in the 1840s. The example of a local Methodist preacher who beat his scolding yet hardworking wife revealed this community's acceptance of wife beating. Although this man regularly horsewhipped his wife, their neighbors, Collins stressed, never interfered. Rather than criticize this husband, the community continued to esteem him as a "worthy citizen."[24]

Why did Collins' neighbors view a man who horsewhipped his wife as a "worthy citizen" and not an abusive bully? Collins herself provided an answer to this question. She declared that a consensus on wives' marital subordination promoted this response to wife beating. According to Collins, even South Bristol's battered wives were resigned to their "hard lot," viewing marital chastisement as a husband's legal "privilege" and Biblical "duty."[25]

These remarks indicate that Collins' neighbors had a patriarchal view of marriage, one which believed that a wife belonged to her husband and was subject to his will. The obverse side of this view of wifely subjection, of course, was the belief that husbands ruled their wives in much the same way that they ruled their children. In both cases a man could allegedly inflict a limited, controlled amount of violence in order to "correct" a child's or a wife's misconduct.

In this context it is significant that the South Bristol community, including Collins, viewed the chastised preacher's wife as a scold. Given their patriarchal view of marriage, Collins' neighbors may well have concluded that a scolding wife provoked and perhaps even deserved her husband's violence.

By contrast, Collins viewed the preacher who beat his wife as an abusive tyrant. Collins' response, of course, is not surprising. As a feminist, she rejected the patriarchal view of marriage which girded her community's toleration of wife beating. Significantly, feminists who emerged as the most outspoken antebellum critics of wife beating were the most vehement critics of husbands' conjugal authority. Starting in the 1850s radical feminists, particularly Amelia Bloomer, Susan B. Anthony, and Elizabeth Cady Stanton, declared that wife beating was symptomatic of women's general oppression within marriage.[26] Stanton's feminist analysis of wife beating became particularly evident when she urged the New York State legislature to grant wives divorces from physically abusive husbands. In her 1861 address to the legislature, Stanton stressed that wives historically had been viewed as the "toy of man" and lived in "legalized slavery," defenseless against their husband's tyranny and cruelty. To remedy this injustice, Stanton urged the legislature to give wives a long overdue "deed to themselves" by broadening the grounds for divorce.[27]

Wife beating evoked different responses in the antebellum United States. In some communities like South Bristol, New York, entrenched patriarchal views toward marriage promoted tolerance for husbands who beat their wives. At the same time, antebellum feminists viewed wife beating as inherently abusive and symptomatic of women's oppressive domination within marriage. These varied responses to wife beating ultimately indicated fundamental differences of opinion regarding the legitimacy and extent of husbands' conjugal authority over their wives.

Keeping these latter differences in mind, let us discuss how Northern, middle-class Americans viewed the problem of wife beating in the antebellum period. A sketch of the changing nature of middle-class marriage provides the context for this discussion.

In the post-Revolutionary period, the marital relationship between middle-class husband and wife underwent a significant, if gradual, transformation. As Jay Fliegelman has most recently noted, various changes undermined a husband's patriarchal authority within the home, including his traditional conjugal authority.[28] Paralleling this development was the emergence of a companionate view of marriage, one which saw wives as their husbands' helpmates and partners, rather than as their subordinates. The changing nature of eighteenth-century New England funeral sermons suggests this shift from a patriarchal to a companionate model of marriage. Lonna Meyers Malmsheimer in her analysis of these sermons found that ministers in the late eighteenth century increasingly stressed mutual bonds of friendship and love between spouses rather than a wife's deference and subjection in marriage.[29] Changing marriage patterns during the post-Revolutionary period also indicate the development of a more companionate view of marriage. According to Daniel Scott Smith, free mate selection, based on romantic love and mutual compatibility, rather than arranged marriages, based on patriarchal authority, increasingly characterized late-eighteenth-century Hingham, Massachusetts.[30] In a similar vein, Herman R. Lantz in his content analysis of popular eighteenth-century New England magazines has suggested the erosion of a patriarchal view of marriage in the post-Revolutionary period. He found that a growing number of magazine articles during the 1741–94 period, especially those after the Revolution, stressed the importance of romantic love and personal happiness in marriage.[31] The conjugal bond between husband and wife was increasingly depicted as a loving partnership rather than an arranged hierarchical relationship.

How did Northern, middle-class Americans in the antebellum period regard these changes in the marital relationship? The popular didactic literature on marriage and domesticity suggests an answer to this question. Aimed primarily at Northern, middle-class readers, this literature simultaneously articulated as well as influenced the views of its audience. It therefore provides a particularly good index to its readers' attitudes toward marriage and domesticity.

Ambivalence about the decline of men's conjugal authority characterized most didactic works on marriage and domesticity. On the one hand, these works continued to uphold men's traditional authority over their wives. Catherine Beecher, for example, declared that women must take a "subordinate station" in domestic affairs since men were the "natural" heads of their families.[32] In a similar vein, William Alcott in his popular marriage manuals, *The Young Wife* and *The Young Husband,* declared that the patriarchal family was the "natural" and God-given state of society. In an early chapter entitled "Submission" in *The Young Wife,* Alcott particularly stressed the need for wifely submission to a husband's patriarchal authority. He declared that "reason, revelation, and nature" decreed a wife's obedience and submission to her husband.[33]

Although ostensibly committed to preserving a husband's traditional supremacy within the home, didactic writers on marriage and domesticity actually undermined a wife's submission by prescribing a companionate view of marriage. Beecher, for instance, popularized this latter view of marriage when she declared that women, including wives, were "intelligent, immortal being[s], whose interests and rights are *every way* equal in value to that of the other sex." Wives, therefore, were entitled to their husbands' respect, confidence, and love.[34] William Alcott's marriage manuals expressed similar views. Despite his injunctions on wifely submission, Alcott repeatedly portrayed wives as their husbands' helpmates, companions, and advisors.[35]

Through this latter view of wives Alcott transmuted the husband's traditional role of ruler into the more democratic one of guide. While discussing men's control over their wives in *The Young Husband,* for example, Alcott declared that the "art of bearing rule ... is to govern as if we governed not." In fact a husband's authority "hardly deserve[d] the name of *ruling*." Rather than being a ruler, a husband should suggest, not dictate, family affairs.[36]

By popularizing a companionate view of marriage antebellum family reformers promoted a high standard of conjugal conduct for husbands. Men were never to nag, much less tyrannize their wives into obedience but rather to treat their spouses with respect, consideration, and love. Husbands were also to consult their wives in all important matters. William Alcott's *The Young Husband* offered representative advice to newly married men. Convinced that the wife should be a "companion, an adviser, an educator . . . [and] a partner" to her husband, Alcott urged men to consult their spouses in the choice of a career, place of residence, and in all religious, moral, and family affairs. He also urged husbands to treat their wives with gentleness, patience, and affection.[37]

In a chapter entitled "Contests for Superiority" Alcott advised husbands to avoid quarreling with their wives, even when the latter wrongfully sought to govern her mate. Confident that "an uninterrupted gentleness, kindness, and gospel forebearance" would overcome a wife's desire "to bear rule," Alcott urged husbands to practice St. Paul's injunction to the Ephesians:

I beseech you . . . that ye walk worthy of the vocation wherewith ye are called; with all lowliness and meekness, with long suffering, forbearing one another in love; endeavoring to keep the unity of the Spirit in the bond of peace.[38]

In short, husbands, especially those of bickering, domineering wives, were to preserve domestic tranquility by practicing a "spirit of forebearance."

Although he offered representative marital advice, Alcott was one of the few didactic writers who discussed husbands' *actual* domination and mistreatment of their wives. In language that suggested a husband's sexual as well as domestic tyranny, Alcott declared that many men "devour[ed]" their wives' "personal identity." Rather than "deny themselves a momentary gratification," these men transformed their wives into the "merest slaves and drudges." In return for servile submission, overbearing husbands, continued Alcott, gave their wives only a "few caresses" and a "few kind words," just as some masters "patt[ed] and rubb[ed]" their "favorite horse ... after a day of the most abject and perhaps abusive treatment." Alcott concluded that these patronizing and infrequent gestures of thanks were a "poor return for high-handed robbery—the robbery of the immortal spirit."[39]

The persistence of a traditional patriarchal view of marriage allegedly underpinned husbands' continued mistreatment and tyranny of their wives. Alcott graphically illustrated this point when he cited the example of a gentleman acquaintance who viewed his wife merely as a "slave" and a servant to his wants. While discussing marriage with Alcott, this anonymous husband upheld a man's traditional patriarchal prerogatives within the family. For him, the sole duty of a wife was "to submit to the will of Providence and of her husband" in all things. A husband's unquestioned and complete authority within the home was the obverse side of this view of marriage. According to Alcott's acquaintance, the husband was to have supreme control over his family. Within the family domain, a man should be able to "eat or drink, ... to correct his children or to caress his companion," without outside interference. Given this view of patriarchal authority, the overbearing husband resented Alcott's marital advice to view a wife as a "helpmeet" rather than as a "slave." Such advice allegedly represented an unwarranted "meddling" into "things which an individual ought to be allowed to call his own."[40]

Throughout *The Young Husband* Alcott stressed that such a patriarchal view of marriage transformed what was normally a tranquil and loving conjugal bond into a tyrannical power relationship, much like that between master and slave. Patriarchal homes such as that of Alcott's acquaintance often became turbulent, unhappy, and occasionally violent. To illustrate these evil consequences, Alcott cited the example of Mr. L. Recall that Mr. L was a demanding tyrant at home who "brook[ed] no delay" in his domestic commands. Whenever his children did not readily obey him, Mr. L screamed and threatened them. At times this verbal abuse escalated into physical violence. Alcott recalled seeing Mr. L "fly into quite a rage" and "beat, strike and use

profane language" against his children. Not content with be-
rating his children, Mr. L also screamed at his wife, calling her
a "good-for-nothing trollop." Once he even threatened her with
physical violence, saying: "Eleanor, if you don't do better, I'll beat
you!"

Significantly, Alcott described Eleanor L as a model of Victorian femininity. She was a "delicate, sensible, well-intentioned
and virtuous woman."[41] By portraying Mrs. L in these terms,
Alcott helped to gain public sympathy for the mistreated wife.
Idealized views of women also encouraged readers to view husbands like Mr. L as petty tyrants or cruel bullies.

Not surprisingly, Alcott believed that husbands who physically
chastised their wives were inherently abusive. Such men allegedly degraded themselves to the level of savages or brutes. Husbands "who will inflict bodily pain on those whom it should be
their highest interest to treat with tenderness" were "brutes in
the shape of men."[42]

Alcott's description of violent husbands as "brutes" suggests
that middle-class Americans viewed wife beating as a horrible
deviation from the social norm popularized by didactic works
on marriage, namely, that husbands were the "natural" protec-
tors of their wives. What accounted for the allegedly unnatural
spectacle of husbands beating their wives?

Reform critics of corporal punishment believed that early exposure to violence promoted wife beating. Cobb, for example,
linked punitive school and parental discipline with marital violence. He rhetorically asked:

> Would any man, either drunk or sober, ever beat the *wife of his
> bosom*, if he had not been previously *HARDENED* by the sight of
> *whipping*, at home or at school? NEVER. How many men, who have
> been accustomed to see girls *beaten*, the same as boys were *beaten*
> by their fathers or teachers, have, in their angry moments, . . . *beaten*
> their wives, just as they would beat *men* with whom they may
> have difficulty, trouble or quarrel!"[43]

Cobb's remarks suggested that the persistence of a masculine
ethos of violence, one nurtured through the continued use of

corporal punishment in schools and homes, warped boys' moral character. These boys then became sadistic bullies governed by "evil passions." Wife beating was the tragic culmination of this vicious process of socialization.

Like other antebellum reformers, Cobb saw a close connection between violence and intemperance. Indeed he believed that "all *wicked men* ... when *drunk*, almost invariably *whip* [their] *wives* or *children*."[44] Wife and child abuse, therefore, reflected the persistence of an intemperate as well as violent male subculture in American society.

These comments illustrated the cultural context in which antebellum middle-class Americans viewed the problem of abusive domestic violence. Wife and child abuse allegedly occurred because there was a tragic deviation from the Victorian social ethic which viewed inner moral restraints as the essence of civilization. Liquor, of course, precipitated this breakdown in the moral order by depriving men of any control over their emotions and passions. Once bereft of self-discipline, men became capable of violent and cruel acts, including wife and child abuse. Alcott's description of abusive husbands as "brutes" underscored the Victorian belief that men who lacked control over their violent impulses had been degraded to the level of animals.

This belief, of course, also prompted public criticism of cruel schoolmasters, naval officers, and prison guards as "brutes." An idealized view of the family as the center of love and tranquillity, however, made a father's abuse of his children a particularly distressing occurrence. The image of a cruel, enraged father beating his child dramatically contradicted the cherished view of the parent-child relationship as a loving bond.

Antebellum middle-class Americans were even more appalled by husbands who beat their wives. Idealized views of domesticity and especially of women made wife beating a particularly repugnant example of abusive violence. Significantly, antebellum critics of wife beating invoked these idealized views to gain sympathy for battered wives. The writings of the most outspoken critics of abusive domestic violence—temperance advocates and feminists—illustrated this point.

Although most temperance writings did not explore how drunkenness precipitated abusive domestic violence, there was one group of temperance writers who did discuss this issue in the mid-nineteenth-century period. These were the Washingtonians, a society of reformed drunkards formed in 1840 and dedicated to the prohibition of alcohol. Significantly, the Washingtonians depicted abused wives as models of Victorian femininity. The testimonials of former drunkards, narrated in T.S. Arthur's *Six Nights with the Washingtonians*, provided typical descriptions of these women. A physician and former alcoholic, for example, praised his abused wife as a kind, gentle, pure, stoic lady who continually prayed for his redemption. Another former alcoholic recalled how he beat his "gentle, uncomplaining" wife. Eventually this martyr-like woman died of a broken heart.[45]

Portraying battered wives in such idealized terms, of course, helped to gain public sympathy for their plight. Feminists, the most outspoken public critics of wife beating, were well aware of this fact. Although critical of their society's prescribed role for women, feminists invoked an idealized view of their sex as "gentle" and "pure" to demand legal protection for battered wives.

Elizabeth Cady Stanton's campaign for liberalized divorce laws particularly illustrated feminists' ironic use of Victorian beliefs. As the foremost champion of both women's rights and divorce reform, Stanton skillfully intertwined feminist arguments with an idealized view of women to urge passage of laws which would grant divorces for cruelty and habitual intemperance. Recall that Stanton in her 1861 legislative address on behalf of divorce reform viewed wife beating as a blatant example of women's oppression within marriage. Wives allegedly lived in "legalized slavery," subject to their husbands' tyranny and cruelty.

Recognizing that feminist arguments might alienate an all-male legislature, Stanton shrewdly invoked idealized views of women and of the home in her legislative address. She portrayed battered wives as virtuous, gentle, and long-suffering women. Stanton stressed, for example, that cruel men often beat their virtuous wives as well as helpless children. Morally outraged by such cases of abuse, Stanton urged the legislature to emancipate gentle, defenseless women from unhappy, violent marriages.[46]

An idealized view of the family as well as of women suffused Stanton's advocacy of divorce reform. She repeatedly depicted restrictive divorce laws as a threat to the alleged sanctity and morality of family life. After rhetorically asking how the legislature could hope to build up "the family—that great conservator of national virtue and strength . . . in the midst of violence, debauchery, and excess," Stanton exclaimed:

> Can there be anything sacred, at that family altar, where the chief priest who ministers, makes sacrifices of human beings—of the weak and innocent? . . . Call that sacred, where innocent children, trembling with fear, fly to the corners and dark places of the house, to hide from the wrath of drunken, brutal fathers, but forgetting their past sufferings, rush out again at their mother's frantic screams, "Help! oh help!" Behold the agonies of those young hearts, as they see the only being on earth they love, dragged about the room by the hair of her head, kicked and pounded, and left half dead and bleeding on the floor! Call that sacred, where fathers like these have the power and legal right to hand down their natures to other beings, to curse other generations with such moral deformity and death!

Having posed these questions, Stanton quickly answered them. Concluding that only an atmosphere of "purity and peace" preserved the alleged sanctity of domesticity, Stanton viewed divorce reform as a way to further family stability.[47]

The efforts of antebellum feminists to help abused wives by invoking prescribed views of femininity and domesticity should not obscure several crucial facts. First, these prescribed views ultimately imposed a very constrictive ideology on women in general and abused wives in particular. The latter *had* to model their behavior after a narrow and distorted view of femininity in order to gain public sympathy and legal help. Even then abused wives gained only a partial and limited protection from their husbands. At most legal aid meant a separation or a divorce.*

---

*In the case of antebellum New York, the state legislature in 1860 narrowly rejected a liberalized divorce law. See Blake, *The Road to Reno*, pp. 76-79, for a discussion of New York legislative debates over divorce in the 1850s and 1860s.

Although these acts enabled *individual* wives to escape from abusive marriages, they did not confront, let alone resolve, the *social* problem of wife beating.

Feminist efforts to help battered wives should also not obscure another crucial fact. In comparison with reform efforts on behalf of chastised seamen, convicts, slaves, and children, there was relatively little public criticism of wife beating during the antebellum period. Idealized views of marriage and women imposed a crucial ideological barrier to widespread public discussion of wife beating. Unlike their attitudes toward other social relationships, most antebellum Americans idealized marriage as a sacred, natural, and indissoluble bond. *New York Tribune* editor Horace Greeley's response to Stanton's plea for divorce reform demonstrated this latter attitude toward marriage. Stanton's alleged view of marriage as "just another contract," asserted Greeley in a May 14, 1860 editorial, ignored the innate sacredness of this bond. "The thought that the marriage tie is of the same nature as a mere business relationship," continued Greeley, "is so objectionable, so dangerous, that we do not care to draw attention from that one point."[48]

Greeley's remarks highlighted the continued, widespread belief in the sanctity and indissolubility of marriage. This belief made most antebellum Americans reluctant to tamper with the institution of marriage, even if it was to redress the plight of abused wives. As free lovers Thomas and Mary Gove Nichols bitterly noted:

> Thousands of women suffer [abuse] where one complains. The ministry, the physician, or sometimes an intimate friend, hears of these things; but there is a deep *hush!* Respectability, and the sacredness of the marriage institution demand silence.[49]

In short, a view of marriage as a sacred ordinance and a basis for "respectability" blunted public discussion of marital violence.

The allegedly private nature of the domestic, especially marital, bond also hindered widespread public discussion of wife beating. Recall that most middle-class antebellum Americans viewed the home as a haven or sanctuary from the outside, public world. Given this view of the family, middle-class Americans were less likely to perceive, much less confront, the existence of *abusive* violence within this private institution.[50]

Committed to idealizing marriage and the family, domestic reformers must have been particularly unable to discuss the issue of marital violence. By its very nature the problem of wife beating threatened to explode the cherished myths cultivated by the canon of domesticity. It particularly contradicted this canon's idealized views of marriage. Violent husbands and their battered wives were a far cry from the loving, gentle, and happy spouses depicted in popular domestic works. Instead of strengthening this idyllic image of domesticity, wife beating graphically illustrated how an allegedly sacred, natural, and benevolent bond—that between husband and wife—could degenerate into a blatantly cruel power relationship.

Wife beating also refuted conventional marital advice to women. Popular works on domesticity and marriage had repeatedly portrayed wifely obedience and virtue as the key to women's happiness and authority within marriage. Pious, benevolent, and obedient wives almost invariably gained their husbands' respect, affection, and confidence in domesticity literature. Wife beating, however, contradicted this popular belief in wifely submission as a means of domestic influence. Gentle and virtuous, yet abused, wives poignantly revealed how husbands continued to misuse their marital authority. Despite the persuasive arguments of domestic reformers, abusive husbands treated their gentle and obedient spouses with violence and anger, rather than with tenderness and respect. Wife beating, therefore, highlighted the limitations and failures of domestic reformers' prescribed marital role for wives.

An underlying fear of man's uncontrolled, especially sexual, passions may also have hindered widespread public discussion of the problem of wife beating. Several students of Victorian sexuality, most notably Steven Marcus and Ian Gibson, have detailed Victorians' fascination with the sexual overtones of corporal punishment, especially in the form of whipping. Much of the pornographic Victorian literature, for example, seemed obsessed with sexual flagellation and dwelt on the sadomasochistic whipping of men and women.[51] Although such explicit association between violent punishment and sexuality were rare in "respectable" antebellum periodicals, recall that some reformers did explore how corporal chastisement aroused the sadism of those who administered, watched, and even received punishment.

Given the association of corporal chastisement with sadistic and uncontrollable human passions, the lack of public discussion of wife beating is not surprising. Since marital violence occurred within the context of a conjugal, essentially sexual relationship, the issue of wife beating threatened to make explicit the latent connection between violence and sexuality which most antebellum middle-class Americans either ignored or only obliquely acknowledged.

The failure of most antebellum reformers to discuss the problem of wife beating suggests the boundaries of the anti-corporal punishment crusade in the first half of the nineteenth century. Although critical of corporal punishment in most aspects of American life, most reformers were either reluctant or unable to confront this issue in the most basic social relationship, that between husband and wife. Unlike the corporal punishment of children, seamen, slaves, and prisoners, the issue of marital violence remained a largely unexplored social problem in the antebellum period.

It is important to keep in mind the moderation as well as limits of the antebellum reform crusade against corporal punishment. Recall that most reformers urged the gradual disuse or limitation, but not abolition, of this punishment. Through their moderate approach to disciplinary reform, reformers ultimately sought to straddle a middle ground between institutional officials who defended the unrestricted use of corporal chastisement and Northern public opinion which increasingly demanded the abolition of this punishment. Reformers' views on corporal punishment, therefore, were ultimately part of a spectrum of opinion regarding this punishment.

Chapter 5 will discuss the views of another group who publicly condemned corporal punishment—seamen- and convict-authors. Unlike most reform critics of this punishment, seamen- and convict-authors often experienced themselves the abusive treatment which they graphically depicted. Discussion of these authors' views on punishment and discipline, therefore, offers a comparative perspective from which to view the reform campaigns against corporal chastisement.

Chapter 5
A Victim's Perspective: Nineteenth-Century Seamen and Convict Writings on Punishment

I N AN APRIL 13, 1850 review of *White Jacket* the *New York Tribune* praised Melville for publicizing the cruel punishments administered aboard American men-of-war. Melville allegedly performed an "excellent service" in exposing the "indescribable abomination of naval life" which was "reeking with the rankest corruption, cruelty, and blood."[1] Melville's account of naval discipline seemed almost mild when compared to the writings of other seamen-authors. Former sailors vividly described a litany of cruel, arbitrary, and often illegal punishments inflicted aboard American men-of-war. In an 1841 exposé Solomon Sanborn, for example, detailed how naval officers cursed, beat, and flogged sailors for trivial or vaguely defined offenses such as "looking insolent" or answering an order in a tone louder than usual.[2] Another seamen-author William Murrell graphically described the brutality of Commodore George Read during the *Columbia's* 1838–40 voyage around the world. At one point Read severely whipped thirteen men, seriously ill from dysentery, because they failed to reef the sail quickly.[3]

Convicts offered similar descriptions of harsh, arbitrary punishment. An 1833 exposé of prisons, for example, corroborated Horace Lane's testimony about the abusive punishments administered in Sing Sing. It described how one inadequately fed prisoner suffered 97 lashes when he complained of hunger. Another man who allegedly received over 130 lashes for the same offense, fell to his knees and begged for mercy during punishment. The prison guard then gave him a severe blow across the mouth with a cane.[4]

Such exposés of abusive treatment reflected as well as capitalized on the widespread revulsion against corporal punishment during the antebellum period. The purpose of this chapter is to explore in greater detail these exposés and other published writings of antebellum seamen and convicts. Analysis of these writings enables us to view the issue of corporal punishment from the perspective of the victim. More specifically these writings enable us to explore the following questions: How did antebellum sailors and prisoners respond to the punitive practices of their respective institutions? How did these men regard the antebellum reformers who criticized corporal punishment?

Before exploring these questions a brief discussion of the lives and perspectives of seamen- and convict-authors is in order. First, it is important to remember that exposés such as William McNally's *Evils and Abuses in the Naval and Merchant Service Exposed* and James R. Brice's *Secrets of the Mount Pleasant State Prison* focused primarily on various abuses practiced in their respective institutions. By definition such works neglected other aspects of daily prison and naval life and therefore presented a skewed image of these institutions.

This comment notwithstanding, these exposés generally portrayed an accurate picture of naval and prison punishments. Various sources, including the writings of reformers and the annual punishment records of prisons and American men-of-war, corroborated the frequent use of arbitrary, cruel punishments in these institutions. Exposés written by former sailors and prisoners, therefore, can flesh out the picture of abusive institutional punishments which is emerging from various sources.

The representativeness, if not accuracy, of seamen- and convict-authors remains problematic for the historian. A comparatively high level of literacy distinguished these authors from most sailors and prisoners. Excluding this obvious difference, some writers tended to be more representative of ordinary seamen and convicts than others. Seamen-authors who made naval service a career, for example, were generally more representative of common sailors than were privileged young men like Melville and Dana for whom the navy was a temporary escape from familial and professional responsibilities.

Another factor, of course, which determined the representativeness of seamen- and convict-writers was their social background. Available biographical data suggests that many of these authors, unlike their comrades, came from middle and even upper class backgrounds. The most obvious example was Dana. A member of one of Boston's oldest and most prestigious families and a graduate of Harvard College and Law School, Dana clearly belonged to Boston's Brahmin elite. Although W. A. Coffey, author of an 1823 exposé on the New York State Prison at Newgate, did not come from such a prestigious background, he was a lawyer before being convicted of forgery.[5] Another convict-author, Colonel Levi S. Burr, was an army officer during the War of 1812.[6]

Not all seamen- and convict-authors came from middle let alone upper class backgrounds. Instead some writers came from backgrounds which were more typical of antebellum sailors and prisoners. One such author was Horace Lane. As noted earlier, Lane was a veteran of the British and American navies who subsequently served five years in Auburn and Sing Sing prisons for robbery. Judging from nineteenth-century prison surveys,[7] Lane's background was typical of antebellum convicts, many of whom had been sailors. Indeed his life suggests that both of these groups were drawn from the same social and economic class.

Lane's early life lacked stability or roots. His father was a farmer turned rafting pilot and lost what little money he had by keeping "bad company." Recall that Lane's mother died in 1795 when he was seven-years old. In his autobiography Lane significantly omitted any discussion of religion in his early life, suggesting that the church did not play an important role in his childhood. Lane regarded another institution, the school, as a nuisance. Like Huckleberry Finn, Lane preferred to roam in the woods and raft down the Hudson River rather than attend school.[8]

Lane resented efforts to check his vagabond ways. Significantly, Lane recalled that he was initially happy about his mother's death since all restrictions on his impulsive nature *seemed* to have been removed. His neighbors, recalled Lane, likened him to a young bear who roamed the woods, without a thought about the future.[9]

Not surprisingly, Lane's youthful stint as an apprentice cobbler was unsuccessful as were his efforts to farm or run a country store. It was not until he became a sailor at the young age of ten that Lane found an occupation which suited his restless nature.[10]

Lane's autobiography provides a fascinating insight into why young boys ran off to sea in early nineteenth-century America. Lane's memoirs also illustrate the close connection between intemperance and crime in the antebellum period. An alcoholic, Lane first became drunk on milk punch when he was ten-years old.[11]

Significantly, Lane was usually inebriated when he committed robberies. This pattern was established when he was still in the navy. Lane recalled, for example, that he and two shipmates stole some furniture from the backyard of a Dutch house when they were drunk.[12] Lane's alcoholism precipitated more serious robberies after his discharge from the navy. He spent three years in Auburn State Prison because he robbed a woolen factory while drunk.[13]

After his discharge from prison, Lane tried to become "respectable." He married a reputable young woman and worked at several jobs, including dockwork in Troy, New York. Despite these efforts, Lane quickly became impoverished. "Dull" economic times precipitated his unemployment, and a sick wife added to Lane's troubles. Desperate and distressed, Lane began to drink and steal again. Recognized as an ex-convict, Lane was quickly caught by the authorities and sentenced in 1830 to Sing Sing Prison for two years.[14]

Lane's memoirs poignantly illustrate the vicious cycle of alcoholism, poverty, crime, and imprisonment which marred the lives of so many antebellum laborers. Lane and other seamen-authors also graphically confirm what naval reformers repeatedly stressed—drunkenness and other alcohol related offenses were major causes of naval corporal punishment. The reminiscences of James Garrison, brother of the noted radical abolitionist, particularly illustrated this point. Like Lane, James Garrison was an alcoholic sailor who repeatedly suffered the lash because of drunkenness and other liquor related offenses. On one occasion, for example, Garrison received two dozen lashes because of intoxication. Another time an officer accused Garrison (falsely according to him) of smuggling liquor on board ship. For this offense Garrison received twelve lashes and was placed in double irons for twenty-eight days.[15]

Given the havoc that alcohol played with seamen's lives, one would expect seamen-authors to advocate temperance. In some cases this did occur. Like reformers, McNally, for example, singled out the grog ration as one of the leading obstacles to a sailor's moral reformation and urged its prohibition.[16]

Other seamen-authors, however, defended alcohol as a needed source of comfort and solace for sailors. Lane offered a particularly vivid account of the joys as well as dangers of grog in his autobiography. Alcohol, he contended, made a sailor's "heart leap for joy." Liquor also enabled a sailor to "drown" his loneliness. Lane recalled that he himself began drinking to escape feelings of depression and loneliness. Alcohol also provided an "ecstatic" escape from the hardships of seafaring life. A drunken sailor was able to feel his "soul ... expand its wings and rise from the earth."[17] No wonder, then, that sailors like Lane and Garrison did not support reform efforts to abolish the navy's grog ration.

Reform efforts to "uplift" sailors through religion and education also provoked a range of responses from seamen-authors. An individual's social background colored, if not determined, his response to these reform efforts. Seamen-authors who came from the middle or upper class were particularly likely to support reform programs. Dana, for example, not only supported but also participated in reform efforts to improve seamen's moral character through education, temperance, and especially religion. While praising religious services aboard seafaring ships, he declared that: "If there is on earth an instance where a little leaven may leaven the whole lump, it is that of the religious shipmaster."[18]

The upper-class bias behind these remarks became particularly evident when Dana declared that the gradual moral improvement of sailors must precede, not follow, their more just treatment by naval officers and the courts. "An intelligent and respectable man of the lower class," confidently predicted Dana, "almost always" got just treatment from his superiors.[19]

Seamen-authors who came from "lower class" backgrounds were less likely to share Dana's sanguine view of naval justice or middle-class reform. Jacob Hazen, who was an impoverished journeyman shoemaker before he joined the navy, bitterly resented reform efforts to "uplift" sailors. The sight of "lady" missionaries distributing religious tracts to seamen particularly upset him. These ladies, resentfully asserted Hazen, were incapable of understanding the "injustice and degradation" which ordinary sailors experienced. Seeking to shock, if not enlighten, one lady, Hazen told her that his soul was damned and that officers' frequent cursing contributed to a sailor's degradation.[20]

Hazen's example notwithstanding, seamen-authors did not have to come from impoverished backgrounds to resent reform efforts to "uplift" them. Harvard graduate Nathaniel Ames, who shipped out to sea at the age of nineteen and later authored several books on seafaring life, resented reformers' condescension toward sailors. He particularly resented the patronizing tone of reform journals like the *Sailor's Magazine*. This periodical, declared Ames, was written in a style which was "too puerile [and] too silly" for five-year-old children, let alone sailors.[21]

The comments of Ames and Hazen suggest that they regarded reformers as patronizing, ill informed, and insensitive. Convict-author John Reynolds, who published an 1839 exposé of Vermont's Windsor Prison, viewed reformers as cruel and inhumane. These reformers' advocacy of solitary confinement, declared Reynolds, vehemently condemned convicts to lives of mental anguish and unrelieved loneliness. Reformers also allegedly neglected discharged convicts.[22]

Significantly, Reynolds also accused prison reformers of promoting the very punishment which they publicly opposed—

flogging. This accusation underscored Reynold's dislike of the penitentiaries which reformers helped to establish. By separating convicts from one another and from the public, penitentiaries allegedly placed prisoners at the mercy of cruel guards who frequently whipped them. "Solitary cells and flogging," stressed Reynolds, "go hand in hand."[23]

Convict- and seamen-authors did not always share the perspective of reformers. Not surprisingly, important differences in tone and emphasis distinguished these two groups' writings on corporal punishment. Whereas reformers stressed how this punishment hindered effective social discipline, seamen- and convict-authors emphasized humanitarian objections to chastisement.

These authors stressed that flogging humiliated its victims. Burr, for example, recalled that whipping crippled a man's spirit as well as his body. Burr poignantly illustrated his point when he described one prisoner after punishment. "The man was humbled, his spirit was broken, he was dejected and cast down, his ambition was gone, and he appeared to fail very fast."[24]

Convict- and seamen-authors also stressed the humiliation which they and their comrades felt while witnessing punishment. Seaman-author Charles Nordhoff, for example, recalled the "feeling of dark humiliation" which he experienced when he saw "the manhood ... scourged out of a fellow creature."[25] The fact that sailors traditionally enjoyed a reputation for "manliness"* undoubtedly exacerbated Nordhoff's sense of humiliation while witnessing punishment.

Seamen- and convict-authors also paid particular attention to the excruciating pain which flogging caused. Hazen, unjustly whipped because of a case of mistaken identity, gave a vivid description of his punishment:

I heard only a confused murmur, and a rushing sound, while a heavy blow descended on my back, suspending my breath, and

---

*For a more detailed discussion of how the concept of manliness shaped attitudes toward naval flogging, see chapter 6.

penetrating every fibre of my body with a pain more excruciating than if molten metal had been poured upon me, seething and scorching my flesh to the very marrow.[26]

A range of responses characterized the men who endured this painful punishment. Melville recalled that one sailor named Peter screamed "My God! Oh! My God!" during punishment and "howled, leaped, and raged in unendurable torture." Peter's shipmate Antone cursed loudly during his flogging and later threatened to kill the captain; while a third victim named John, endured the lash with defiant bravado, declaring: "D—n me! It's nothing when you're used to it! Who wants to fight?"[27]

In discussing the reactions of men who witnessed punishment, seamen- and convict-authors occasionally noted what reformers also observed, namely, that whipping aroused the sadistic impulses of some spectators. Recall that Dana felt "excited" as well as horrified by witnessing flogging. Hazen's shipmates also *seemed* to experience sadistic pleasure during punishment. After watching a particularly bloody flogging, these sailors eagerly awaited the next victim, which was Hazen himself.[28]

Like reformers, seamen- and convict-authors also explored how harsh, frequent corporal punishment "hardened" an individual's sensibility toward human suffering. Hazen noted that when he first witnessed punishment he was "deeply agitated." Indeed he almost cried during the whipping of a young deserter. Hazen significantly added, however, that he gradually became inured to the sufferings of lashed victims, and could witness punishment with the "stoicism of an American Indian."[29]

Although Hazen's ultimate reaction to corporal punishment seems callous, it might also have been prudent. Seamen and convicts who sympathized too closely with lashed victims risked getting punished themselves. Dana's captain, for example, flogged a sailor named John because he asked why his friend Sam was punished.[30]

The fact that John intervened on Sam's behalf illustrates another point which seamen- and convict-authors repeatedly stressed: compassion, not callousness, characterized the response of *most* sailors and prisoners toward whipped victims. Sing Sing convict James Brice, for example, sympathized with fellow prisoners who had been whipped until their flesh was "as raw as a piece of beef" and their backs "smelled of putrefaction."[31] Similarly, Murrell felt compassion for a "poor marine" whose back was "absolutely cut to pieces" for some trivial offense.[32]

Compassion for flogged men seemed to lessen, if not transcend, whatever class differences existed between victim and spectator. This was certainly the case with convict-author W. A. Coffey. A former attorney, Coffey was often hostile and patronizing toward his fellow prisoners. Most convicts, he declared, were "debased and profligate in the extreme" and therefore beyond any hope of reformation.[33] Coffey also contemptuously noted that convicts were generally "ignorant and unlettered" men who stood in awe of those who possessed the most basic knowledge. For this reason one prisoner who had a "smattering of English Etymology" acquired the reputation of being an "eminent grammarian" even though he knew as much about syntax as "the most enlightened monkey in the island of Borneo."[34]

Despite Coffey's contempt for his fellow inmates, he was still able to sympathize with their sufferings. Coffey admitted that his "feelings of indignation and compassion" were aroused by the sufferings of men who were subjected to cruel punishments such as the lash, the yoke, and the block and chain. When he witnessed such punishments, recalled Coffey, he forgot the convicts' "vices" and instead remembered that they were "human" and therefore entitled to sympathy.[35]

Although reformers had expressed similar sentiments, convict- and seamen-authors did so from a different perspective. Irrespective of their social backgrounds, these authors shared the same rank and status of their fellow sailors and prisoners. They were therefore subject to the same abusive treatment as their comrades. This was true even in cases where a man could expect protection from punishment because of his familial or social connections. While in Sing Sing, James Brice, for example, enjoyed the protection of General Van Courtland who regularly visited him and also got him extra rations. Despite Van Court-land's protection, however, Brice still suffered the lash.[36]

Often enduring the very punishments which they described, convict- and seamen-authors could draw on their own personal experiences when they described the sufferings of flogged victims. Understandably compassionate toward these victims, seamen- and convict-authors usually described the inflictors of punishment in angry and bitter terms. Seamen-authors felt particularly hostile toward midshipmen who summarily whipped sailors and therefore ignored naval regulations which prohibited punishment without the explicit approval of the commanding officer. Writing under the pseudonym Tiphys Aegyptus, one sailor, for example, denounced midshipmen as tyrannical, incompetent, arrogant, and spoiled youngsters.[37] Nathaniel Ames shared these sentiments and wondered why sailors should have to suffer the "pain and disgrace" of the lash "at the hands of every little tyrannical brat of a midshipman that the naval service is . . . disgraced with."[38]

Not surprisingly, the cruelty and sadism of officers was a particularly prominent theme in the writings of seamen- and convict-authors. Recall Dana's graphic description of his captain's sadism or Lane's description of the cruel guards in Sing Sing.[39] The sadism of prison guards and naval officers allegedly prompted them to inflict punishment without any provocation or cause. Brice, for example, recalled that a guard named Joseph Perry devised a particularly bizarre daily ritual of punishment. Perry would arbitrarily select one or two prisoners for public whipping. Several other inmates would then drag the intended victim into the prison hall and flog him for allegedly winking or smiling.[40]

Convict- and seamen-authors also stressed that officers often combined cruel punishments with humiliating ones. James Garrison offered a graphic illustration of how naval officers humiliated sailors when he recalled the actions of Matthew C. Perry aboard the *North Carolina* in 1824. Then a young lieutenant, Perry allegedly devised a particularly humiliating punishment for two men found guilty of urinating on deck. Both sailors not only received thirteen lashes each but were forced to rub human excrement into their own face and eyes.[41]

The revulsion which seamen- and convict-authors felt toward punitive officers like Perry cut across class lines. Dana and Melville, as well as Garrison and Hazen, angrily condemned naval officers who whipped and humiliated sailors. Similarly, convict-authors, irrespective of their social background, vehemently denounced the cruelty of prison guards.

This last comment notwithstanding, class sentiments did color the attitudes of some convict-authors toward prison guards. Coffey, for example, hated his prison guards because he perceived them as social inferiors* as well as cruel. Seemingly more contemptuous of guards than convicts, Coffey described the former in particularly vicious terms. Prison guards were allegedly

impudent and ignorant rustics, just escaped from some filthy cowyard, or *infected* debauchees, or *daily-wasting* drunkards, but one solitary remove from the poisonous reptile, that grovels from life ... into an ... unlamented nihility ... and who are acquainted with nothing but the grossest vulgarity.[42]

Coffey's remarks underscore how class sentiments fueled his hatred of prison guards. Indeed Coffey believed that the brutality and cruelty of these guards reflected their lower-class background. Since he was "the sewer-menial of the people ... disgusting in aspect [and] pitiful in conduct," a guard was therefore "sanguinary in heart."[43]

Like other convict- and seamen-authors, Coffey also portrayed lash-wielding officers as intemperate and debauched men. Indeed Coffey contended that guards often whipped convicts while under the "revelry of brandy and water."[44] Seaman-author Sol-

---

*Available biographical evidence on prison keepers indicates that most were farmers, laborers, and artisans before becoming guards. See, for example, "Examination and Evidence, Accompanying Assembly Document No. 135, made to the Legislature, January 29, 1839," esp. pp. 1–26, in New York State Assembly, *Report of the Commissioners Appointed Under the "Act Concerning State Prisons,"* Assembly Document No. 135, vol. 2, 58th sess.

omon Sanborn also stressed the connection between the cruelty and intemperance of officers. Somewhat smugly Sanborn noted that an alcoholic lieutenant who regularly cursed and flogged men became so "beastly" drunk that he fell overboard and drowned.[45]

Reformers, of course, had also noted the existence of debauched and certainly cruel naval and prison officers. They were usually reluctant, however, to publicize the failings and vices of officers in general. By contrast, seamen- and convict-authors stressed that cruelty and depravity were the rule, not the exception, among their respective groups of officers.

The way that these authors and reformers depicted officers revealed a great deal about their respective attitudes toward the navy and penitentiary. Recall that prison and naval reformers ultimately sought to improve, not undermine, these institutions. They were therefore understandably reluctant about portraying prison and naval officers as *generally* cruel, depraved men. To do this would tarnish the reputation of institutions which reformers sought to enhance. Significantly, reformers often tempered their criticism of individually abusive officers by declaring that such men blemished the record of institutions which were basically sound and useful.

Compared to reformers, seamen- and convict-authors were much more critical of their respective institutions. These writers often portrayed the navy and penitentiary as *inherently* tyrannical and cruel institutions. Indeed they believed that the alleged tyranny of these institutions made cruel, abusive punishments inevitable. Recall, for example, John Reynold's condemnation of prisons. The unrestrained power which these institutions gave to guards, stressed Reynolds, made the abusive treatment of convicts inevitable since men always misuse absolute authority.[46] Penitentiaries, therefore, were inherently cruel as well as despotic. Perhaps Burr best captured this dual criticism of penitentiaries when he described Sing Sing Prison as a "cat-ocracy and cudgel-ocracy."[47]

In a similar vein, seamen-authors depicted the navy as a despotic as well as cruel institution. Significantly, these writers often described the navy as an absolute monarchy. James Durand expressed representative sentiments when he declared that "no monarch in the world is more absolute than the captain of a man-of-war." Consequently captains were free to indulge whatever tyrannical or sadistic desires they had.[48]

Seamen- and convict-authors obviously resented the tyranny and cruelty which allegedly pervaded their respective institutions. The writings of these two groups suggest that sailors and prisoners responded in different ways to mistreatment. Convict-authors usually stressed the suffering and endurance, rather than rebellion, of their fellow prisoners. They did this not only to gain public sympathy for the convict but also because they realized that prisoners could do relatively little to protest or escape their condition. Separated from one another at night, forced to labor in silence during the day, and surrounded by heavily armed guards, convicts found it difficult to plan, let alone execute, escapes or mutinies. Since all mail was censored and visits from outsiders either prohibited or carefully monitored, convicts rarely publicized their mistreatment while still in prison. Most of them would probably not have wanted to in any case since they would then be subject to persecution by prison officers.

The writings of seamen-authors suggest that sailors had more opportunity to protest, escape, and rebel against their mistreatment. Unlike convicts, seamen could desert while on furlough. Sailors also had a legal way out of their seamanship. They could simply refuse to reenlist. Nordhoff, who chose this option, recalled his initial reaction after finishing his first term of duty and arriving home:

> *Free* at last. Then first came the full realization . . . that I was once more my own master, and with the feeling, I half involuntarily straightened myself, and threw back my shoulders, as though to fling off the long-borne yoke.

Deciding that he "had had a surfeit of bondage," Nordhoff resolved never to join the navy again.[49]

Nordhoff's decision, of course, illustrated what naval reformers worriedly noted, namely, that punitive, despotic treatment discouraged Americans from joining the service. Like reformers, seamen-authors stressed that the allegedly "slavish" punishment of flogging particularly dissuaded Americans from joining the navy. Sailor Roland Gould expressed representative sentiments when he denounced the cat-o'-nine tails as a "species of torture" which degraded American freemen to slaves. Gould then rhetorically asked:

> What American, who feels the noble impulse of freedom throbbing in his bosom, would ever consent to rivet the chains of slavery upon himself? The clanking of the chains which have been riveted on the few native seamen, who are found in naval service, has served to deter others from selling their birthright for a mess of pottage.[50]

The remarks of other seamen-authors confirmed reformer's fears that frequent or harsh use of the lash provoked mutiny. Durand, for example, recalled how frequent punishment transformed the well behaved crew of the *Constitution* into sullen, rebellious men. With the ship near Malta, angered by junior officers' frequent abuse of the lash, the crew stopped a lieutenant from beating a sailor who had refused to strip for punishment. When the enraged lieutenant ordered the ships' marines to fire upon the rebellious crew, the former refused. Officers then got their swords and pistols and stood guard. Only the return of the captain prevented bloodshed. Crew members complained to their captain that during his absence men had been flogged even though their time of service had expired. The crew then gave the captain an ultimatum: they would proceed quietly back to the United States under his direction or else they would take over the ship![51]

In sharp contrast to reformers, seamen-authors often approvingly noted sailors' rebellion against cruel officers. Indeed some of these authors participated in and even led such rebellions. Hazen, for example, was the alleged ringleader of one crew which protested frequent floggings by refusing to do any work.[52]

Hazen's actions highlight an important point: unlike reformers, seamen- and convict-authors often subordinated the issue of order to that of humane and just treatment for themselves and their comrades. Richard Henry Dana, one of the few seamen-authors whose concern with order ultimately outweighed his humanitarian objections to the lash, underscored how an individual's social background, as well as institutional rank, shaped his response toward corporal punishment. Recall that Dana, despite his privileged background, had been able to feel a sense of camaraderie with his fellow seamen aboard the 1834–36 voyage of the *Pilgrim*. This camaraderie was evident when Dana angrily noted how his captain flogged a man "whom I had lived with and eaten with ... as a brother."[53]

Dana's attitudes toward flogging and seamen, however, were ultimately quite complex. Abused seamen evoked his condescension as well as sympathy. Meanwhile a desire to punish abusive captains while upholding their authority characterized Dana's response to naval punishment. These paradoxical views became particularly apparent in Dana's first published work, an October 1839 article in the *American Jurist* which condemned Judge Joseph Story's leniency in a much publicized incident of cruelty, the Nichols Case. In 1839 the captain of a Massachusetts merchant ship, Captain William Nichols and his first mate William Couch beat to death the ship's former cook, Henry Burr, because the latter failed to "lay hold" of a reef-tackle. Upon their return to Massachusetts Nichols and Couch were arraigned, tried, and convicted of "unjustifiably beating" Burr with "malice, hatred, and revenge." Judge Story, the presiding Justice, however, gave Nichols and Couch extremely light sentences. Citing Nichols' youth, reputed good character, and family responsibilities, Story gave the convicted captain a ninety-day sentence and a one-hundred-dollar fine. Couch received a thirty-day sentence and a ten-dollar fine.

Although Story was one of Dana's instructors at Harvard Law School, Dana's article in the *American Jurist* criticized Story's ruling in the Nichols Case. Dana declared that this ruling did not sufficiently punish Nichols. Several concerns lay behind Dana's demand for more severe punishment of the cruel commander. First, Dana's comments reflected a humane concern for abused sailors and their families. Story's Court, noted Dana, cited Nichols' family responsibilities as a basis for lenient sentencing, yet disregarded the poverty and sorrow endured by families of maimed or killed sailors.

These remarks also suggested Dana's concern for judicial impartiality. Dana believed that the Story Court harbored an unjust bias against common seamen. To substantiate his point, Dana cited the Court's lack of confidence in seamen's testimony as well as its leniency toward abusive commanders. Ironically Dana's article in the *American Jurist* revealed his own bias against sailors. He patronizingly argued that seamen were usually reliable court witnesses because they were too "ignorant to be artful." Dana, therefore, viewed Jack Tar with condescension as well as sympathy.

Fears that abused sailors might threaten naval order also characterized Dana's response to the Nichols Case. Like naval reformers, Dana feared vigilante justice by disaffected seamen. He warned that cruel commanders must be legally punished in order to prevent vengeful sailors from committing mutiny.[54]

Dana's commitment to naval order, as well as his view of seamen, made him reluctant to abolish flogging altogether. Recall that Dana warned against "ignorant foreigners" who were as familiar with the "knife" as with the "marline-spike." Since these sailors allegedly understood only force, Dana believed that captains must retain the right to use corporal punishment. Indeed Dana in his 1840 book, *Two Years Before the Mast*, declared that he did not want to diminish the captain's authority by "an iota."[55]

Dana's remarks suggest an important caveat: historians should not assume that all seamen- and convict-authors necessarily favored the immediate prohibition of flogging and other forms of corporal punishment. Various factors, including an individual's social background, his length of naval service or imprisonment, and his attitudes toward his fellow sailors or prisoners, shaped a man's response toward the abolition of physical chastisement.

This caveat notwithstanding, convict- and especially seamen-authors were more likely to demand the complete prohibition of the lash, than reformers were.[56] This fact in turn underscores the moderation of reformers who generally sought the limitation or gradual disuse, but not immediate abolition, of corporal punishment.

Despite their professed moderation, reform critics of corporal chastisement provoked opposition from institutional officials, most of whom resisted efforts to restrict this punishment. In an 1846 letter to prison reformer Louis Dwight, Elisha Johnson, warden of the Connecticut State Prison at Wethersfield, expressed representative views among his colleagues. Johnson warned against the development of a uniform code of prison discipline which would limit the use of corporal punishment. He stressed that wardens and keepers must be able to administer a wide range of punishment in order to fit the disciplinary needs of particular institutions and prisoners.[57] Charles Northend, principal of a local school in Salem, Massachusetts, offered similar advice in a lecture before the American Institute of Instruction. Northend declared that the widely diverse conditions of local schools demanded that teachers retain broad discretion in matters of discipline.[58] Naval officers also defended their right to inflict punishment. Significantly, most of the eighty-six officers who responded to a January 1850 naval circular on corporal punishment strongly favored the continuation of existing naval regulations on flogging and warned against interference with their traditional prerogative to whip seamen.[59]

Although parents sought advice on childrearing and discipline, they too resented any encroachment on their traditional authority to chastise their children. Recall that an acquaintance of William Alcott resented the "meddling" of domestic reformers. Within the family domain, a man should allegedly be able "to correct his children" without outside interference.[60]

Those who resented reform efforts to regulate or limit corporal punishment were not necessarily cruel or tyrannical. Instead hostility to disciplinary reform indicated particular institutional and cultural concerns. What were these concerns and how did they foster a defense of corporal punishment? Chapter 6 explores these questions by focusing on particular antebellum controversies over corporal punishment.

Chapter 6
A House Divided:
Public Debates Over
Corporal Punishment,
1843–1852

I N 1843 THIRTY-ONE Boston Schoolmasters formed an Association to protest the educational reforms proposed in Mann's *Seventh Annual Report*, especially his advice to substitute moral suasion for corporal punishment in public schools. Although they shared Mann's belief that the development of internalized moral restraints was the primary aim of school discipline, these thirty-one teachers viewed corporal punishment as a way to achieve this goal. Corporal punishment, they argued, was a "moral act" which initiated "reflection, . . . self-examination and finally conviction of wrong-doing."[1]

While the Association of Boston Schoolmasters defended the use of schoolroom corporal punishment, Southern legislators advocated the continued practice of flogging in the United States Navy. During a series of 1848–50 and 1852 Congressional debates over naval flogging, Southern legislators declared that this punishment was an effective and necessary way to discipline sailors.[2]

Favorable remarks on corporal chastisement provoked rejoinders from critics of this punishment. Mann, for example, engaged in a vituperative debate with the Association of Boston Schoolmasters during the period 1843 to 1845. Similarly, Northern Congressional critics of naval flogging, led by New Hampshire Senator John Parker Hale, debated this issue with their Southern colleagues.

Both sets of debates merit detailed investigation for several reasons. First, each debate illuminated different dimensions of the anti-corporal punishment crusade. The debate between Mann and the Association illustrates how the desire to safeguard traditional local autonomy in the face of emerging centralized, bureaucratic institutions shaped discussions of discipline and punishment in antebellum America. The controversy over school discipline also indicated how sectarian differences between orthodox Calvinists and liberal Christians, especially Unitarians, shaped attitudes toward punishment. Meanwhile the 1848–50 Congressional debates over the abolition of naval flogging, as well as the 1852 debates regarding Southern legislative efforts to reinstate this punishment, illuminate how sectional and political divisions over slavery shaped discussions of corporal punishment.

Although two seemingly disparate controversies, the antebellum debates over naval flogging and school punishment merit comparative analysis. Such analysis reveals that Boston Schoolmasters and Southern legislators shared common ideals, emotions, and worries when they defended corporal punishment. The debates over naval and school punishment, therefore, reveal the underlying cultural concerns of those who favored as well as those who opposed corporal punishment in antebellum America. More specifically, these debates illustrate how differences over the nature of man, God, and society suffused questions of discipline and punishment. Finally, a comparative analysis of publicized debates over school and naval discipline highlight the extent of public opprobrium against corporal punishment. To appreciate the wider significance of these debates, however, we must first discuss the immediate contexts in which they occurred.

On one level the corporal punishment debate between Mann and the Boston Schoolmasters reflected a wider dispute over educational reform. Members of the Association were masters of Boston's secondary writing and grammar schools. Joshua Bates, Jr., the recognized leader of the Association, for example, was master of the prestigious Brimmer School in Boston for over a third of a century.[3]

The common school reform movement, however, threatened these teachers' traditional prestige and authority. By stressing the need for professionally trained teachers, educational reformers implicitly questioned the adequacy of an earlier generation of schoolmasters, including members of the Association. Reformers' attempts to centralize and streamline the public school system also jeopardized the traditional status of local teachers. An 1845 Boston School Committee Report on schools, for example, recommended the abolition of Boston's traditional "double headed" system of instruction, which taught reading and writing under different masters.[4] The implementation of this recommendation would abolish the positions of several of the "thirty-one," while increasing the workload of the others.

Not surprisingly, the Boston Schoolmasters ardently opposed reforms which threatened their professional status. Bates and his colleagues criticized various educational reform programs during their pamphlet war with Mann. Mann's pet projects, infant and monitorial schools,* were allegedly "vain" and "worthless" experiments which undermined a student's deference and subordination.[5] The Thirty-one schoolmasters, however, reserved their harshest criticism for reformers' efforts to professionalize teachers. They claimed that the current emphasis on Normal School training was undermining public confidence in "old time," "practical" teachers.[6] Somewhat defensively, the Association denied the need for professionally trained educators. The "sturdy lad . . . who *teams it, farms it, peddles, keeps a school* . . . [and] feels no shame in not studying a profession" was worth a hundred "city Dolls" with their "untried theories."[7] The Association also opposed the impetus towards a centralized school system. In 1845 they spearheaded the formation of the Massa-

---

*Infant schools were popularized by Robert Owens in Great Britain in the early 1800s. These schools were designed for small children, aged two to five, and taught the uses of common things by conversation rather than by books. Monitorial schools used older children as monitors to teach and watch younger children.

chusetts Teachers Federation which sought a "local" and "voluntary" solution to educational problems.[8]

The "Thirty-One" viewed disciplinary reform as the climax of an insidious conspiracy against nonprofessionally trained local schoolteachers like themselves. By stressing the frequent use of corporal punishment in Boston schools, Mann was allegedly "poisoning" the public mind against "teachers of the *old* school."[9]

A valid perception lay behind these accusations. Critics of corporal punishment did call into question the professional competency of those who inflicted punishment. An anonymous 1845 defender of Mann, for example, accused Association members of professional incompetency. The thirty-one schoolmasters and their supporters were "narrowed down conservative[s], obsolete in matter and manner; by nature and by habit ... opposed to progress in knowledge, lest it should disturb [their] antiquated notions of truth and propriety."[10] Since they were allegedly incompetent, the "Thirty-One" were unable to govern a classroom, except by widespread reliance on corporal punishment. One of their grammar schoolteachers, the author pointedly asserted, exceeded an average of sixty-five floggings per day.[11]

The corporal punishment debate between Mann and the Boston Schoolmasters crystallized and exacerbated educational disputes over teachers' professional competency and local autonomy. This debate also intensified the ongoing denominational feud between liberal Christians and orthodox Calvinists for control of the public schools. Members of the Association were staunch supporters of orthodox Calvinism. Religious orthodoxy played a particularly prominent role in Bates' background. His father, Reverend Joshua Bates, Sr., was a well-known Congregationalist minister and President of Middlebury College in Vermont. In 1803 he received some notoriety for defending his colleague and friend, Reverend John Coldman, when the latter refused to exchange his pulpit with a clergyman of liberal views. Like his father, Bates, Jr. was a staunch Calvinist who became a Congregationalist minister in later life.[12]

The Association's staunchest supporters were also ardent Calvinists. One such supporter, Reverend Leonard Withington, for

example, was a noted Congregationalist minister who defended
Calvinist theology in various books and essays.[13] Another supporter of the Association was Reverend Matthew Hale Smith, a
former Universalist minister who became an outspoken expo-
nent of Calvinism after his conversion in 1829.[14]

Horace Mann's Unitarian beliefs, of course, were in sharp contrast to the religious views of the Association and their supporters. Significantly, Mann's staunchest supporters in the 1843–
45 pamphlet war shared his religious views. Educator George
Barrell Emerson, author of a pamphlet defending Mann's *Seventh Annual Report*, espoused a vague, liberal Christianity which
stressed God's benevolence in nature;[15] while Mann's other leading supporter, Dr. Samuel Gridley Howe, was a Unitarian.[16]

The Unitarian beliefs of Mann and other educational reformers
angered orthodox Calvinists. Apprehensive about the erosion of
religious orthodoxy in New England, Calvinist ministers and educators viewed Mann's appointment to the Massachusetts Board
of Education with alarm. Religious hostility between Mann and
Calvinists formally began over the issue of sectarian schoolbooks
in the common schools. The controversy started when Mann
refused the offer of Frederick A. Packard, editor of the American
Sunday School Union publication, to insert doctrinal Calvinist
texts in the common school libraries. Although an 1827 law specifically prohibited the use of sectarian books in public schools,
orthodox Calvinists attacked Mann's decision as illegal and anti-
religious. Stressing Mann's Unitarian affiliations, Calvinists condemned his position as sectarian. In banning books that taught
the concept of innate depravity, Mann was allegedly foisting
Unitarian ideas on the common schools.[17]

From the beginning, the larger controversy over sectarianism
shaped the debate over punishment and discipline. The Association and their supporters repeatedly denounced Mann's proposed reforms in school discipline as a sectarian conspiracy
against orthodox Calvinism. Reverend Matthew Hale Smith was
particularly adamant about this point. Equating liberal Protestantism with irreligion, Smith denounced common school reformers, especially Mann, as atheists who blasphemously sought
to spread "impiety and irreligion" by banning the rod and the

Bible in the schools.[18] Smith reiterated these charges in an exchange of letters with Horace Mann. Mann's "theory" of punishment, argued Smith, was based on a blasphemous "sectarian assumption." Mann assumed "the native purity of children in opposition to the Bible, which asserts that our race are 'by nature children of wrath.'" This blasphemy merited God's righteous and awful retribution. Smith contended that an angry "avenging Jehovah" would punish meddling reformers who had presumptuously set his "ark upon a new cart," just as he had "smote" Uzzah for touching the ark.[19] In short, dire consequences awaited Mann and other advocates of disciplinary reform.

Angered by these charges of blasphemy, Mann quickly denounced Smith, portraying him as a dogmatist who tried to impose his sectarian beliefs on others. Common schools, Mann asserted, should instill "not my religion, nor yours as *such*, nor the religion of any class or sect, but the religion of the Bible."[20] While ostensibly taking a nonsectarian approach, Mann refuted Smith's views on punishment by attacking his Calvinist beliefs in human depravity. After stressing that Smith based his defense of the rod "on [the] strict Calvinist grounds . . . of total depravity," Mann urged a more benevolent view of human nature. Although he conceded that children were not ultimately pure, Mann stressed that they did have the "capacity for all that is good and noble." Without this capacity, men could never be saved. How could anyone, Mann asked rhetorically, be "the recipient of truth, if he has not the capacity to receive it . . . ?" After impaling Calvinism on the horns of this dilemma, Mann posed another one. If *all* children were *totally* depraved, they must all be flogged. To except the obedient child meant thwarting God's law.[21] The Calvinist doctrine of human depravity, therefore, inevitably produced frequent and universal floggings. Since this practice violated common sense, Calvinist views on human depravity must be abandoned.

Disputes over religious orthodoxy and educational reform suffused the 1843–45 controversy over corporal punishment. This latter controversy, however, was not merely a continuation of other conflicts. Disagreements over the professional training of teachers, the emergence of an educational bureaucracy, and the erosion of religious orthodoxy were ultimately symptomatic of a more fundamental dispute over social change. A closer look at the Association's views of antebellum reformers will clarify the nature and significance of this latter dispute.

The Association and their supporters repeatedly accused Mann of being a "come outer," one who rejected all external authority as an obstacle to individual perfectionism. "Scholiast," the anonymous critic of the 1845 Boston School Committee Report, for example, declared that Mann's theories of discipline were a "virtual endorsement of [the] system of social, civil, and religious licentiousness [of the] . . . 'come outers' [who] are now endeavoring to subvert all authorities."[22] In a similar vein, Reverend Leonard Withington accused Mann of being a "nonresistant" and "no-government" man who sought to abolish all jails and sheriffs as well as corporal punishment.[23]

Such remarks were ironic given Mann's fervent commitment to an orderly, stable society. On one level of course these remarks served a polemical function. They were designed to discredit an influential critic of the Boston Schoolmasters by raising the spectre of anarchism. A particular vision of social order, however, also promoted the Association's charges against Mann. The Boston Schoolmasters and their supporters viewed "unconditional surrender" to hierarchical authority as the only safeguard against widespread insubordination. Man's "highest duty," they emphasized, was to worship God and to obey all "rightful authority, wherever it exists in the great chain, from the highest to the lowest." This obedience must be an "entire, unqualified submission." In fact the "subjection of the governed to the will of one man" was to be so complete that the former's will was ideally submerged within the "will of the ruler."[24]

Important differences in emphasis, if not in kind, distinguished such a view of order from that of Mann's. Unlike the Association, Mann tempered his commitment to order with a concern for the rights of children. He preferred a voluntary compliance, rather than an abject submission, to legitimate authority. Such views were heretical to Association members. Mann's concern for an individual's rights as well as for his duties undermined the belief that "true obedience" meant "unconditional surrender." Mann's "theories" of discipline, then, were allegedly anarchistic because they threatened to undermine a hierarchical view of absolute authority.

This charge of anarchism illustrated another belief of the Boston Schoolmasters, namely, that external, punitive restraints were essential to the preservation of order. The legacy of Calvinism, with its belief in innate human depravity, was crucial in promoting this attitude toward discipline. Unlike Mann, Association members did not believe that moral suasion could effectively govern either children or adults. Convinced that human beings, including children, were born with a "lower nature" of "base" passions, the Association believed that natural inclination to evil had to be repressed through physical punishment. For this reason the "Thirty-One" urged teachers to "save" "bad boys" from the "dungeon and the halter in maturer life" by dutifully punishing them now.[25]

Ironically the Association's staunch advocacy of a hierarchical order based on absolute submission and enforced through corporal punishment suggested the increasing defensiveness of their world view. In their pamphlet war with Mann, the "Thirty-One" and their supporters denounced various social and cultural changes which were undermining their beliefs. Smith's *The Bible, the Rod and Schools* perhaps best illustrated this hostility to change. Often reading like a Puritan jeremiad, Smith's sermon perceived a dangerous decline in American morals. He argued that the spread of intemperance, gambling, prostitution, theatregoing, and "Sabbath desecration" was transforming New England, especially Boston, into a sinful and dissipated society. Ironically the professed foes of this immorality, "pseudo philanthropists," promoted rather than checked this dissipation. To illustrate his point Smith singled out for criticism the rapidly growing temperance movement. Temperance societies had allegedly become the "handmaid of impiety," filled with members who "desecrated" the Sabbath by holding their meetings on Sunday and who denounced "old friends" as "sectarian" when the latter rightfully argued that God would damn sinful drunkards. Horrified by these developments, Smith concluded that the temperance movement was now identified with "sabbath desecration" rather than with pious moral reform.[26]

Smith also accused social reformers of disregarding the "whole weight of tradition [and] history." Reformers were destroying "all that is stable, tried, and true" by arrogantly substituting their untried "visionary theories" for the "sound doctrines" of antiquity.[27] Such a process allegedly threatened the social order. Elaborating on this point, Smith blamed the "extravagant innovations" of reformers for the apparent increase in crime. Forgetting man's innate depravity, reformers now sympathized with the criminal rather than with the victim and denounced the parent, teacher, or judge who rightfully sought to punish the offender. As a result of this misguided philanthropy, "bad men" brazenly committed offenses at the expense of law-abiding citizens. The future was even grimmer. Smith dolefully predicted that America would soon become a "paradise for rogues" and a haven for atheists.[28]

Smith's pessimistic vision of the world ultimately suggested a deep alienation from the changes occurring in the antebellum Northeastern United States. The very changes which Smith decried—the trend towards a more anthropocentric Christianity, the evolution of evangelical societies into mass reform movements, the rise of various urban leisure activities, and the increase of social problems—highlighted the United States' transformation into an increasingly secular, urban, and complex society. Given their commitment to a hierarchical and theocentric world view, Boston Schoolmasters and their supporters viscerally condemned this transformation, equating change and instability with moral decline.

It was in this context that Smith and the Boston Schoolmasters attacked Mann's efforts to substitute moral suasion for corporal punishment in the classroom. Mann's proposed reforms allegedly furthered as well as reflected the social and cultural changes which Smith and the Association decried. The latter's defense of corporal punishment, therefore, represented a defense of an eroding social order, one characterized by a belief in innate human depravity, submission to hierarchical authority, and the systematic use of corporal punishment.

The Boston Schoolmasters and their supporters were not the only ones who viewed reform campaigns against corporal punishment as an insidious attack on traditional notions of order, authority, and human nature. The Southern legislators who defended naval flogging during the 1848–50 and 1852 Congressional debates over this issue expressed similar sentiments. An analysis of these debates, therefore, is in order.

From the beginning, the Congressional debates over naval flogging revealed the increasing sectional hostility between North and South over the issue of slavery. The success of the United States' nationalistic foreign policy of "Manifest Destiny" generated sectional tensions in the mid-1840s. America's acquisition of Southwestern territories, especially Texas, after the Mexican War, invariably raised the issue of the expansion of slavery into the newly acquired territories. The controversial Wilmot Proviso of 1846 which sought to prohibit slavery from any of the territories acquired in the Mexican War and the ensuing public debates over the annexation of Texas and California brought to the fore unresolved political and moral issues regarding slavery. Increasing sectional rivalry between the North and South in the late 1840s was particularly evident in the United States Congress, where representatives began to divide along sectional, not party, lines on the question of the expansion of slavery. The 1846–47 Congressional debates over the organization of the new territories especially illustrated this sectional division. While Northerners such as Columbus Delano of Ohio warned the South that a cordon of free states would ignite the "fires of liberty" in slave territories, Southerners threatened to secede from the Union rather than jeopardize the institution of slavery.[29]

The Congressional debates over naval flogging occurred in this context of sectional rivalry. Significantly, Hale and other leading Congressional critics of naval flogging were antislavery Northern Democrats and Free Soilers, many of whom later became Radical Republicans. Recall that Hale was a particularly staunch and controversial antislavery advocate. After being read out of the Democratic Party in 1845 because of his refusal to vote for the annexation of Texas, Hale became a Free Soiler and later a well-known Radical Republican. As the first United States Senator to be elected on an antislavery ticket, Hale was a particularly outspoken critic of slavery in the Senate. In 1847, for example, he moved to abolish slavery in the District of Columbia, denounced the Mexican War as a Southern conspiracy to expand the institution of slavery, and condemned the gag rule prohibiting the introduction of antislavery petitions in Congress.[30] Besides Hale, the leading Congressional critics of the lash included Hannibal Hamlin, the Democratic Senator from Maine who later served as Lincoln's Vice President during the Civil War; Salmon P. Chase, a Free Soiler from Ohio and later a leader of the Radical Republicans; John M. Niles, Democratic Senator from Connecticut who joined the Republicans in the early 1850s.[31]

As noted earlier, these Senators denounced naval flogging in much the same way that they condemned slavery. Corporal punishment on the high seas was a "relic of feudalism and barbarity," a "barbarous custom," a "bloody record of legalized brutality from the past." Like the institution of slavery, naval flogging was a "reproach" to civilization and Christianity, a "stumbling block" to the progress of an "enlightened humanity."[32]

A particular world view suffused Northern legislators' objections to both flogging and slavery. They generally envisioned society as a collection of free individuals operating within a highly competitive, democratic, market oriented economy. According to Eric Foner, Radical Republicans such as Hale were particularly committed to an ideology of "free labor" which viewed an individual's freedom from external constraints either in economics or politics as the sine qua non of economic growth, upward mobility, and republican liberty.[33]

This ideology of free labor had an important impact on Northern Republicans' attitudes toward discipline. Committed to a belief in individual freedom, Republican leaders advocated a particular kind of social control, one based on internalized, voluntary restraints rather than on external coercion. Like a growing number of middle-class antebellum Northerners, Republican leaders generally equated individual freedom with self-government. Voluntarily imposed self-restraints were the "web of civilized society."[34]

It was in this context that Northern legislators denounced flogging. Like slavery, this punishment represented a coercive system of discipline which a democratic society had allegedly outgrown. It was such a perspective which lay behind repeated condemnations of flogging as a "relic of barbarism."

The Congressional debates over the abolition of this punishment revealed important sectional differences of opinion regarding naval punishment. Significantly, Southern legislators such as the head of the Naval Appropriations Committee, Senator David Yulee of Florida; former Naval Secretary and North Carolina Senator George Badger; and North Carolina Representative Abraham Watkins Venable were Hale's leading opponents in the 1848–50 and 1852 Congressional debates over naval flogging.[35]

Like their Northern counterparts, Southern legislators injected the issue of slavery into these Congressional debates. Venable, for example, viewed Hale's efforts to abolish corporal punishment in the navy as part of a broader "species of fanaticism" and "hyperphilanthropy" currently "rife" in the North.[36] Similarly, Representative Thomas Stanhope Bocock from Virginia declared that the campaign against naval flogging represented another radical "ism" from the North, similar to "socialism, . . . Fourierism . . . [and] abolitionism. . . ."[37]

Like the Association's description of Mann as a "come outer," these comments served an obvious polemical function. Southern legislators sought to discredit critics of both flogging and slavery by portraying them as fanatical radicals. Southerners who portrayed their opponents as radicals, however, also revealed a good deal about their own attitudes toward human nature and social order. Like the Boston Schoolmasters, Southern legislators who defended flogging advocated a hierarchical society, one characterized by submission and deference. Yulee, for instance, stressed that life consisted of a series of reciprocal relationships between superiors and inferiors; between parent and child, teacher and student, master and apprentice, slaveowner and slave, commander and sailor. Envisioning these relationships in essentially authoritarian terms, Yulee declared that naval commanders, like the "master of a school or the father of a family," must have "arbitrary power" over their subordinates in order to fulfill their respective responsibilities.[38]

A pessimistic view of human nature lay behind these remarks. Echoing the sentiments of the Boston Schoolmasters, Southern legislators declared that fear and punishment were necessary to restrain innate human depravity. Convinced that punishment was needed to check a "spirit of evil," Badger, for example, declared that "all wise and just governments, act by the double influence of hope and fear, by the application at one time of reward, at another time of punishment.[39]

Pessimistic about human nature in general, Southern legislators had a particularly low opinion of sailors. South Carolina Senator Andrew P. Butler characteristically declared that many seamen had "vicious and wicked" natures.[40] Many sailors were allegedly lazy as well as depraved. Venable, for example, argued that sailors, like the newly arrived Irish immigrants, were often lazy men who needed the threat of severe punishment in order to work. In a pointed criticism of an often cited substitute for corporal punishment, confinement in irons, Venable declared that seamen often welcomed this latter punishment since it excused them from hard work.[41]

Venable's association of sailors with Irishmen indicated not only a bias against Jack Tar but also against foreigners. Often these biases fused together since a growing number of American seamen in the antebellum period were newly arrived immigrants. While defending the naval lash, Maryland Representative Alexander Evans stressed that a growing number of seamen were not native-born Americans but rather foreigners. Many of these "foreign" sailors were allegedly "worthless men, scandalous jailbirds ... who require the strong hand of power laid upon them continually."[42]

Southern legislators' nativist bias against foreign-born seamen exacerbated their concern for naval discipline. They warned that abolition of flogging would seriously undermine, if not destroy, this discipline. Evans, for example, argued that a relaxed code of naval discipline inevitably encouraged individual disobedience. This insubordination could quickly escalate into wide-spread mutinous behavior among the crew. According to Evans, "each mutinous man [was] a pestilent plague spot, spreading his miasma until at length the whole crew becomes corrupted." Insubordination, therefore, was a "terrible and dangerous contagion" which must be suppressed at its "very inception" through harsh punishment.[43]

Evans and his Southern colleagues believed that flogging was necessary to maintain not only naval discipline but also social order. Opponents of this punishment, therefore, were anarchists bent on subverting all order and stability. Venable succinctly expressed these views when he accused critics of naval flogging of "pour[ing] contempt on those institutions which . . . restrain the unholy passions of men." Venable warned that if these critics succeeded, the republic would "dissolve in its own filth and corruption."[44]

Venable's remarks highlighted Southern legislators' commitment to established institutions and practices. Not surprisingly, these legislators invoked the shibboleth of military tradition to justify the continuation of naval flogging. Both Yulee and Badger stressed that the naval cats were sanctioned by "long usage." They had existed "for more than half a century" and had allegedly stood the test of time and experience.[45] Senator Butler shared these views. Equating change with moral declension, Butler viewed the proposed reforms in naval discipline as a sign of America's growing corruption and "sickly sentimentality." The "false philanthropy" of the present age, declared Butler, was a far cry from the "practice of our hardy ancestors."[46]

Butler's comments underscored the resonance between Southern legislators' defense of naval flogging and the Association's defense of school corporal punishment. Filiopietistic views of the past, fear of impending anarchy, and the association of reform with moral corruption characterized both of these groups.

Butler's praise of America's "hardy ancestors" also suggested another important theme in Southern legislators' defense of flogging. These legislators believed that the lash was a "manly" punishment, particularly suited to disciplining proud, hardy, and

virile men. According to Senator Jefferson Davis from Mississippi, sailors resented reform efforts to prohibit the lash since
this was a distinctly masculine and therefore appropriate punishment for seamen: "Tell the sailor that he is unable to endure
the punishment of a sailor, and he resists with . . . manly pride."[47]

Underlying these comments was a traditional concept of masculinity which historians have yet to fully discuss.[48] For our purposes it is important to note one particular aspect of this concept
of masculinity, namely, the belief that virile or "manly" men sto-
ically endured physical pain. Not surprisingly, soldiers and sailors, traditional models of virility, were expected to display a
particularly high degree of stoicism in the face of painful punishments or injuries.[49]

It is important to note that antebellum discussions of "manly"
behavior occurred in a context of anxiety over the loss of masculine strength and virility. This anxiety, of course, was apparent
in popular advice manuals to young men which warned against
the loss of male virility through sexual overindulgence.[50] Popular
plays, songs, and novels which juxtaposed effeminate, foppish
men to hardy farmers or frontiersmen also suggested Americans'
underlying anxiety about the loss of manliness. One stanza from
the nostalgic nineteenth-century broadside "Adam And Eve"
evoked this anxiety:

The dandies now look slim and pale,
Once they look'd hearty, fresh and hale;
Their voices sound like a squeaking fiddle,
And they're small as a wasp around the middle!
Singing, Heigho, I grieve, I grieve, for the
  good old days of Adam and Eve.[51]

Recent scholarship suggests that antebellum Southerners may
have been particularly concerned with the issues of effeminacy
and manliness. Recall that the Southern code of honor placed
particular stress on cultivating the "manly" virtues of physical
prowess, strength, valor, and aggression. As Bertram Wyatt-Brown
has most recently observed, anxiety about the lack or loss of
manliness and therefore of honor shaped every aspect of an-

tebellum Southern life. Fear of effeminacy, for example, shaped Southern childrearing patterns. Parents encouraged their young male children to behave in an aggressive, even belligerent manner. The masculine code of honor, with its underlying fear of effeminacy, also prompted Southern men to participate in traditional male activities like hunting, drinking, dueling, and wenching.[52]

Southern anxieties about emasculating and therefore dishonoring American men shaped the Congressional debates over naval flogging. Significantly, Southern legislators associated the anticorporal punishment campaign with effeminacy. This association became particularly evident when Senator James Alfred Pearce from Maryland discussed one proposed substitute for naval flogging—public ridicule of sailors by dressing them up as women. "Manly" sailors allegedly preferred the lash to this emasculating and therefore humiliating punishment. To demonstrate this point, Pearce noted how one old sailor committed suicide rather than subject himself to the disgrace of wearing women's clothes.[53]

Northern legislators vehemently denied that sailors preferred the lash to other punishment. Significantly, these legislators argued that sailors opposed the lash precisely because they were men. Hale, for example, declared: "I know that the sailor is a man, and that I am a man; and knowing these things, it would be enough to demonstrate to me that the sailors do not want it [flogging]."[54]

Underlying these remarks was a particular ideal about what constituted "manly" behavior. Hale ultimately believed that no "manly" sailor would ever voluntarily relinquish his basic personal freedom and rights. Indeed a true man would valiantly fight to keep his personal liberty, even if it meant rebelling against lawful authority. For this reason Hale declared that as long as "sailors are men, and have the feelings of men," they would mutiny against tyrannical, abusive treatment.[55]

The association of manliness with personal freedom promoted condemnation of flogging. The lash was a distinctly unmanly punishment because it completely deprived a sailor of any liberty. Publicly stripping, spread eagling, and whipping a man dramatized his complete and humiliating subservience to another individual in much the same way that slaves or domesticated animals were subservient to their respective masters. Given this perspective, it is not surprising that critics of the lash noted how flogging whipped the "manhood" out of a sailor.[56]

During the Congressional debates over naval flogging Northern legislators argued that the alleged emasculation of Jack Tar seriously impaired the navy's military effectiveness. Sailors who lost their sense of manhood through whipping acted like cowards, not brave fighting men. New Jersey Senator and former naval commander Robert F. Stockton articulated this belief when he declared: "Degrade a man by an infamous punishment, which destroys his personal honor and self-respect, and you do all that human ingenuity can to make him cowardly."[57]

Stockton's comments suggest that Northern legislators invoked the traditional concept of masculinity espoused by their Southern opponents. Far from rejecting the need for the allegedly masculine virtues of courage, strength, and fortitude, Northern legislators argued that these qualities were essential to maintain military prowess. Unlike their Southern colleagues, however, these legislators contended that the lash destroyed, rather than cultivated, these "manly" qualities.

Stockton and Hale sought to discredit their Congressional opponents by portraying the lash as an unmanly punishment. Other critics of corporal chastisement, especially those in educational and domestic reform, associated this punishment with masculinity, if not manliness. Unlike Southern legislators, however, these critics believed that the allegedly masculine nature of corporal chastisement discredited, not vindicated, this punishment. Hostility toward traditional notions of masculinity fueled reformers' critical view of chastisement. Recall, for example, domestic reformers' advice to substitute gentler, feminized forms of discipline for the allegedly masculine and barbaric "iron rule" of punishment.

Underlying this advice was an exuberant vision of moral progress. Antebellum reformers believed that the spread of allegedly feminine values like gentleness and pacifism would further a glorious, civilized era. Not surprisingly, antebellum reformers urged women to lead campaigns against not only corporal punishment but other forms of violence. *The Moral Advocate*, for example, declared that women were the "ministers of Grace and Peace" and therefore should lead campaigns against war and slavery.[58]

Openly advocating the spread of allegedly feminine principles like pacifism, of course, was particularly problematic for Hale and his Congressional supporters. Given the widespread belief that "manly" virtues were essential in the military, Northern legislators had to persuade the public that the abolition of naval flogging would strengthen, not undermine, these virtues.

Despite different public responses to conventional notions of masculinity, critics of corporal chastisement did agree on one crucial point: this punishment was a cruel and outdated method of discipline, a "relic of barbarism." The common ground which different critics of corporal punishment shared enabled them to respond in similar ways to those who defended this punishment. Significantly, both Mann and Hale accused their respective opponents of thwarting progress toward a more civilized way. Mann, for example, declared that the Association's philosophy of "Authority, Force, Fear, [and] Pain" threatened to transform a progressive society into a "frozen midnight where the light of love is extinguished and all moral sentiments and humanity are congealed."[59] Similarly, Hale declared that those who invoked a "hoary headed" tradition, "covered with cobwebs of age," merely thwarted needed social reforms and human progress. Exasperated by his Southern colleagues' filiopietism, Hale declared:

> I am sick to death of going back to the dusty and dead past, digging among the monuments of the Government from which we spring [sic], to find and bring up causes and apologies for trying to keep up these remnants of barbarity still longer.[60]

Tradition, therefore, did not offer a legitimate argument for maintaining corporal punishment.

In answering their critics, Mann, Hale, and their supporters reiterated an important theme in reform writings: a system of discipline based on moral suasion was the key to human progress because it cultivated the moral character of individuals. By contrast, corporal punishment undermined order by arousing the proscribed emotions of anger and revenge.

Paraphrasing his earlier writings on punishment, Mann, for example, declared that corporal chastisement instilled only a superficial obedience since it repressed but did not reform students. In fact physical punishment undermined order by arousing the proscribed emotions of "sullenness, irreverence, fraud, [and] lying." In short, corporal punishment promoted rather than prevented disorder by making students more disobedient and unmanageable.[61] Similarly, Senator John M. Niles declared that the feelings of "mortification [and] degradation" aroused by flogging "tended to produce mutiny and combination." "What acts of cruel and fearful retribution," rhetorically asked Niles, could vengeful sailors "not commit upon [their] superiors?"[62]

These arguments revealed the full scope of Hale's and Mann's opposition to their critics. Ultimately these men and their supporters believed that defenders of corporal punishment posed a double threat to American society. The continued defense of this punishment threatened the nation's progress toward a more orderly as well as more humane and enlightened society.

To summarize, both critics and defenders of corporal punishment viewed controversies over this issue as conflicts about the nature and future of society. Mann and Hale ultimately envisioned themselves as waging a crucial battle against the foes of civilization. At the same time, their critics saw themselves engaged in a fundamental struggle against anarchistic radicals, bent on promoting widespread chaos through disciplinary reform. In other words, both sides believed that they were engaged in a moral crusade, the outcome of which would spell either disaster or triumph for their nation.

The highly publicized debates over school and naval punishment underscored the extent of popular support for disciplinary reform. In his pamphlet war with the "Thirty-One" Mann emerged as the victor, receiving widespread educational and public support for his views. The growing number of anti-corporal punishment articles in leading educational journals as well as Cobb's *The Evil Tendencies of Corporal Punishment* (1847) indicated educators' growing sympathy with Mann's proposed reforms in school discipline. Anti-corporal punishment resolutions passed in various teachers' conventions throughout the mid-1840s also revealed the increasing popularity of Mann's disciplinary theories. During its annual May, 1844 meeting the New York State Convention of County Superintendents, for example, resolved to substitute "moral for physical punishment" as rapidly "as the preservation of good order . . . will allow";[63] while a similar convention, held two years later in Albany, New York, urged teachers to use "all mild and persuasive means . . . before resorting to corporal punishment."[64] Numerous teacher testimonials, addressed to Horace Mann and other educational reformers during Mann's controversy with the Association, expressed similar sentiments. After three years of teaching, Boston educator Martha Ann Dudley, for example, testified that she had never used the rod to govern the three hundred children under her tutelage.[65]

Mann enjoyed widespread public as well as educational support in his controversy with the Association. While leading periodicals such as the *North American Review* condemned the Association as "conspirators,"[66] major New York and Boston newspapers supported Mann's stand on corporal punishment. Both the *Boston Post* and the *Boston Daily Advertiser,* for example, defended Mann's proposed reforms in school discipline and urged Boston's "practical teachers" to benefit from his criticism. The *Boston Post* was especially critical of the Association of Boston Schoolmasters, contending that their harsh and despotic reliance on the rod alienated the majority of parents from public education.[67] At the same time, several 1845 issues in the *Boston Atlas* pointedly criticized the harsh discipline meted out in Boston's grammar and writing schools,[68] while letters to the editors of the *Boston Courier* and *Boston Olive Branch* denounced grammar schoolmasters' "barbaric" reliance on the "brutal" lash and rattan.[69]

New York newspapers were equally critical of both school-room corporal punishment and its defenders. New York support for Mann's campaign against the "Thirty-One" was particularly evident when both the *Brooklyn Evening Star* and the *Brooklyn Daily Eagle* reprinted an 1846 article by Walt Whitman on class-room punishment. After praising Mann's campaign against the rod, Whitman denounced teachers who flogged their students into a "sullen and spiteful endurance." Convinced that corporal punishment was a degrading and cruel punishment, Whitman argued that punitive schoolmasters were fit to be "dog whippers" but not teachers.[70]

Public support for Mann's disciplinary reforms resulted in the 1845 defeat of four entrenched Boston school committee members in their bid for reelection.[71] Mann's conflict with the Association also garnered monetary support for his educational projects. In January 1845 a group of thirty-four leading Bostonians publicly expressed their confidence in Mann by giving him $5,000 towards the building of two normal schools in Westfield and Bridgewater, Massachusetts. Sensitive to public opinion, the Massachusetts state legislature quickly matched the generous contribution.[72]

Northern public opinion also supported Congressional efforts to abolish naval flogging. On April 22, 1850 the *New York Tribune* approvingly described how a circus clown, in a parody of campaigning politicians, promised to abolish naval floggings and initiate this punishment in Congress. With tongue in cheek, the *Tribune* declared that if sailors could be flogged for drunkenness, insolence and a "thousand" other infractions, Senators could justly be whipped for drawing pistols at each other. This punishment was particularly appropriate for violent Senators who continued to defend corporal punishment on the high seas. These "blackguards" richly deserved the punishment which they so cavalierly upheld for minor offenses.[73]

Although these editorial remarks registered the *Tribune's* disapproval of the recent violent confrontation between Mississippi Senator Henry Stuart Foote and Missouri Senator Thomas Hart Benton (who had recently drawn pistols at each other on the Senate floor), they also revealed the public's growing exasperation with prolonged Congressional debates on the issue of naval whipping. This exasperation was particularly evident in the growing number of memorials and resolutions which urged the immediate prohibition of naval flogging. As noted earlier, the United States Senate in 1850 received 271 such petitions from citizens of various states, including Pennsylvania, New Hampshire, New York, and especially Massachusetts.[74]

At the same time, the legislatures of Rhode Island and Indiana formally instructed their representatives in Congress to support the campaign against naval flogging.[75] Public meetings on behalf of disciplinary reform also suggested the widespread animosity against naval flogging. In 1850 William Seward, who would later become a leading Radical Republican, presented to the Senate the proceedings of several public meetings held in Troy, New York and Hartford, Connecticut which demanded the immediate abolition of both the naval cats and the grog ration. Similarly, Hale noted that numerous public meetings of citizens in Buffalo, Rochester, Syracuse and other New York cities passed resolutions condemning both naval flogging and grog.[76]

Public condemnation of the naval lash had important repercussions for the Congressional debates on flogging. As criticism of the lash increased, Hale and his supporters invoked the force of public opinion to pressure Congress into abolishing this punishment. Citing the growing number of anti-corporal punishment petitions before Congress, Hale predicted that naval flogging would not long withstand the "vehemence of public scorn and indignation." Convinced that public opinion would inevitably abolish this punishment, Hale urged his Southern colleagues to follow the popular will and prohibit the lash immediately.[77]

Growing criticism of corporal punishment in schools, homes, prisons, and reformatories also provided legislative critics of the lash with important ammunition. These critics stressed that the continuation of whipping in the navy was at odds with the general disuse of this punishment in other American institutions. Niles, for example, noted that the abolition of corporal punishment in the army and in many schools and prisons highlighted the exceptionally backward conditions of naval discipline. Arguing that the navy must keep up with the "progress of reform in society," Niles urged the abolition of naval flogging.[78] Hale also viewed the continuation of corporal punishment as a glaring affront to the trend towards more humane forms of punishment. "Why is it," asked Hale, "that, while humanity is lifting up her voice, and that successfully, too, for every other class of the unfortunate and oppressed, the sailor alone shall be left to have the finger of scorn pointed at him forever, as the only man, as the only creature that walks erect with the image of God upon his countenance that is still subjected to this degradation?"[79]

Ironically Hale's remarks seemed to confirm Southerners' worst fears about disciplinary reform. Keenly aware that slaves were still subject to the lash, Southern legislators viewed with alarm the growing momentum of the anti-corporal punishment crusade. In their continued defense of flogging, Southern legislators pointedly noted that it was Northern, not Southern, public opinion which demanded the abolition of corporal punishment in different institutions. Venable particularly stressed this point when he discussed the sanguinary penal code of his home state North Carolina. He proudly declared that North Carolina citizens regularly whipped larceners, counterfeiters, and thieves and placed "those who deserve it in the pillory or jail." Venable significantly noted that such practices enjoyed widespread support in North Carolina.[80]

These comments highlight an important point about antebellum Southern culture, one which recent historical scholarship has stressed: antebellum Southerners were more likely to tolerate, if not condone, institutionalized forms of violence than their Northern counterparts.[81] Southern legislators who defended the practice of flogging, therefore, enjoyed the support of their constituents.

By contrast, the Boston Schoolmasters were at odds with public opinion in their region. Recognizing this fact, the Association and their supporters became increasingly defensive about their views. Indeed they portrayed themselves as martyrs. In a plaintive note, the schoolmasters argued that Mann had mercilessly maligned them when they pointed out some shortcomings in his educational theories.[82] Similarly, Leonard Withington declared that the "Thirty-One" were "doomed to immortal infamy" merely because they had dared to speak out on behalf of their own convictions.[83]

The Boston Schoolmasters attempted to recoup some educational support for their position by establishing the Massachusetts Teachers Federation in 1845. Committed to a decentralized approach to educational improvement, the Massachusetts Teachers Federation offered "sympathy and support" for teachers who enforced the "wholesome restraints of the rod when necessary."[84] Ironically, however, the Federation underscored Mann's triumph over the Association. Although the opening meeting of the Federation supported schoolroom corporal punishment, later lectures qualified their staunch defense of corporal punishment. An 1845 lecture entitled "First Principles of School Government," for example, rejected both "despotism" and "foolish" "nursery government" in school government. Only a judicious mixture of love and fear "perfectly exemplified" the "natural and moral system under which we live." Fear would check man's "strong appetites" and prevent insubordination, while love would obtain the "cheerful and affectionate compliance" of students.[85] Several articles for the *Massachusetts Teacher*, a journal edited by the Federation, gave even stronger support for moral suasion. One 1849 article urged teachers to replace "the debasing and repulsive bond of fear" with the "silken cord of love."[86] Members of the Massachusetts Teachers Federation, therefore, increasingly shared common school reformers' reservations about corporal punishment.

Public condemnation of corporal punishment gained momentum in the North, especially urban Northeast, during the mid to late 1840s. This fact raises important questions for the historian: Did public criticism of corporal chastisement significantly affect the disciplinary practices of antebellum institutions? What disciplinary measures and techniques did reformers advocate as substitutes for corporal punishment?

Chapter 7
From Theory to Practice: The Decline of Corporal Punishment in Antebellum America

P REVIOUS CHAPTERS have discussed different dimensions of the antebellum naval, educational, prison, and domestic reform campaigns against corporal punishment. Chapter 7 will explore how changes in the theory of punishment affected the actual disciplinary practices of antebellum institutions. In exploring this issue, historians must first grapple with a crucial question: What kinds of available sources document or illustrate changes in the way institutions actually disciplined their inmates?

These sources differ for each institution under consideration. Recall, for example, that most antebellum schools and certainly most parents did not keep detailed records of punishment. Historians who wish to explore changes in antebellum domestic or educational discipline, therefore, must use various kinds of impressionistic evidence. These include the personal correspondence, diaries, and reminiscences of former children, parents, and teachers.

Extant annual punishment records of various state prisons and the navy enable the historian to explore changes in the disciplinary practices of these institutions. Fortunately, the Prison Association of New York and the Prison Discipline Society of Boston, as well as various state legislatures, regularly reprinted these records in their own annual reports. In a similar vein, the Secretary of the Navy, in his annual reports to Congress, reprinted the punishments inflicted aboard American men-of-war.

127

The extant evidence demonstrates two crucial facts: (1) There was a significant decline in the actual use of corporal punishment during the antebellum period, especially during the latter half of the 1840s. (2) Parents, teachers, naval and prison officials increasingly experimented with a range of disciplinary techniques which were psychologically, if not physically, punitive. Significantly, reformers often advocated the use of these techniques as well as the use of various positive incentives.

Analysis of the disciplinary practices of the antebellum navy, penitentiary, school, and middle-class home will flesh out these points. The last section of this chapter will summarize the major themes and assess the historical significance of the various antebellum reform campaigns against corporal punishment.

During the 1830s and '40s navy officials sought to mollify public opinion against flogging by regulating and restricting this practice. These efforts began when Naval Secretary Levi Woodbury in a September 26, 1831 circular urged captains to substitute "pecuniary fines, badges of disgrace, and other mild correction" for the "humiliating practice of whipping." The circular also forbade captains to exceed the number of lashes allowed by law, when punishing a seaman for two offenses at once. To check the abuse of power by junior officers, the circular also noted that punishment must be administered in the "presence and under the sanction of the commander officers."[1]

In 1840 President Van Buren further regulated the practice of naval corporal punishment by requiring the navy to make quarterly reports on this subject. According to a May 29, 1840 General Order, issued by Van Buren's Secretary of the Navy James K. Paulding, all punishment

> shall be entered on the Log Book and a quarterly return made to the Secretary of the Navy, stating the names of the persons punished, their offences, and the extent of the punishment inflicted, together with such explanations or remarks as the commanding officer may deem necessary to a proper understanding of the case. . . .[2]

These quarterly returns became the basis for more extensive reports on naval punishment. Congress in an August 3, 1848 naval appropriations act instructed the Secretary of the Navy to give detailed annual reports, starting with the years 1846 and 1847, on naval punishment. Specifying the number of seamen flogged on individual ships, their offense and sentence, and the number of lashes inflicted, these reports provided an invaluable source of information for anti-corporal punishment advocates.[3]

Hale made especially wise use of the statistics on flogging. He noted, for example, officers' frequent use of the whip for minor or vaguely defined offenses. On one ship, seamen were severely flogged for committing the "unpardonable sin" of stealing officers' champagne.[4] Hale also used the statistics on flogging to illustrate the lack of uniformity in inflicting corporal punishment. Although the commander of the *Cyane* inflicted only fifty-seven lashes during a three month period in 1847, the captain of another ship inflicted over nine hundred lashes for the same period.[5] Hale also cited the statistics on punishment to deny that corporal punishment was inflicted only on a "few skulking and cowardly rascals." Noting that there was hardly one name recorded twice in these statistics, Hale declared that a wide range of seamen suffered the lash.[6] Finally, Hale argued that naval records on punishment conclusively proved the close connection between flogging and liquor. He pointed out that the navy's grog ration, not the natural insubordination of seamen, was the major cause of flogging on seafaring frigates. The navy was wrongly intoxicating seamen with whiskey and then punishing these sailors for drunkenness or insolent behavior. To eradicate this unjust inconsistency Hale urged the abolition of the grog ration. Once this ration was prohibited, the need for corporal punishment would vanish.[7]

Hale's comments triggered continued Congressional debates over naval flogging. Finally, on September 28, 1850 the Senate narrowly abolished flogging in the navy by a vote of twenty-six to twenty-four. The voting pattern underscored the sectional overtones of the anti-corporal punishment campaign. Twenty-four of the twenty-six Senators who voted to abolish the naval lash came from Northern states while the other two Senators came from the border states of Missouri and Kentucky (Senators Thomas Hart Benton and Joseph R. Underwood respectively).[8]

The prohibition of flogging in the navy ironically promoted the increased use of other forms of corporal punishment. The most common punishments included gagging seamen by placing a rod of iron across their mouths; "bucking" or "bagging" which consisted of "placing a bar or rod or iron . . . crosswise beneath the hams and in front of the elbow joints, after the wrists and ankles have been put in irons"; "tricing up" which meant that a sailor's hands were confined in irons, raised in front and with a rope triced up so that the feet barely touched deck; and keelhauling, the practice of hauling a sailor through water under the keel of a ship from one side to the other.[9]

The use of these punishments indicated most naval officers' continued commitment to corporal punishment. This commitment became particularly apparent in an official report on corporal punishment which Secretary of the Navy William A. Graham presented to Congress on December 23, 1851. Seeking to study the aftereffects of the abolition of flogging on the navy, Graham had asked commanding officers to comment on efficiency, morals, and discipline aboard men-of-war. The consensus among the twenty-three officers who answered Graham's questionnaire was that order and efficiency in the navy had significantly deteriorated since the abolition of the lash. Commodore F. Engle, for example, noted a decline in subordination and prompt obedience to orders on board his ship the *Princeton* following the abolition of the lash.[10] Similarly, Commodore William Salter declared that the abolition of the cats had been "extremely injurious" to naval discipline. Elaborating on this point, Salter noted that the crew of the *Brandywine* had remained in a "good state of discipline" until they learned that Congress had abolished naval flogging. According to Salter, a change in discipline occurred "immediately." A day after receiving the news about corporal punishment, the *Brandywine* crew, contended Salter, was practically in a "state of open mutiny." Salter declared that a similar decline in discipline occurred on board the *Constitution*. Upon hearing that commanding officers could no longer flog sailors, the *Constitution's* crew became so rebellious that the captain was unable to comply with an order directing him to take his ship to Boston. Convinced that the abolition of the lash precipitated widespread insubordination among seamen, officers such as Salter urged the restoration of this punishment.[11]

Their recommendation provided Southern Congressmen with the needed ammunition to demand the reinstatement of naval flogging. In a January 15, 1852 Congressional speech Florida Senator Stephen Mallory, for example, extensively quoted officers' opinions on the bad aftereffects of disciplinary reform. After noting that commanders denounced the recent abolition of the lash, Mallory urged restoration of this punishment.[12]

As noted earlier, the efforts of Southern legislators and naval officers to reinstate naval flogging failed. Instead Congress passed an "Act to Provide a More Efficient Discipline for the Navy" on March 2, 1855. This Act provided the navy with a comprehensive and uniform code of discipline, one which combined rewards with punishments. Any seaman honorably discharged from the service, for example, received a bounty if he reenlisted. Commanders were also to reward model sailors by granting them more liberty on shore. Besides encouraging good behavior through positive incentives, the 1855 code established a system of summary courts-martial which could mete out the following punishments for minor offenses:

First. Discharge from the service with bad conduct discharge . . .

Second. Solitary confinement in irons . . . on bread and water, or diminished rations, provided no such confinement shall exceed thirty days.

Third. Solitary confinement in irons, single or double, not exceeding thirty days.

Fourth. Solitary confinement not exceeding thirty days.

Fifth. Confinement not exceeding two months.

Sixth. Reduction to next inferior rating.

Seventh. Deprivation of liberty on shore on foreign station.

Eighth. Extra police duties, and loss of pay, not to exceed three months, may be added to any of the above-mentioned punishments.[13]

What is significant about this list of prescribed punishments is the omission of traditional forms of naval punishment such as flogging, gagging, bucking, and keelhauling. Although some commanders continued to inflict these latter punishments, their actions were no longer sanctioned by law. As of March 2, 1855 the only *legal* form of naval corporal punishment was solitary confinement in irons and diminished rations.

Important changes in penal as well as naval discipline occurred in the mid-nineteenth century. The annual reports of prison officers and inspectors, as well as those of the Prison Discipline Society of Boston and the Prison Association of New York, reveal an important fact: the *total* amount of corporal punishment, especially floggings, administered in Northeastern penitentiaries declined in the latter half of the 1840s. The reports of the Prison Association of New York are particularly important since the New York State legislature in 1846 authorized this organization to inspect all New York state prisons and to annually report their findings to the legislature.

New York prison inspectors, for example, noted a decline in the total number of punishments inflicted in Clinton State Prison—40 punishments in 1845, compared with 36 in 1846.[14] Clinton State Prison, which opened in 1845, usually punished convicts with the whip, dungeon, shower bath, or head shavings. As stated earlier, the inspectors of Auburn Prison noted that 1,279 punishments occurred in this penitentiary during the years 1844 and 1845. Significantly, however, 844 punishments were administered in 1844, while the following year the number of punishments declined to 435.[15] Except for one case of solitary confinement, all Auburn convicts were punished with the lash. The 1846 *Report* of the Prison Association of New York significantly noted that 259 Auburn convicts were whipped in 1846, compared with a total of 1,278 in the preceding two years.[16]

Nowhere, however, was the disuse of penal corporal punishment, especially flogging, more dramatic than in Sing Sing Prison. Recall that this prison was notorious for its cruel punishments, especially under the regimes of Robert Wiltse and Elam Lynds. Lynds' harsh and frequent use of the lash, however, resulted in his permanent dismissal from Sing Sing Prison in 1844.[17] After his departure the amount of corporal punishment declined significantly. In 1847 the Prison Association of New York printed the following table extracted from Sing Sing Prison's annual report:[18]

Years	Average No. of violations per month	Average no. of lashes per month
1843	115¾	1,121
1844	73⅓	787
1845	64⅔	366
1846	65⁷⁄₁₂	144⅚
1847	66	38

Note that the average number of lashes per month declined from 1,121 in 1843 to 38 in 1847.

The Association's own inspection of Sing Sing Prison corroborated the disuse of whipping in this penitentiary. According to the Association's 1846 *Report*, the *aggregate* number of stripes administered in Sing Sing declined from 4,400 in 1845 to 2,421 in 1846.[19]

Despite the significant decline in the total amount of whipping administered in New York prisons, individual cases of abusive flogging continued to occur. One particularly controversial case of abuse involved a disruptive and insane Auburn convict named Charles Plumb. During the month of January, 1846 Plumb committed various offenses. He tore up his bed clothes and Bible, smashed windows in the prison's shoe shop, and attacked a guard. During the course of several days Plumb received from 360 to 600 stripes with the lash for these offenses. On January 24 he died in a feverous delirium. A formal inquest into Plumb's death concluded that the cause of death was a "bilious fever, aggravated, not superinduced, by severe flagellation."[20]

The whipping and subsequent death of Plumb provoked a public uproar, one which precipitated the prohibition of corporal punishment in New York prisons. On December 14, 1847 the state legislature passed a law which declared that "no keeper in any State Prison shall inflict any blows whatever upon any convict unless in self-defence or to suppress a revolt or insurrection." If wardens "must inflict unusual punishment," declared the legislature, they must now do so through solitary confinement and stinted rations.[21]

Despite this law some prison guards continued to beat and club, if not whip, convicts. They also continued to punish convicts through use of the ball and chain, bucking, and especially the shower bath. In its 1854 *Report* to the state legislature, the Prison Association of New York, for example, angrily noted that 223 Auburn and 247 Sing Sing convicts had been showered during the preceding year.[22]

The continued use of corporal punishment in New York State prisons, however, should not obscure an important fact. The December 14, 1847 statute made it illegal, if not impossible, to inflict corporal punishment in New York penitentiaries. Passage of this law also ended the most common and traditional form of penal corporal punishment —flogging—in New York State prisons.

In 1849 the Massachusetts State Legislature followed New York's example and prohibited all forms of corporal punishment in its penitentiaries. Solitary confinement was now the only permissible way to punish convicts interned in Massachusetts.[23]

With the notable exception of Frederick Robinson,[24] Massachusetts prison officials condemned the prohibition of corporal punishment. Inspectors of the Massachusetts State Prison, for example, declared that corporal chastisement, especially the lash, was needed to restrain the "hundreds of unprincipled, turbulent and refractory" men crowded in prison.[25]

The summary abolition of corporal punishment, continued the inspectors, provoked widespread insubordination among convicts. To substantiate this charge, the inspectors noted that corporal punishment was inflicted on 19 convicts during the first six months of 1849. During this same period 34 convicts were punished by solitary confinement, amounting to a total of

137 days. During the last six months, when only solitary confinement was permissible, the number of violations and therefore punishments had risen dramatically: 89 convicts were confined for a total of 545 days.[26] The inspectors also noted that the increased amount of solitary confinement had deprived the state of convict labor and therefore needed income. Convinced that solitary confinement was an unprofitable as well as ineffective way to punish convicts, the inspectors urged the reinstatement of corporal punishment.[27]

Their petition touched a responsive chord in the Massachusetts State Legislature for several reasons. During the late 1840s various factors, including increased immigration and the return of Mexican War veterans, precipitated a crime wave in Massachusetts, especially in urban areas.[28] Michael Hindus has explored how the substantial increase in crime strained Massachusetts' penal system. Prisons became dangerously overcrowded and increased revenues were needed to construct a new state penitentiary.[29]

Hoping to increase the efficiency as well as profitability of prisons, the Massachusetts State Legislature reinstated penal corporal punishment on May 3, 1850. It is important to note, however, that the legislature restricted the use of this punishment. The warden now needed the permission of one or more inspectors in order to inflict punishment. The former was also to chastise convicts *only* as a "last resort" and keep a careful record of all cases of punishment. These records were then subject to inspection by the state legislature.[30]

Like Massachusetts, most states were reluctant to prohibit penal corporal punishment altogether. Responsive to public pressure, however, prison officials in various states voluntarily limited their actual use of corporal punishment. The actual disuse, if not legal prohibition, of corporal punishment, for example, characterized the State Prison in Maine during the late 1840s. Out of the forty-five punishments administered in 1847, forty-three were in the form of solitary confinement. One convict suffered four days solitary confinement and eleven stripes; while another received twenty-two stripes and the chain and clog. (The clog being a heavy piece of wood attached to a prisoner's leg or neck which hindered his movement). Out of the fifty-one convicts punished in 1848, only one suffered any form of corporal punishment—twenty-four stripes, the chain and clog for stabbing four fellow inmates. Out of the eleven punishments inflicted in the first six months of 1849, only one convict suffered the chain and clog when he assaulted a deputy warden with a club.[31]

The disuse, if not abolition, of corporal punishment in Northeastern state penitentiaries and the complete prohibition of this punishment in the United States Navy occurred concurrently with another important development. As several scholars have noted, there was a discernible trend away from corporal punishment in Northeastern urban public schools and middle-class homes during the first half of the nineteenth century. Teachers and parents increasingly sought to discipline children, particularly middle-class Anglo-Americans, through "moral suasion," not corporal punishment.[32]

The decline in schoolroom chastisement was particularly apparent in the latter half of the 1840s. During this period school committees and administrators increasingly regulated and restricted a teacher's traditional right to punish. An 1846 bylaw, for example, admonished public school teachers in New York City to chastise students only with "great discretion" and in "special cases."[33] It also required teachers to record all cases of punishment (though unfortunately these records have not survived).

This bylaw precipitated a decline in the amount of schoolroom punishment. The 1847 Report of the Public School Society of New York City noted that out of a total of fifty-nine Primary Schools, two teachers had dispensed with corporal punishment from six to eleven months; ten had dispensed with it for one month; and the remainder from one to three weeks at a time.[34]

In Boston, Mann's controversy with the Association promoted passage of a school ruling which required Boston teachers to record their use of classroom punishment. According to Mann, this ruling helped to decrease the amount of corporal punishment in Boston public schools by 25 percent.[35] The reports of local school committees throughout the state, declared Mann in 1846, showed that 500 schools taught without the infliction of corporal punishment. Although Mann was aware that local school committees probably exaggerated the disuse of punishment in their official reports, he nevertheless concluded that there had been a significant decline in schoolroom chastisement during the 1840s.[36]

Like prison and naval officers, school officials restricted their use of corporal chastisement in order to check public demands to abolish this punishment altogether. This tactic usually worked for school and prison officials. In these institutions corporal punishment was restricted and regulated but rarely abolished altogether, whereas parental corporal punishment, unless abusive, was not legally restricted or regulated in any way. In the case of the navy, however, flogging was prohibited by Congressional statute. Why was this punishment completely and summarily prohibited only in the United States Navy?

In exploring this question, it is important to recall that most antebellum Americans associated flogging with slavery. The use of the "slavish" whip on seamen was particularly objectionable since most sailors, unlike prisoners or children, were free, white adult males. The fact that sailors suffered degrading punishment while in the service of the United States heightened public animosity against naval flogging.

Neglecting the growing number of foreign and black sailors in the United States Navy, Northern legislators significantly portrayed seamen as not only free, white males but also citizens of a proud republic. New Jersey Senator Robert F. Stockton described seamen in this manner during an 1852 Congressional speech. Stockton, who had been one of the few naval commanders to publicly criticize flogging, stressed that whipping violated the citizenship rights of American seamen. Indeed, the crucial question for Stockton became whether or not the American sailor "shall ... be scourged like a slave ... or ... American citizen as he is ... be entitled to all his rights as a ... freeman." For his own part, Stockton declared that he would rather see the "navy abolished and the stars and stripes buried with their glory in the depths of the ocean" than see Americans subjected to the "ignominious and brutalizing whip."[37]

Revulsion against whipping free, white citizens dovetailed with another objection to naval corporal punishment. Like naval reformers, Northern legislators declared that the continued use of harsh punishments frustrated efforts to alleviate the navy's acute manpower shortage. Stockton, for example, predicted that as long as naval flogging continued, "good men" would shun this branch of the service.[38]

Several concerns, then, prompted Congress to prohibit flogging and later all forms of corporal punishment in the United States Navy. On one level, this prohibition reflected the ideological belief that free, white citizens should not be subject to "slavish" punishment. On another level, Congress' action revealed a desire to make the navy more attractive to prospective recruits by abolishing all corporal punishment.

The prohibition of this punishment in the navy and its restriction or disuse in prisons, schools, and homes raised an important question: what kinds of substitutes could one devise for corporal chastisement? In grappling with this question, antebellum reformers underscored their commitment to an internalized code of discipline.

Antebellum reformers devised various ways to reform and even prevent deviant behavior. These ways often employed methods which contemporary child psychologists have labeled "love oriented" or "nonpower assertive." These techniques seek to discipline children in a nonovertly punitive manner and try to keep a child oriented positively towards the parent. Psychologists usually include in this broad category:

a) "Cognitive structuring" or the use of reason and suasion to convince a child of his wrongdoing and point out to him the harmful consequences of his actions for others;

b) "Empathy arousing" techniques, which cultivate a child's identification with and sympathy for authority figures;

c) The use of warm, gentle authority figures, whom psychologists call "nurturant agents." These usually refer to loving parents or teachers.[39]

Antebellum educational and domestic reformers advocated all three methods in disciplining children. T. H. Gallaudet, head of the American Asylum for the Deaf and Dumb, used "cognitive structuring" to quell the bad temper of a deaf boy. Impervious to his teacher's admonitions and punishments, this boy was finally "subdued" when Gallaudet quietly reasoned with him and declared that the former's violent temper "offended" God.[40]

Reformers also devised methods to cultivate a child's identification with authority figures. John Griscom, for example, urged teachers to use the monitorial system in their classrooms. Placed in a position of authority, school monitors soon learned to empathize with teachers and to recognize the "importance of self-government."[41] Noted educator and prolific children's writer Jacob Abbott shared Griscom's views. While describing his experiences as principal of a private boys' school, Abbott noted that his students voluntarily set aside a study period at the beginning of each semester. Having established this rule themselves, the students conscientiously obeyed it. Children who participated in school government, therefore, sympathized with teachers and readily obeyed authority.[42]

Abbott and other didactic writers also urged parents and teachers to gain children's friendship and confidence. Bonds of affection, however, were ultimately means to an end. They encouraged children to internalize the values of their teachers and parents. For this reason Cobb declared that beloved parents and teachers enjoyed an *"unlimited* control over their [children's] minds and conduct."[43]

Although they advocated various ways to discipline children, educational and domestic reformers expressed misgivings about one proposed substitute for corporal punishment: rewards in the form of extra treats, medals, or badges. The systematic use of rewards, feared reformers, socialized children toward competition and greed. Even more importantly, rewards encouraged children to behave correctly out of a desire to receive tangible compensation, rather than out of an intrinsic love of goodness.[44]

Reservations about rewarding young children for good conduct underscore an important point: educational and domestic reformers ultimately sought to cultivate an individual's inner moral conscience, not simply condition his outward behavior. This goal also shaped naval and prison reformers' discussions of proposed substitutes for corporal punishment. Like their counterparts in educational and domestic reform, these reformers advocated the use of kindness, friendship, and reason. Recall Edmonds' belief that kindness and rational suasion reformed seemingly incorrigible convicts.[45]

Naval and prison reformers also sought to cultivate an adult's moral conscience through religion and education. Not surprisingly, naval and prison chaplains particularly stressed the importance of religion in reforming depraved men. Naval chaplain Edward McLaughlin expressed representative views when he declared that the Bible and an "enlightened, discreet, evangelical and efficient chaplain" would transform every ship's company into a "moral, christian and orderly" community. In this moral atmosphere, the "handcuffs, cats and colts" could safely be thrown overboard.[46]

Education was allegedly another effective way to reform and even prevent social deviancy. Naval chaplain Charles Rockwell, for example, believed that improved educational facilities aboard seafaring ships, particularly a well stocked library, made men more virtuous and orderly.[47] Reverend John Luckey shared Rockwell's sentiments. In 1845 Luckey praised a resolution passed by Sing Sing's board of prison inspectors which distributed "good" books to convicts. Since this resolution, declared Luckey, the number of convicts who expressed penitence for their crimes had "greatly increased."[48]

Despite the optimistic tone of these comments, reformers ultimately believed that convicts and sailors were less malleable and therefore less reformable than children. Given this belief, naval and prison reformers had fewer reservations about rewarding good conduct than their counterparts in educational and domestic reform. Seeking to cultivate proper behavior, if not proper motives, naval and prison reformers advocated various rewards and incentives. Gideon Haynes, for example, believed that convicts who were model prisoners should receive good conduct marks in their records. These marks would then result in a reduction of their prison sentences.[49] Meanwhile Hale advocated a range of incentives to induce good behavior in sailors. These included higher pay, more promotions, and increased shore leave.[50]

Antebellum reformers, however, did not attempt to govern individuals only through rewards and "love oriented" techniques. Adumbrating the work of modern day psychologists, they also experimented with psychological punishments. Perhaps the most frequently advocated punishment was solitary confinement. This punishment, which was increasingly used as a substitute for corporal chastisement aboard American men-of-war and in prisons, allegedly reformed "hardened" men.

It was this belief, of course, which prompted proponents of the separate system of prison discipline to advocate the complete isolation of convicts. In an 1822 report on American penitentiaries the Society for the Prevention of Pauperism declared that "complete and entire solitude . . . is the inquisition of the soul and the tyrant of every vice. It may be regarded as scarcely possible that the guilty prisoner can long inhabit a cell where darkness and silence reign, undisturbed arbiters of his doom . . . without . . . some real penitence of heart."[51] A crucial assumption lay behind these comments. Like many other antebellum writings on punishment, this report assumed that isolation encouraged human beings to recognize and more importantly to renounce their deviant behavior.

This assumption prompted didactic writers on childrearing to urge the emotional and physical isolation of disobedient children. A classic story of discipline graphically illustrated this punitive technique. Educational periodicals repeatedly cited the story, originally narrated in Catherine Sedgwick's popular didactic novel *Home*, of Wally Barclay, who angrily threw his sister's kitten into a caldron of boiling water and was then banished from the warm and happy family circle. Wally's father believed that his son had "forfeited" the "right" to domestic protection through his violent, uncontrollable temper: "creatures who are the slaves of their passions . . . are like beasts of prey, fit only for solitude." "Quarantined" from his family for several weeks,

Wally was finally readmitted into the family, but only after he repented his behavior and learned to control his violent temper.[52]

Sedgwick's story underscored reformers' desires to discipline an individual's mind, not punish his body. Significantly, the 1822 report on penitentiaries declared that felons should have their "minds . . . broken on the rack and wheel, instead of their bodies."[53]

In their efforts to discipline an individual's mind, antebellum reformers experimented with psychological punishments which induced a mixture of shame and guilt* in their victims. Transcendentalist educator Amos Bronson Alcott was particularly innovative in his use of these punishments. In his own experimental Temple School, Alcott regularly cultivated his students' sense of shame and guilt through encouraging a ritualistic confession of wrongdoing. On one occasion he asked a little girl to relate her latest act of disobedience at home and then asked the class if they had been as "bad" as this little girl.[54] Not content with these disciplinary techniques, Alcott also devised an unusual way to induce guilt and shame in recalcitrant students. He forced two persistently disobedient students to hit him as punishment for their own misbehavior! Ashamed and mortified

---

Webster's New World Dictionary of the American Language, 2nd college edition, defines "shame" as the "painful feeling of having lost the respect of others because of the improper behavior . . . of oneself." Shame also means "dishonor or disgrace." "Guilt" is a "painful feeling of self-reproach resulting from a belief that one has done something wrong or immoral." Various psychologists, including Freud, have traditionally argued that "guilt, or self-reproach, is based on internalization of values, notably parental values—in contrast to shame, which is based upon dissapproval coming from outside, from other persons." In recent years psychologists have drawn other kinds of distinctions between shame and guilt. According to Dr. Gerhart Piers, for example, "the crucial distinction between guilt and shame is not that between self-criticism and criticism by others but between transgression of prohibitions [which precipitates a sense of guilt] and failure to reach goals or ideals [which precipitates a sense of shame]." In a similar vein, Dr. Franz Alexander argues that a "sense of guilt arises from a feeling of wrongdoing, a sense of shame from a feeling of inferiority." See Helen Merrell Lynd, *On Shame and the Search for Identity* (New York: Science Editions, Inc. 1961), pp. 20–26, for a particularly helpful summary of psychological and also literary discussions of the concepts of shame and guilt. For quotes see pp. 21–22.

at having to hit their respected and beloved schoolmaster, these boys burst into tears and promised to reform.[55]

Despite Alcott's desire to reform rather than merely repress children, the evidence is ultimately ambiguous over whether or not he accomplished his goal. Like other reformers and many modern psychologists of punishment, Alcott mistakenly equated the inhibition of undesirable behavior with a child's internalization of prescribed values. He proudly viewed public confession of wrongdoing as automatic evidence of students' highly developed moral consciences. Alcott's students, however, may well have been motivated by a fear of discovery and anxiety over anticipated punishment. These latter motives especially came into play when Alcott asked individual students to single out schoolmates who had misbehaved during his absence.[56]

Alcott's request suggested how educators used peer group pressure in order to ostracize and shame pupils. An 1828 article in the *American Journal of Education* offered a particularly graphic example of this process. It described how a child accused of theft was placed under "arrest" and judged by his peers. School monitors were the jury, and the whole proceeding ran like a criminal court, complete with "depositions" and a "defense of the accused." When he was "convicted and condemned," the "guilty" child burst into tears and confessed his "crime."[57]

Punishments which publicly shamed and ridiculed individuals in front of their peers were also used to discipline adult offenders. In 1839 controversial Jewish commander and naval reformer Uriah Phillips Levy substituted badges of disgrace for corporal punishment aboard the *U.S.S. Vandalia*. Levy forced drunken seamen to wear a black wooden bottle around their necks while sailors found guilty of petty thievery had to wear a badge proclaiming their crime. Levy devised a particularly unusual punishment for John Thompson, a sixteen-year-old mess boy caught mimicking a junior officer. While the entire crew looked on, Thompson was strapped to a gun, his trousers were lowered, and a small amount of tar and parrot feather was applied to his buttocks.[58]

Although the *Norfolk Herald* praised Levy's innovative approach to discipline as more humane than corporal punishment,[59] his actions angered many fellow officers. In fact, Levy's first Lieutenant George Mason Hooe formally charged his commanding officer with "scandalous and cruel conduct." Hooe stressed that Levy's punishment of Thompson was particularly cruel because it humiliated and degraded a sailor in front of his peers.[60] The ensuing naval court martial of Levy upheld Hooe's charges. The Court declared that Levy's punishment of Thompson was not only "unusual but wholly unlawful and at the same time exceedingly cruel," since it was designed to "dishonor and degrade" its victim.[61] Not content with formally reprimanding Levy, the Court stripped him of his command and dismissed him from the navy.[62]

Although personal animosities and anti-Semitism played a role in these proceedings,[63] Levy's harsh sentence also indicated officers' belief that ridicule was indeed a cruel and humiliating punishment. In their 1850 *Reports on Corporal Punishment* most naval officers denounced badges of disgrace in these terms.[64] Like most prison officials, these officers also declared that flogging was a more humane and just punishment than solitary confinement. The latter punishment unfairly increased the workload of obedient men. At the same time, prolonged solitary confinement cruelly separated a man from his comrades and precipitated serious illness, including insanity.[65]

Those who defended corporal punishment ironically invoked the very arguments which reformers had hurled against them. The former accused the latter of using cruel and humiliating punishments. This accusation served not only a rhetorical purpose but also had intrinsic merit. The psychological punishments which reformers advocated were often as cruel and humiliating as corporal chastisement, sometimes even more so. The fact that reformers countenanced the use of ridicule and shame is particularly ironic. Recall that one of their major arguments against corporal chastisement was that it degraded and humiliated its victims.

Reformers' advocacy of psychologically coercive and shaming punishments highlights a crucial tension in their approach to social discipline. These reformers' desire to alleviate human degradation and suffering was ultimately at odds with their desire to develop efficient, effective techniques of social discipline. Like their toleration of corporal chastisement as a "last resort," reformers' advocacy of other kinds of punishment demonstrated that the latter goal ultimately outweighed the former.

This fact, however, should not obscure an important point: most antebellum reformers did not perceive their goals—the development of more humane as well as effective means of discipline—as mutually exclusive. Viewing both goals as attainable, reformers sought to establish a rough equilibrium between them.

Underlying their efforts was the conviction that moral suasion usually reformed deviant behavior. This optimistic belief muted inherent tensions in reform goals and galvanized public opposition against corporal punishment. Significantly, public criticism of this punishment became particularly pronounced during the late 1840s, a period when the antebellum belief in human perfectibility through moral reform reached its zenith.

Having reached a high point in the late 1840s, the antebellum reform crusade against corporal punishment lost its momentum in the 1850s. A decline in both the amount and intensity of public criticism against this punishment became particularly evident in the latter half of the 1850s. One obvious reason for this decline was the nation's growing concern with the problem of slavery and the threat of disunionism. By the late 1850s Americans increasingly focused their attention on these issues and neglected earlier reform concerns, including the crusade against corporal punishment.

In the 1850s Americans also became disillusioned with the basic premise of antebellum reform, namely, the belief that moral, voluntary means reformed, even perfected, human nature. As John L. Thomas has observed, reformers increasingly viewed this belief as a sentimental illusion, not an attainable goal.[66] This shift in perceptions undermined reformers' optimism in moral suasion and therefore helped to dissipate the antebellum momentum against corporal punishment.

The waning of public criticism against corporal chastisement in the 1850s should not obscure the significant changes which occurred in both the theory and practice of punishment during the antebellum period. By 1860 public opinion in the Northern United States condemned the corporal chastisement of various groups of Americans, including children, seamen, slaves, and prisoners. Although few Americans in the antebellum period explicitly and publicly focused on the issue of wife beating, various sources—didactic works on marriage and the family, with their emphasis on gentle, domestic rule; liberalized divorce laws; and temperance tracts—suggested the public's opposition to wife beating.

The growth of public aversion to corporal punishment had important repercussions for the disciplinary practices of American schools, homes, armed services, and penal institutions. In the late 1840s various Northeastern state legislatures regulated and restricted, if not abolished, the use of corporal punishment in penitentiaries. In 1850 Congress prohibited the use of flogging in the United States Navy. Five years later the only permissible form of punishment in the navy was solitary confinement and stinted rations. Extant school regulations and records, as well as impressionistic evidence, indicate that the use of corporal punishment declined in Northeastern urban public schools and middle-class homes.

Various concerns motivated the antebellum reformers who led the organized opposition against this punishment. Personal, especially childhood, experiences with physical chastisement promoted some reformers' opposition to this punishment. Antebellum reformers also campaigned against this punishment out of a desire to improve the reputation, efficiency, and productivity of their respective institutions. Cultural concerns also fueled the antebellum reform campaigns against corporal chastisement. These campaigns were ultimately part of a broad reform movement against various kinds of violent practices, including war, slavery, and dueling.

Underlying these different reform concerns was a common commitment to a particular ethic of social discipline, one which sought to reform deviant behavior by disciplining the mind, not punishing the body. Antebellum reform critics of corporal punishment, therefore, were ultimately experimenting in new ways to discipline social deviancy, ways which were not necessarily less coercive or humiliating than physical chastisement.

Antebellum reform experiments in punishment adumbrated the work of present day psychologists, penologists, and educators. Like their earlier counterparts, these professionals seek to reform, not simply punish, chronic offenders by substituting psychologically punitive techniques of discipline and positive incentives for corporal chastisement. Contemporary "experts" on deviancy and punishment are also grappling with the crucial challenge posed by antebellum reformers, namely, how to balance a commitment to institutional efficiency and order with a concern for individual rights and sufferings. Unless this balance is struck, the goal of reformation will remain as elusive as ever.

Appendixes

Appendix A: List of fifteen leading reform critics of corporal punishment.

Reformer	Lifespan & Birthplace	Father's Occupation	Religious Affiliation	Paid Work or Occupation	Major Reform Activities
Alcott, William A.	1798–1859 Wolcott, Conn.	farmer	Episcopalian	educator; author; physician	educational, domestic & health reforms
Arthur, Timothy Shay	1809–1885 Orange County, N.Y.	farmer	Swedenborgian	editor; author	domestic & temperance reform
Cobb, Lyman	1800–1864 Lenox, Mass.	unknown	Episcopalian	educator; author	educational reform
Colton, Walter	1797–1851 Rutland County, Vt.	weaver	Congregationalist	theologian, journalist, author	naval reform
Dana, Richard Henry	1815–1882 Cambridge, Mass.	lawyer; poet & essayist	Episcopalian	author; lawyer	antislavery, naval reform
Dix, Dorothea Lynde	1802–1887 Hampden, Mass.	farmer; minister	Unitarian	teacher; Civil War superintendent of army nurses	treatment of the mentally ill & prison reform
Edmonds, John Worth	1799–1874 Hudson, N.Y.	merchant	Spiritualism	lawyer, judge, author	spiritualism & prison reform
Emerson, George Barrell	1797–1881 Wells, Maine	physician	Episcopalian	naturalist, educator; author	educational reform

Name	Dates/Location	Father's occupation	Religion	Occupation	Reform interests
Farnham, Eliza Wood	1815–1864 Rensselaerville, N.Y.	farmer (foster father)	Freethinker	author; lecturer; prison matron	prison reform, phrenology, advocate of female superiority
Griscom, John	1774–1852 Hancock Bridge, N.J.	farmer	Quaker	educator; chemist	educational & prison reform
Hale, John Parker	1806–1873 Rochester, N.H.	lawyer	Unitarian	lawyer, politician, diplomat	antislavery, naval, & temperance reform
Hall, Samuel Read	1795–1877 Croyden, N.H.	teacher, businessman, minister	Congregationalist	minister; educator; author; lecturer	educational reform
Mann, Horace	1796–1859 Franklin, Mass.	farmer	Unitarian	lawyer; political office holder; educator	educational, temperance, and antislavery reform
Peirce, Cyrus	1790–1860 Waltham, Mass.	farmer	Unitarian	minister; educator	educational & temperance reform, pacifism
Sedgwick, Catherine	1789–1867 Stockbridge, Mass.	legislator & jurist	Unitarian	author	domestic & prison reform

* Major Biographical Source: *Dictionary of American Biography*

Appendix B: Available Biographical Data on Members of the Association of Masters of the Boston Public Schools.

Name: Joshua Bates Jr (1810–1888).
Source of Biographical Data: Obituary: *Boston Evening Transcript*, 26 June 1888; *Memorial of Joshua Bates, LL.D., Late Master of Brimmer School, Boston*, ed. by Granville B. Putnam, Franklin School, Boston, reprinted in *Education*, September 1888.
Born: Dedham, Massachusetts; father was a Congregational minister and President of Middlebury College, Vermont.
Formal Education: Phillips Andover Academy; Middlebury College—B.A., LL.D.
Professional Experience: Taught in several Massachusetts schools; for over one-third of a century Bates was Master of Brimmer School in Boston, Massachusetts; he was also the leader of the Association; one of the first vice-presidents of the Massachusetts Teachers Federation and a well-known critic of the common school reforms initiated by Horace Mann. See, for example, Bates, "Our Common Schools," *Boston Herald*, 30 November 1879.
Religion: Congregationalist; in later life Bates received his LL.D. degree and was a minister.

Name: Albert Bowker (1815–1898).
Source of Biographical Data: Obituary: *Boston Evening Transcript*, 29 July 1898.
Born: Walpole, Massachusetts.
Formal Education: Obituary merely notes that Bowker received a "liberal education."
Professional Experience: Taught school in several Massachusetts towns; 1837–45—Master of Lyman School, Boston; 1845–50—President of Maverick Mutual Insurance Company; 1851—became President of North American Insurance Company; was later on the executive Board of Fire Underwriters; treasurer of East Savings Bank and on the board of East Boston Board of Trade; 1848—State Legislature; 1860–62—member of Common Council.
Religion: Active in Congregational Church.

Name: Josiah Fairbank (1794–1878).
Source of Biographical Data: Obituary: *Boston Daily Advertiser*, 21 March 1878.
Born: No data
Formal Education: Westford Academy in Massachusetts.
Professional Experience: Employed in numerous Massachusetts schools before becoming Master of Milton School, Massachusetts; later taught in Adams School, Boston. 1845—opened private academy in Boston.
Religion: No data available.

Name: Barnum Field (1796–1851).
Source of Biographical Data: Arthur Brayley, *Schools and Schoolboys of Old Boston*, p. 67.

Born: Taunton, Massachusetts.

Formal Education: No data available.

Professional Experience: Field taught in several secondary Boston schools, especially Hawes School where he was noted for his severe discipline; 1829–36—Master of Hancock School; 1836–51—Teacher and Master of Franklin School; Field authored a geography text and an atlas and was writing a history of the public schools when he died in 1851.

Religion: No data available.

Name: Abner Forbes (1797–1877).

Source of Biographical Data: Obituary: *Boston Daily Advertiser*, 27 October 1877.

Born: Buckland, Massachusetts.

Formal Education: Williams College, Massachusetts—B.A.

Professional Experience: Taught in several private academies in Massachusetts; also a private tutor as a young man for a Virginia Senator's family; usher and teacher in Franklin and Adams Schools in Boston; Forbes was also one of the leading young men in Hartford Convention; and also active in the antislavery movement.

Religion: No data available.

Name: Josiah Atherton Stearns (1812–1883).

Source of Biographical Data: *The New England Historical and Genealogical Register* 39 (Boston: New England Historic Genealogical Society, 1885): 401; obituary: *Boston Evening Transcript*, 10 September 1883.

Born: Bedford, Massachusetts.

Formal Education: No data available.

Professional Experience: Stearns was originally in the bookselling and publishing business; circa 1840 he became an usher in the Adams School, Boston, under the care of two other members of the Association, Samuel Barrett and Josiah Fairbank. He later was a Master in Mather School in South Boston and then in Lawrence and Norcross Schools in Boston until his retirement in 1882.

Religion: No data available.

Name: Ruben Swan Jr.

Source of Biographical Data: Data on the Swan family is available in a biographical sketch of Swan's son Reuben Samuel Swan (b. 1850), in: *Representative Citizens of the Commonwealth of Massachusetts—New England Library of Genealogy and Personal History* (Boston: New England Historical Pub. Co., 1902), pp. 559–60.

Born: No data.

Formal Education: No data.

Professional Experience: Ruben Swan Jr. was a "well-known educator" who served as submaster of the Wells School in Boston and later became a bookkeeper.

Religion: Swan family were members of the Congregational Church.

Name: William Draper Swan (1809–1864).

Source of Biographical Data: *Appleton's Encyclopedia of American Biography*
6:4; see also *Representative Citizens of Commonwealth of Massachusetts—
New England Library of Genealogy and Personal History*, pp. 558–59.

Born: Dorchester, Massachusetts.

Formal Education: *Representative Citizens* notes that Swan received a "good
education."

Professional Experience: For many years Swan was principal of Wells School,
Boston, Massachusetts; later he was a bookseller; in 1862—served in Massachusetts Senate; Swan published a series of readers for schools with his
brother Robert, principal of Winthrop School in Boston and Daniel Leach,
superintendent of the schools in Providence, Rhode Island. Swan was also
author of a series of arithmetic texts. He was a member of the Old School
Boys Association in Boston.

Religion: No data.

Name: Cornelius Walker (d. 1875).

Source of Biographical Data: Obituary: *Boston Daily Advertiser*, 9 November
1875.

Born: Bedford, Massachusetts.

Formal Education: Dartmouth College.

Professional Experience: Obituary referred to Walker as one of the "last of the
old Grammar Schoolmasters." He introduced Latin into a grammar school
in Charlestown, Massachusetts. He was Master of Wells School in Boston
for twenty-five years; elected to state legislature several times.

Religion: No data available.

Appendix C: Sampling of the Records on Naval Corporal Punishment

Returns of Punishment on board the *Potomac* are found in *Annual Report of the Secretary of the Navy, with Returns of Punishment in the Navy*, 30th Cong., 2nd Sess. (House of Representatives), Executive Document No. 51, pp. 138–39.

Returns of punishments on board the *United States* are found in ibid., pp. 202–203.

Returns of punishments on board the *Brandywine* are found in ibid., 31st Cong., 1st Sess. (House of Representatives), Executive Document No. 26, pp. 42–43.

Returns of punishments on board the *Dale* and *Bainbridge* are found in ibid., pp. 36–37.

Appendix C: Returns of Punishment on board the Potomac

Quarterly return of punishments inflicted on board the United States ship Potomac, Captain J. H. Aulick, from September 1 to November 30, 1846, inclusive: made in conformity to general order from the Navy Department of May 29, 1846.

Date.	Names.	Rank.	Offences.	Punishment.
Sept. 1	Enoch B. Fields	Seaman	Sleeping in top as lookout	6 lashes with a piece of 9-thread rattling.
	Thomas Taylor, 2d	Landsman	Sleeping on lookout	9 lashes with a piece of 9-thread.
3	Edward Harding	Boy	Skulking	8 do
	H. M. Fadden	Marine	Cursing sentry on post	8 do
	Nelson Olds	Ordinary seaman	Disobedience of orders	6 do
	Edward Harding	Boy	Stealing	6 do
9	Wm. O'Brien, 1st	..do	Skulking	6 do
	Joseph Mitchell	Ordinary seaman	..do	6 do
	Wm. Frazier	Boy	..do	6 do
	Wm. Young	Ordinary seaman	..do	6 do
	Charles Pembroke	..do	..do	6 do
10	John Weston	..do	Disobedience of orders	10 do
	John Johnson, 3d	..do	..do	10 do
	Oliver McLean	..do	Neglect of duty	12 do
13	Fras. Madden	Landsman	Disobedience of orders	6 do
	James Bancroft	Boy	..do	6 do
15	Wm. Sunny	Ordinary seaman	..do	6 do
24	James Tucker	..do	Fighting	6 do
	Louis Villar	..do	Carelessness in rigging out conductor	6 do
	John Francis	..do	Gross misconduct to boys	12 lashes with cats.

	Name	Rating	Offense	Punishment
	Fras. Brown	..do	Drunkenness	12 lashes with 9-thread.
	John Thompson	Seaman	..do	12 do.
	Wm. A. Cavanaugh	..do	..do	12 do.
	Edward Doyle	Ordinary seaman	..do	12 do.
	Thomas McGlue	Seaman	..do	12 do.
	Aug. F. Mason	Ordinary seaman	..do	12 lashes with a piece of 9-thread.
12	Wm. Squires	..do	Desertion	12 lashes with cats.
	Wm. Benson	..do	..do	12 do.
	John Curry	Seaman	Drunkenness	12 lashes with 9-thread.
	Henry Watson	..do	Insubordination and drunkenness	12 lashes with cats.
	Lewis Thompson	Ordinary seaman	Disobedience of orders	6 lashes with a piece of 9-thread.
	Charles Himmelwright	..do	..do	6 do do.
18	Joseph Ward	..do	Drunkenness and abusive language to an officer	12 lashes with cats.
	James Darrow	Landsman	Drunkenness and fighting	6 lashes with a piece of 9-thread.
20	Nathaniel Dow	Ordinary seaman	Disobedience of orders	6 do
	John Eagan	..do	Fighting	6 do
	John Givens	Boy	..do	6 do
25	Wm. Squires	Ordinary seaman	Stealing	12 lashes with cats.
29	J. F. Smith	Seaman	Disobedience of orders	9 lashes with a piece of 9-thread
	Daniel Smith	..do	..do	9 do.
	Wm. Henry, 1st	Landsman	..do	9 do.
	John Tookey	..do	..do	9 lashes with 9-thread
	George Wells	Ordinary seaman	..do	9 do.
	R. W. Roberts	Landsman	..do	9 do.
	Joseph Webster	..do	..do	8 do.

Date	Name	Rating	Offense	Lashes	Instrument
Nov. 1	Thomas Brown	1 C. M.	...do...	8	do.
3	Miles Haskell	Landsman	...do...	9	lashes with a piece of 9-thread
	Fras. Earle	Boy	...do...	6	do
	Wm. O'Brien	...do	...do	6	do
	Jackson Bruley	...do	...do	6	do
4	Fras. Earle	...do	...do	6	do
5	Wm. Henry, 1st	Landsman	Neglect of duty	8	do
	R. W. Roberts	...do	...do	8	do
11	D. G. Baltimore	...do	Fighting	9	do
	Samuel E. Smith	Boy	...do	9	do
12	George Wells	Ordinary seaman	Neglect of duty	12	do
	Edward Doyle	...do	Drunkenness	6	do
13	Z. N. Hall	...do	Neglect of duty	6	do
15	Nich'l Contis	Boy	Skulking	6	do
	John Bennon	Ordinary seaman	...do	6	do
19	John Johnson	...do	Neglect of duty	6	do
21	William Treat	...do	Abusive language to an officer	6	do
23	Wm. Young	...do	Neglect of duty	7	do

UNITED STATES SHIP POTOMAC, *Off Tampico, December 1, 1846.*

J. H. AULICK, *Captain.*

Appendix C: Returns of Punishment on board the United States

Quarterly report of persons punished on board the United States frigate United States, bearing the broad pennant of Commodore George C. Read, Joseph Smoot, esq., commanding, from Aug. 18 to Nov. 18, 1847, inclusive.

Date.	Names.	Rank.	Offences.	Punishment.
Aug. 19	George Robinson	Ordinary seamen	Making noise on gun deck	12 lashes with the cats.
	Wiliam Melville	..do....do	Disobedience of orders	12 do.
	Peter Arthur	..do....do	Attempting to desert	12 do.
	James Nutter	Landsman	..do....do	12 do.
	Peter Noland	..do	Drunk on duty	12 do.
	Thomas A. Hamilton	Seaman	Disobedience of orders and staving a boat	12 do.
	Hiram D. Henderson	Ordinary seaman	..do....do....do	12 do.
	Solomon Alexander	..do	..do....do....do	12 do.
	Hugh McCarran	Boy	..do....do....do	6 do.
	James Sullivan	Seaman	Desertion	12 do.
	John Kerr	Ordinary seaman	..do	12 do.
	Alexander Barkley	Landsman	..do	12 do.
	William Carlton	Ordinary seaman	Abuse to the sentry	12 do.
	Richard Squires	..do....do	Disobedience of orders	12 do.
	Edward Marmly	..do....do	..do....do	12 do.
26	Thomas Ford	Seaman	Drunk, desertion, and mutinous conduct	36 do. (Sentenced)
Sept. 1	Richard Griffith	Marine	False accusation and drunk	12 do.
	Severn Ross	Landsman	Drunk on duty	12 do.
	John Forrester	Ordinary seaman	Smuggling liquor	12 do.
	William G. Stevenson	..do....do	Striking a man	12 do.
	James Creighton	..do....do	Drunk on duty	12 do.

Date	Name	Rating	Offense	No.	Vessel
	John Caffray	Landsman	do.	12	do.
	Joseph Campbell	Seaman	do.	12	do.
	James Denio	Landsman	Skulking	12	do.
	Edward Marmly	Wardroom steward	Disobedience of orders	6	do.
	Chris Haines	Ordinary seaman	Striking a man	6	do.
	Ennel Adams	Seaman	Cursing the sentry	12	do.
10	Williams Yates	Ordinary seaman	Disobedience of orders of the boatswain and drunk	12	do.
	James Livingston	Seaman	Smuggling liquor	12	do.
	Smith Newell	Landsman	Disobedience of orders of boatswain's mate	12	do.
18	John Francis	Ordinary seaman	Disobedience of orders	12	do.
	Robert D. Barry	Seaman	Drunk on duty	12	do.
	James M. Preston	do.	do.	12	do.
	Joseph McCarty	Ordinary seaman	do.	12	do.
	Frederick White	Seaman	Procuring liquor for boat's crew	12	do.
	Horace Bucklin	Landsman	Refusing duty	12	do.
25	John Baxter	Seaman	Theft	9	do.
	James McMullen	Ordinary seaman	Drunk on duty and fighting	12	do.
	William Edwards	Seaman	Drunk on duty	12	do.
	Thomas Crosby	do.	Smuggling liquor	12	do.
	John Welsh	Musician	Disobedience of orders	9	do.
Oct. 9	Henry Hookery	Seaman	Drunk and cursing the boatswain	12	do.
	William Barnett	do.	Drunk and mutinous conduct	12	do.
	Thomas Hartley	do.	Attempting to smuggle liquor	12	do.
14	Thomas Owens	Captain's cook	Drunk and fighting	12	do.
	Samuel Ramsdale	Captain foretop	Disobeying boatswain's orders	7	do.
	Anthony Van Allen	Captain hold	Insolence	5	do.
	John Reichert	Marine	do.	12	do.
26	John McDonald, 1st	Seaman	Drunk on duty and abusing the American flag	12	do.

Date	Name	Rating	Offense	No.	
	Isaac N. White	Ordinary seaman	Drunk and stealing liquor	12	do.
	Avod Briggs	do.	Fighting	6	do.
	Lewis D. Clark	do.	do.	6	do.
	Joseph Campbell	Seaman	Drunk and fighting	9	do.
	William Shields	do.	Drunk and disobedience of orders	5	do.
	James Doyle	do.	Drunk	12	do.
	Severn Ross	do.	do.	12	do.
	William G. Stevenson	Ordinary seaman	do.	12	do.
	Horace Bucklin	do. . . . do.	Choking a man	12	do.
	John Francis	do. . . . do.	Disobedience of orders	12	do.
	James Denio	Landsman	do. . . . do.	9	do.
	George H. Whitmore	Ordinary seaman	Drunk and fighting	9	do.
Nov. 6	Otto C. Brown	do. . . . do.	Skulking	12	do.
	Thomas Castello	Seaman	Fighting	12	do.
15	John Kyle	Ordinary seaman	do.	12	do.
	Edward Walch	Boy	Abuse to a boatswain's mate	12	do.
	William G. Stevenson	Ordinary seaman	Striking a man	12	do.
	James Livingston	Seaman	Drunk on duty	12	do.
	John Anderson	do.	fighting	9	do.
	Alanson Mills	do.	Attempting to smuggle liquor	12	do.
	Otto C. Brown	Ordinary seaman	Disobedience of orders	12	do.
	Anthony Williams	Seaman	Drunk on duty	12	do.
	Andrew J. Percey	Landsman	Cheating his mess of ration money	12	do.

Appendix C: Returns of Punishment on board the Brandywine

Bimensal return of punishments on board the Brandywine (frigate) from
July 1 up to August 31, 1849.

Offence.	Punishment.	
Allowing H. Drake to take his place in the launch, for the purpose of getting drunk	9 lashes.	
Drunkenness	9	do
Do.	6	do
Disobedience of first lieutenant's orders	12	do
Smuggling liquor aboard	12	do
Disobedience of orders in not turning out for post, and abusing sergeant	12	do
Drunkenness	12 lashes, and disrated	
Detected smuggling on board	12 lashes	
Sleeping on post	9	do
Drunkenness	12	do
Do.	12	do
Do.	9	do
Insolence at gangway	12	do
Drunkenness	9	do
Drunk and striking sergeant of guard in execution of his duty	12	do
Drunkenness	12	do
Detected smuggling liquor aboard	12	do
Drunkenness	12	do
Do.	9	do
Do.	12	do
Do.	9	do
Do.	12	do
Drunkenness and fighting	12	do
Insolence and disobedience of first lieutenant's orders	9	do
Drunkenness and insolence to first lieutenant	12	do
Drunkenness	12	do
Drunkenness and insubordination	12	do
Disobedience of first lieutenant's orders	9	do
Drunkenness and fighting	6	do

CHAS. BOARMAN, *Captain.*

Appendix C: Returns of Punishment on board the Dale

Return of punishments on board the Dale, (sloop,) from
October 19
up to December 5, 1848.

Offence.		Punishment.
Desertion		*50 lashes with cats.
Drunk and impertinent	9	do
Breaking drum and sticks intentionally	8	do
Selling clothes without leave	12	do
Quarrelling and fighting	6	do
Do. . . . . do.	12	do
Abusive language to a petty officer	8	do
Smuggling liquor.	10	do
Drunkenness, insolence to doctor, and neglect of duty	12	do
Do. . . . .do. . . . .do	12	do
Abusive language.	6	do
Drunk and insolent	12	do
Do.	12	do
Mutinous conduct	12	do
Do.	8	do
Drunk and noisy.	12	do
Do.	12	do
Drunkenness	12	do
Smuggling liquor.	9	do
Theft	15	do

*Sentence of court-martial.

JOHN RUDD, *Commander.*

Return of punishments on board Dale, (sloop,) from
July 3, 1848, up to September 16, 1848.

Offence.		Punishment.
Drunkenness		9 lashes with cats.
Insolence and abuse of captain of forecastle	8	do
Disobedience and quarrelling	12	do
Do. . . . .do	9	do
Quarrelling and fighting	12	do
Drunkenness and abusive language	12	do
Drunk on duty.	6	do
Insolence to an officer and drunkenness	12	do
Drunk on duty.	6	do

JOHN RUDD, *Commander.*

Appendix C: Returns of Punishment on board the Bainbridge

Bimensal return of punishments on board Bainbridge, (brig,) from
August 1 up to September 30, 1849.

Offence.		Punishment.
Neglect of duty and abusive language		12 lashes with the cats
Disobedience of orders and staying ashore all night without leave	9	do
Do.....do.....do.....do	9	do
Do.....do.....do.....do	9	do
Disobedience of orders and leaving boat without leave	6	do

A. G. SLAUGHTER, *Commander.*

Bimensal return of punishments on board Bainbridge, (brig,) from
June 1 up to July 31, 1849.

Offence.		Punishment.
Molesting one of the kroomen		12 lashes with the cats
Negligence in duty	9	do
Do....do	9	do
Do....do	9	do

A. G. SLAUGHTER, *Commander.*

Bimensal return of punishments on board Bainbridge, (brig,) from
April 1 up to May 31, 1849.

Offence.		Punishment.
Sleeping on lookout		6 lashes with cats.
Sleeping and neglect of discharge of duty	9	do
Fighting	12	do
Do	12	do
Drunk on duty	9	do
Do	9	do
Selling his clothes	6	do
Neglect of duty	6	do
Remaining out of vessel 36 hours without permission	12	do
Disobedience of orders	6	do

A. G. SLAUGHTER, *Commander.*

Notes

Notes to Introduction

1. Carl Kaestle, "Social Change, Discipline, and the Common School in Early Nineteenth-Century America," *Journal of Interdisciplinary History* 9 (Summer 1978):1–17.

2. David J. Rothman, *The Discovery of the Asylum: Social Order and Disorder in the New Republic* (Boston: Little, Brown and Company, 1971), esp. pp. 101–103; 231–235.

3. Harold Langley, *Social Reform in the United States Navy, 1798–1862* (Urbana, Chicago: University of Illinois Press, 1967), pp. 131–206.

4. Michael Ignatieff, *A Just Measure of Pain: The Penitentiary in the Industrial Revolution, 1750–1850* (New York: Columbia University Press, 1978); Lawrence Stone, *The Family, Sex and Marriage in England, 1500–1800* (New York: Harper & Row, 1977), pp. 439–444; Eugene L. Rasor, *Reform in the Royal Navy: A Social History of the Lower Deck, 1850 to 1880* (Hamden, Conn.: Archon Books, 1976).

5. David Brion Davis, "The Movement to Abolish Capital Punishment in America, 1787–1861," *American Historical Review* 63 (October 1957):23–46; idem, *The Problem of Slavery in Western Culture* (Ithaca, N.Y.: Cornell University Press, 1966); James Turner, *Reckoning with the Beast: Animals, Pain and Humanity in the Victorian Mind* (Baltimore: The John Hopkins University Press, 1980).

6. Michel Foucault, *Discipline and Punish: The Birth of the Prison*, trans. Alan Sheridan (New York: Pantheon Book, 1977).

7. For discussions of contemporary distinctions between "moderate" and "abusive" corporal punishment, see Ralph S. Welsh, "Severe Parental Punish-

ment and Aggression: The Link between Corporal Punishment and Delinquency," in Irwin A. Hyman and James H. Wise, eds., *Corporal Punishment in American Education: Readings in History, Practice and Alternatives* (Philadelphia: Temple University Press, 1979), p. 140; Jeanne M. Giovannoni and Rosina M. Becerra, *Defining Child Abuse* (New York: The Free Press, 1979), esp. pp. 243–244.

Notes to Chapter 1

1. Horace Lane, *The Wandering Boy, Careless Sailor, and Result of Inconsideration. A True Narrative* (Skaneateles, N.Y.: Luther A. Pratt, 1839), esp. pp. 7–10.

2. Ibid., p. 44.

3. Ibid., esp. pp. 33–39.

4. Ibid., pp. 197–200. See also Lane's *Five Years in State's Prison; or, Interesting Truths, Showing the Manner of Discipline in the State Prisons at Sing Sing and Auburn, Exhibiting the Great Contrast between the Two Institutions . . . Represented in a Dialogue between Sing Sing and Auburn*, 3rd ed. (New York: Luther Pratt & Son, 1835).

5. Benjamin Wadsworth, *The Well Ordered Family; or, Relative Duties Being the Substance of Several Sermons . . . Duties of Husbands and Wives; Duties of Parents and Children; Duties of Masters and Servants* (Boston: B. Greven, 1712), esp. pp. 55; 94–95.

6. *Dorchester. Town Records, 1632–1686, Reports of the Record Commissioners*, vol. 4, City Document No. 9, March 14, 1645, p. 56. I am grateful to Charles R. Lee for bringing this citation to my attention.

7. *The Laws and Liberties of Massachusetts Reprinted from the Copy of the 1648 Edition in Henry E. Huntington Library* (Cambridge, Mass., 1929), p. 38, as cited in Edmond S. Morgan, *The Puritan Family: Religion and Domestic Relations in Seventeenth Century New England*, new ed., rev. and enl. (New York: Harper & Row, 1966), pp. 113–114.

8. Edwin Powers, *Crime and Punishment in Early Massachusetts, 1620–1692. A Documentary History* (Boston: Beacon Press, 1966), provides a particularly good introduction to colonial forms of penal discipline. See pp. 163–194 for a discussion of bodily punishments, especially whipping. See also Alice Morse Earle, *Curious Punishments of Bygone Days* (1896; reprint ed., Detroit: Single Tree Press, 1968), pp. 70–85; William Andrews, *Old-Time Punishments* (1890; reprint ed., Detroit: Single Tree Press, 1970), pp. 146–163.

9. Russell F. Weigley, *History of the United States Army* (New York: Macmillan Co., 1967), p. 63; Earle, *Curious Punishments*, pp. 119–137.

10. For a concise summary of naval regulations on flogging, see Leo F. S. Horan, "Flogging in the United States Navy; Unfamiliar Facts Regarding Its Origins and Abolition," *United States Naval Institute Proceedings* 76 (1950):969–975.

11. Ibid., pp. 971–972.

12. The following sources are useful in exploring the historical development of the loco parentis argument: Emma Jane Hirschberger, "A Study of the Development of the *In Loco Parentis* Doctrine: Its Application and Emerging Trends." (Ph.D. diss., University of Pittsburgh, 1971); Theodore Alvin Faulkner, "The History of Legal Action in Corporal Punishment Cases in New York State, 1812–1965. An Investigation of Judicial Decisions Arising from Punishment of Pupils by Teachers in Public and Private Schools of New York State." (Ed. D. diss., New York University, 1967).

13. The best introduction to post-Revolutionary developments in penal reform is still Orlando F. Lewis, *The Development of American Prisons and Prison Customs, 1776–1845. With Special Reference to Early Institutions in the State of New York* (Albany: J. B. Lyon Co., 1922). For early prison developments in Pennsylvania, see pp. 11–35. On the establishment of Newgate, see pp. 43–44. See also W. David Lewis, *From Newgate to Dannemora: The Rise of the Penitentiary in New York, 1796–1848* (Ithaca: Cornell University Press, 1965), pp. 1–53.

14. For a discussion of these legislative acts see New York State Senate, *Report of the Committee on State prisons, on petitions praying for a law abolishing the use of the whip in our penitentiaries*, Senate Document No. 120, vol. 4, 69th sess., April 11, 1846, pp. 3–6. See also Lewis, *From Newgate to Dannemora*, pp. 45–46.

15. Lewis, *The Development of American Prisons*, p. 68.

16. Ibid., pp. 220–223, discusses the use of these and other punishments in the Eastern Penitentiary at Philadelphia during the late 1820s and '30s.

17. For a discussion of the introduction of this punishment in the Massachusetts State Prison in 1840, see Gideon Haynes, *Pictures from Prison Life. An Historical Sketch of the Massachusetts State Prison with . . . Suggestions on Discipline* (Boston: Lee & Shepard, 1869), pp. 58–60.

18. For a brief survey of Quaker involvement in post-Revolutionary prison reform, see Blake McKelvey, *American Prisons: A Study in American Social History Prior to 1915* (Chicago: University of Chicago Press, 1936), pp. 6–11; M. J. Heale, "Humanitarianism in the Early Republic: The Moral Reformers of New York, 1776–1825," *Journal of American Studies* 2 (1968):161–175. See also the works cited in Footnote 13.

19. See Webster's 1788 essay "On the Education of Youth in America," reprinted in Noah Webster, *A Collection of Essays and Fugitive Writings on Moral, Historical, Political and Literary Subjects* (Delmar, N.Y.: Scholars' Facsimiles & Reprints, 1977). See esp. pp. 16–17.

20. Edward Cutbush, *Observations on the Means of Preserving the Health of Soldiers and Sailors; and on the Duties of the Medical Department of the Army and Navy, with Remarks on Hospitals and Their Internal Arrangements* (Philadelphia: Fry & Kammerer, Printers, 1808), pp. 130–131.

21. "Flogging in the Navy," *New York Tribune*, 11 May 1850, p. 1. For other criticisms of naval flogging, see "Brief editorial denouncing the cruel practice

of whipping offenders in the American Navy," *Niles Weekly Register* 57 (September 21, 1839):64; editorial criticisms of naval flogging by numerous newspapers are reprinted in the *Army and Navy Chronicle*. See, for example, "Flogging to Death at Sea," ibid., 3 (December 29, 1836):412; "Editorial Commentary," ibid., 1 (September 17, 1835):299; "Corporal Punishment," ibid., 8 (June 27, 1839):403–404; "Flogging in the Navy," ibid., 10 (January 23, 1840):54–55; "The Navy," ibid., 13 (February 5, 1842):39–40.

22. "Prison Discipline," *United States Magazine and Democratic Review* 19 (August 1846):129–140. For other criticisms of prison corporal punishment, see "Influence of Penal Laws," ibid. 22 (March 1848):233–240; Francis Wayland, "Prison Discipline," *North American Review* 49 (July 1839): 1–43; "Flogging in Prisons," *New York Daily Tribune*, 4 February 1846, p. 2; "Sing Sing State Prison," ibid., 25 February 1847, p. 1.

23. This editorial is reprinted in Lyman Cobb, *The Evil Tendencies of Corporal Punishment as a Means of Moral Discipline in Families and Schools, Examined and Discussed* (New York: Mark H. Newman & Co., 1847), pp. 267–268.

24. See the May 13, 1847 editorial of the *New York Daily Globe* reprinted in ibid., pp. 266–267. See also "Editorial Commentary," *Boston Post*, 11 December 1844, p. 1; "Mr. Mann and the Teachers of the Boston Schools," *North American Review* 126 (January 1845):224–246.

25. Bernard Wishy, *The Child and the Republic: The Dawn of Modern American Child Nurture* (Philadelphia: University of Pennsylvania Press, 1968), pp. 42–49, discusses these writers.

26. New York State Senate, *Report of the Committee on State Prisons*, p. 5.

27. *United States Senate Journal*, 31st Cong., 1st sess. (Serial 548), pp. 37, 38, 44, 54, 58, 72, 94, 104, 126, 140, 147, 153, 160, 204, 205, 218, 227, 228, 340, 401. Harold Langley, *Social Reform in the United States Navy, 1798–1862* (Urbana, Chicago: University of Illinois Press, 1967), p. 185, brought these memorials to my attention.

28. Ibid., pp. 50–63, discusses the aims and programs of the American Seaman's Friend Society. See also George Sidney Webster, *The Seaman's Friend. A Sketch of the American Seaman's Friend Society* (New York: The American Seaman's Friend Society, 1932).

29. For an excellent discussion of prison reformers' efforts to establish a more humane penal code in New York prisons, see Lewis, *From Newgate to Dannemora*, especially pp. 201–255; see also David J. Rothman, *The Discovery of the Asylum: Social Order and Disorder in the New Republic* (Boston: Little, Brown & Company, 1971). The annual reports of the Prison Discipline Society of Boston and the Prison Association of New York provide a great deal of information on the prison reform campaign against flogging. So does the *Prisoner's Friend* and the *Journal of Prison Discipline and Philanthropy*, published under the direction of the Philadelphia Society for Alleviating the Miseries of Public Prisons.

30. For a discussion of the leading educational reformers in the 1830–60 generation, see Paul H. Mattingly, *The Classless Profession: American Schoolmen in the Nineteenth Century* (New York: New York University Press, 1975). Perhaps the best introduction to the ideas of educational reformers are Mann's *Annual Reports on Education* (Boston: Horace B. Fuller, 1868). For Mann's views on the rod and birch, see his essay "On School Punishments," *Lectures on Education* (Boston: W. B. Fowle & N. Capen, 1845), pp. 303–338. Cobb, *Corporal Punishment*, Appendix, pp. 222–270, reprinted the opinions of various leading educators who criticized corporal punishment.

31. See, as examples, Catherine E. Beecher, *A Treatise on Domestic Economy for the Use of Young Ladies at Home and at School*, rev. 2d ed. (Boston: Thomas H. Webb & Co., 1842), esp. pp. 228–229; S. F. Goodrich, *Fireside Education* (London: William Smith, 1839), pp. 25–35; Mrs. J. Bakewell, *The Mother's Practical Guide in the Early Training of her Children; Containing Directions for Their Physical, Intellectual and Moral Education* (New York: Pub by G. Lane and P. P. Sandford for the Methodist Episcopal Church 1843), pp. 151–168.

32. For biographical data on leading reform critics of corporal punishment, see Appendix A.

33. For a more detailed discussion of the rise of a specialized regional economy in the United States, see Douglas C. North, *The Economic Growth of the United States, 1790–1860* (New York: W. W. Norton & Co., Inc., 1966), esp. pp. 66–74; on developments in transportation, see George R. Taylor, *The Transportation Revolution, 1815–60* (New York: Rinehart & Co., Inc., 1951); for a discussion of the rise of manufacturing in the antebellum Northeast, see North, pp. 156–176; Taylor, pp. 207–250; Victor S. Clark, *History of Manufacturing in the United States*, 2 vols. (New York: McGraw-Hill Book Co., 1929), 1:529–578.

34. See J. Potter, "The Growth of Population in America, 1700–1860," in *Population in History: Essays in Historical Demography*, eds. D. V. Glass and D.E.C. Eversley (Chicago: Avon Pub. Co., 1965), pp. 631–678, for an excellent discussion of the overall demographic changes during this period. On the rapid urbanization of Northeastern cities, see Allan R. Pred, *Urban Growth and the Circulation of Information: The United States System of Cities, 1790–1840* (Cambridge, Mass.: Harvard University Press, 1973), p. 5; Richard D. Brown, "The Emergence of Urban Society in Rural Massachusetts, 1760–1820," *Journal of American History* 61 (1974):29–51. On immigrants' influx to Boston, see Oscar Handlin, *Boston's Immigrants: A Study in Acculturation* (Cambridge, Mass.: Harvard University Press, 1959), especially pp. 25–53. See also Stephen Thernstrom, *Poverty and Progress: Social Mobility in a Nineteenth Century City* (New York: Atheneum Press, 1973).

35. For a comparative analysis of the relationship between commercial capitalism and the decline of orthodox Calvinism, see Daniel Walker Howe, "The Decline of Calvinism: An Approach to its Study," *Comparative Studies in Society and History* 14 (1972):306–327.

36. For a discussion of industrialization's impact on the family, see Robert Wells, "Family History and Demographic Transition," *Journal of Social History*

9 (1975):1–21; Nancy F. Cott, *The Bonds of Womanhood: "Woman's Sphere" in New England, 1780–1835* (New Haven: Yale University Press, 1977), explores how the family's increasingly specialized role in childrearing fostered cultural domesticity. See especially her chapters on domesticity and work, pp. 19–100. See also Mary P. Ryan, *Cradle of the Middle Class: The Family in Oneida County, New York 1790–1865* (Cambridge, Mass.: Cambridge University Press, 1981).

37. Various students of modernization have noted this shift from "vertical" to "horizontal" and increasingly specialized institutions. See Harold Perkins, *The Origins of Modern English Society, 1780–1880* (Toronto: University of Toronto, 1969), pp. 17–62, for a description of "traditional" preindustrial institutions and pp. 107–133 for a discussion of increasing specialization and complexity of various social organizations; Neil J. Smelser, "The Modernization of Social Relationships," in *Modernization: The Dynamics of Growth*, ed. Myron Weiner (New York: Basic Books, Inc., 1966), pp. 110–122; James A. Henretta, *The Evolution of American Society, 1700–1815: An Interdisciplinary Analysis* (Lexington, Mass.: D. C. Heath & Co., 1973), pp. 206ff.; Richard D. Brown, *Modernization: The Transformation of American Life, 1600–1865* (New York: Hill & Wang, 1976), especially pp. 94–158; and Brown's "Modernization and the Modern Personality in Early America, 1600–1865: A Sketch of a Synthesis," *Journal of Interdisciplinary History* 2 (Winter 1972):201–228.

38. Mann's most recent biographer, Jonathan Messerli, borrows Horace Bushnell's "Age of Homespun" to describe the Mann household. See Messerli, *Horace Mann: A Biography* (New York: Alfred A. Knopf, 1972), pp. 3–27.

39. Ibid., pp. 15-17. For Mann's bitter reaction to the "sedentary occupation" of braiding, see Mary Mann, ed., *Life and Works of Horace Mann*, 5 vols. (Boston: Lee and Shepard, 1891), 1:10.

40. Messerli, *Horace Mann*, pp. 17–20; for a discussion of Mann's college years, see ibid., pp. 28–53.

41. Mann, ed., *Life and Works of Horace Mann*, 1:14.

42. On the evolution of Protestant theology in the first half of the nineteenth century, see Joseph Haroutunian, *Piety Versus Moralism: The Passing of the New England Theology* (New York: H. Holt & Co., 1932). On the emergence of Unitarianism, see Conrad Wright, *The Beginnings of Unitarianism in America* (Boston: Starr King Press, distributed by Beacon Press, 1955).

43. See Appendix A.

44. For biographical data on Colton, see Lieut. William W. Edel, "The Golden Age of the Navy Chaplaincy, 1830–55," *United States Naval Institute Proceedings* (June 1924):875–885. See also "Colton, Walter," *Dictionary of American Biography*, vol. 2, Part II, pp. 323–324 (hereafter cited as *DAB*).

45. See Appendix A.

46. "Hall, Samuel Read," *DAB*, vol. 4, Part II, pp. 142–143. See also Mattingly, *The Classless Profession*, p. 28; "Samuel Read Hall," in Henry Barnard, ed., *Memoirs of Teachers, Educators, and Promotors and Benefactors of Education, Literature, Science* (1861; reprint ed., New York: Arno Press & The New York Times, 1969), pp. 169–181.

47. Two of Hall's teaching manuals which discuss the importance of governing children through reason and suasion are *Lectures on School-Keeping* (Boston: Richardson, Lord & Holbrook, 1829); *Lectures to Female Teachers on School-Keeping* (Boston: Richardson, Lord & Holbrook, 1832).

48. Edel, "The Golden Age of the Navy Chaplaincy," pp. 875–885, discusses these chaplains' reform activities, including their efforts against corporal punishment.

49. Ann Douglas, *The Feminization of American Culture* (New York: Alfred A. Knopf, 1977), pp. 17–43. For Rev. Dewey's comments, see p. 22.

50. Sedgwick advocated the disuse of parental corporal punishment in her popular novel *Home* (Boston: James Monroe & Co., 1835). See also Sedgwick, "A Plea for Children," *Ladies Magazine* 8 (February 1835):93–97; and "A Supplement to a Plea for Children," ibid., 8 (November 1835):597–598. Lewis, *From Newgate to Dannemora*, pp. 237–250, discusses Farnham's views on prison discipline. See also Farnham, "Cruelties in Clinton Prison," *Prisoner's Friend* 1 (September 1846):25–27. For a good introduction to Dix's ideas about prison punishment see her *Remarks on Prisons and Prison Discipline in the United States* (1845; reprint ed., Montclair, N.J.: Patterson Smith, 1967), esp. pp. 13-27.

51. Mann, ed., *Life and Works of Horace Mann*, 1:11–12.

52. Horace Mann, *Fourth Annual Report of the Massachusetts Board of Education, Together with the Fourth Annual Report of the Secretary of the Board* (Boston: Dutton and Wentworth, State Printers, 1841), p. 26.

53. Charles Francis Adams, *Richard Henry Dana: A Biography*, 2 vols (1890; reprint ed., Detroit: Gail Research Co., Book Tower, 1968), 1:2–3.

54. Ibid., pp. 6–7.

55. Ibid., p. 5.

56. Ibid., pp. 9–10.

57. Richard Henry Dana, *Two Years Before the Mast: A Personal Narrative of Life at Sea* (Cleveland: The Fine Editions Press, 1946), p. 120.

58. Eliza Wood Farnham, *My Early Days* (New York: Thatcher & Hutchinson, 1859), esp. pp. 13–29. See also W. David Lewis, "Farnham, Eliza Wood Burhans," *Notable American Women* 1:598–600.

59. "Cyrus Peirce," Barnard, ed., *Memoirs of Teachers, Educators*, pp. 432–433.

Notes to Chapter 2

1. A. B. Muzzey, *The Fireside: An Aid to Parents*, 2nd ed. (Boston: Crosby, Nichols & Co., 1856), pp. 4–5; 9; 17.

2. Kathryn Kish Sklar, *Catherine Beecher: A Study in American Domesticity* (New York: W. W. Norton & Co., 1973), discusses Beecher's efforts to make homemaking a profession. See esp. pp. 151–167.

3. For a good introduction to the efforts of naval Secretaries and officers to reform the navy, see Harold Langley, *Social Reform in the United States Navy, 1798–1862* (Urbana, Chicago: University of Illinois Press 1967), pp. 26-40.

4. Matthew F. Maury [Harry Bluff], "Of Reorganizing the Navy," *Southern Literary Messenger* 7 (1841):3–25, esp. pp. 15–22; see also Abel Parker Upshur's 1841 *Annual Report of the Secretary of the Navy to Congress*, p. 19, and his 1842 *Annual Report*, pp. 544–545. Both *Reports* are reprinted respectively in the *Congressional Globe*, 27th Cong., 2nd sess., Appendix; ibid., 27 Cong., 3rd sess., Appendix.

5. See Upshur's 1841 *Annual Report*, p. 21, and his 1842 *Annual Report*, pp. 40–41; for reform proposals which were similar to Upshur's recommendations, see "Report of the Navy to the President of the United States," *North American Review* 30 (1830):360–389; James K. Paulding's 1839 *Annual Report of the Secretary of the Navy to Congress*, reprinted in the *Cong. Globe*, 26th Cong., 1st sess., Appendix; "Thoughts on the Present Condition of the Navy and Suggestions for its Improvement," *Military and Naval Magazine of the United States*, March 1833–January 1836, pp. 256–265.

6. Langley, *United States Navy*, pp. 21–27, discusses Perry's efforts and the rise and work of these naval magazines.

7. As an introduction to the antebellum common school reform movement the older works in educational history are still useful. See Lawrence A. Cremin, *The American Common School: An Historic Conception* (New York: Bureau of Pub. Teachers College, Columbia University, 1951); for an introduction to revisionist historiography on education, see Michael B. Katz, *The Irony of Early School Reform: Educational Innovation in Mid Nineteenth Century Massachusetts* (Cambridge, Mass.: Harvard University Press, 1968). See also Carl Kaestle, *Pillars of the Republic: Common Schools and American Society, 1780–1860* (New York: Hill & Wang, 1983), pp. 75–135.

8. My account of the political controversy over school centralization is based on the following works: Raymond B. Culver, *Horace Mann and Religion in the Massachusetts Public Schools* (New Haven: Yale University Press, 1929), pp. 22 & 217; George H. Martin, *The Evolution of the Massachusetts Public School System: A Historical Sketch* (New York: D. Appleton & Co., 1901), pp. x–xii; 151–153; 177; Cremin, *The American Common School*, pp. 143–144; see also Michael B. Katz, *Class, Bureaucracy, and Schools: The Illusion of Educational Change in America* (New York: Praeger Pubs., 1971), esp. pp. 56–104; and Kaestle, *Pillars of the Republic*, pp. 151–158.

9. For an excellent study of the professionalization of teachers, see Paul H. Mattingly, *The Classless Profession: American Schoolmen in the Nineteenth Century* (New York: New York University, 1975). See also David B. Tyack and Elizabeth Hansot, *Managers of Virtue: Public School Leadership in America 1820–1980* (New York: Basic Books, Inc., 1982), pp. 15–104.

10. For a sample of the literature which debated the relative merits of each system, see Samuel Gridley Howe, *An Essay on Separate and Congregate Sys-*

tems *of Prison Discipline* (1846; reprint ed., New York: Arno Press, 1974), which defended the former system; and Francis C. Gray, *Prison Discipline in America* (1847; reprint ed., Montclair, N.J.: Patterson Smith, 1973), which defended the Auburn or congregate plan.

11. David J. Rothman, *The Discovery of the Asylum: Social Order and Disorder in the New Republic* (Boston: Little, Brown and Co., 1971), esp. pp. 79-108.

12. Richard Henry Dana, *Two Years Before the Mast: A Personal Narrative of Life at Sea* (Cleveland: The Fine Editions Press, 1946), pp. 125–126.

13. William A. Alcott, *The Young Husband; or, Duties of Man in the Marriage Relation* (1839; reprint ed., New York: Arno Press & The New York Times, 1972), p. 275.

14. Prison Discipline Society of Boston, *Twentieth Report* (1845), p. 86, reprints the comments of Sing Sing prison officials. The Society's reports appear in *The Twenty-nine Annual Reports of the Board of Managers, 1826–1854, with a Memoir of Louis Dwight,* 6 vols. (1855; reprint ed., Montclair, N.J.: Patterson Smith, 1972).

15. New York State Senate, *Annual Report of the Clinton State Prison,* Senate Document No. 10,, vol. 1, 70th sess., January 8, 1847, pp. 27–28.

16. Horace Mann, *Ninth Annual Report of the Massachusetts Board of Education, Together with the Ninth Annual Report of the Secretary of the Board* (Boston: Dutton and Wentworth, State Printers, 1846), p. 98.

17. Lyman Cobb, *The Evil Tendencies of Corporal Punishment, as a Means of Moral Discipline in Families and Schools, Examined and Discussed* (New York: Mark H. Newman, 1847), pp. 47–48.

18. Walter Colton, *Deck and Port; or, Incidents of a Cruise in the United States Frigate Congress to California, with Sketches of Rio Janeiro, Valparaiso, Lima, Honolulu, and San Francisco* (New York: A. S. Barnes & Co., 1850), pp. 23 and 45.

19. New York State Senate, *Report of Luman Sherwood, One of the Inspectors of the State Prison at Auburn,* Senate Document No. 12, vol. 1, 70th sess., January 13, 1847, p. 14.

20. Ibid.

21. See appendix C for a sample of these records. For these records see *Reports of the Secretary of the Navy, Communicating copies of returns of punishment in the navy, in compliance with a resolution of the Senate.* These reports are found in: 30th Cong., 1st sess. (Sen.) Exec. No. 69; 30th Cong., 2nd sess. (House of Rep.) Exec. Doc. No. 51; 30th Cong., 2nd sess. (Sen.) Exec. Doc. No. 23; 31st Cong., 1st sess. (House of Rep.) Exec. Doc. No. 26.

For the punishment returns of the *Vincennes* during this period, see ibid., 30th Cong., 2nd sess. (Sen.), Exec. Doc. No. 23, p. 16; for the returns of the *Columbus* see ibid., pp. 23–24.

22. Ibid., pp. 297 and 301, for punishment records of the *Plymouth* and *Princeton* during this period.

23. The lack of uniformity in punishing children was a major theme in Cobb, *Corporal Punishment*.

24. George K. Behlmer, *Child Abuse and Moral Reform in England, 1870–1908* (Stanford, Calif.: Stanford University Press, 1982), argues that these factors hindered British reform efforts to legislate against child abuse until the last quarter of the nineteenth century.

25. As a result of the efforts of New Hampshire Senator and naval reformer John Parker Hale, for example, naval records on punishment were subject to scrutiny by the United States Congress after 1848.

26. Timothy Shay Arthur, *The Iron Rule; or, Tyranny in the Household* (Philadelphia: T. B. Peterson, 1853).

27. "Paternal Authority in Rome," *Ladies Magazine* 8 (January 1835):42–47.

28. For a recent discussion of these developments, see Mary P. Ryan, *Cradle of the Middle Class: The Family in Oneida County, New York, 1790–1865* (Cambridge, Mass.: Cambridge University Press, 1981).

29. Keith Melder, "Woman's High Calling: The Teaching Profession in America, 1830–60," *American Studies* 13 (1973):19–32.

30. David B. Tyack, *The One Best System: A History of American Urban Education* (Cambridge, Mass.: Harvard University Press, 1974), pp. 61–62.

31. See, for example, Horace Mann, *Fourth Annual Report of the Massachusetts Board of Education, Together with the Fourth Annual Report of the Secretary of the Board* (Boston: Dutton and Wentworth, State Printers, 1841), pp. 45–46.

32. Horace Mann, *Reply to the "Remarks" of Thirty-one Boston Schoolmasters on the Seventh Annual Report of the Secretary of the Massachusetts Board of Education* (Boston: W. B. Fowle & N. Capen, 1844), p. 158. For a discussion of Mann's debate with these schoolmasters, see Chapter 6.

33. Moses Jaquith, *An Appeal to the Public in a Case of Cruelty, Inflicted on a Child of Mr. Jaquith's at the Mayhew School . . . by William Clough . . . Together with Other Matters* (Boston: privately printed, 1832), esp. pp. 3,6, 13–14, 21.

34. Carl Kaestle, "Social Change, Discipline, and the Common School in Early Nineteenth-Century America," *Journal of Interdisciplinary History* 9 (Summer 1978):1–17.

35. Jaquith, *An Appeal to the Public in a Case of Cruelty*, p. 22.

36. Most educators who responded to Cobb's 1847 survey on schoolroom punishment, for example, advocated this approach to disciplinary reform. See Cobb, *Corporal Punishment*, pp. 222–270.

37. "Lynds, Elam," *DAB*, vol. 6, Part I, p. 527.

38. For details of the charges against Lynds, see New York State Senate, *Report of the Majority of the Committee appointed under a resolution of the Senate, of the 25th April, 1839, to investigate the affairs of the Auburn and Mt. Pleasant State Prisons*, Senate Document No. 37, vol. 2, 63rd sess., 1840, esp. pp. 5–12. See also John W. Edmonds, *A Letter from John W. Edmonds, one of the inspectors of the State Prison at Sing Sing to General Aaron Ward in regard*

to the removal of Captain Elam Lynds as principal keeper of that prison (New York: W. G. Boggs, 1844).

39. New York State Assembly, *Report of the Committee on State Prisons, in relation to the Mt. Pleasant Prison,* Assembly Document No. 335, vol.6, 62nd sess., March 30, 1839, esp. p. 17.

40. W. David Lewis, *From Newgate to Dannemora: The Rise of the Penitentiary in New York, 1796–1848* (Ithaca: Cornell University Press, 1965), pp. 204; 208–209; discusses local disapproval of both Lynds and Wiltse.

41. Howe, *An Essay on Separate and Congregate Systems,* p. 20; Dorothea Lynde Dix, *Remarks on Prisons and Prison Discipline in the United States* (1845; reprint ed., Montclair, N.J.: Patterson Smith, 1967), p. 16.

42. "Abstracts of the Reports on Punishments, Presented to the Legislature in Compliance with a Resolution of that Body"; found in the *Second Report of the Prison Association of New York, 1845. Including the Constitution and By-laws and a List of Officers and Members* (New York: Pub. by the Association, 1846), Appendix, pp. 151–152.

43. Ibid., pp. 34–36; "Does the Auburn System of Prison Discipline Depend on Stripes?," Prison Discipline Society of Boston, *Sixteenth Annual Report* (1841), pp. 39–44.

44. Ibid., p. 43.

45. For the comments of both the Committee and Edmonds, see New York State Senate, *Report of the Committee on State Prisons, on petitions praying for a law abolishing the use of the whip in our penitentiaries,* Senate Document No. 120, vol. 4, 69th sess., April 11, 1846, p. 19.

46. For a discussion of the navy's manpower shortage after the War of 1812, see Langley, *United States Navy,* pp. 71–96.

47. William McNally, *Evils and Abuses in the Naval and Merchant Service Exposed; with Proposals for Their Remedy and Redress* (Boston: Cassady & March, 1839), pp. 48–53.

48. See Paulding's 1840 *Annual Report of the Secretary of the Navy to Congress,* reprinted in the *Congressional Globe,* 26th Cong., 2nd sess., Appendix, p. 14. See also Upshur's 1841 *Annual Report,* p. 18.

49. William Elliot Griffis, *Matthew Calbraith Perry: A Typical American Naval Officer* (New York: Houghton Mifflin Co., 1890), pp. 435–439. See also Langley, *United States Navy,* pp. 98–112.

50. John P. Lockwood [Anonymous], *An Essay on Flogging in the Navy; Containing Strictures Upon Existing Naval Laws and Suggesting Substitutes for the Discipline of the Lash* (New York: Pudney & Russell, Printers, 1849), esp. p. 27. This essay originally appeared as "Flogging in the Navy," *United States Magazine and Democratic Review* 25 (1849): 97–115; 225–242; 318–337; 417–432.

51. Various sources discuss the Somers Case. The most useful are Harrison Hayford, ed., *The Somers Mutiny Affair* (Englewood Cliffs, N.J.: Prentice-Hall, 1959); Frederic F. Van De Water, *The Captain Called it Mutiny* (New York: Ives Washburn, Inc., 1954); *Proceedings of the Naval Court Martial in the Case of*

Alexander Slidell Mackenzie, A Commander in the Navy of the United States . . . Including the Charges and Specifications of Charges, Preferred against Him by the Secretary of the Navy, to which is Annexed an Elaborate Review by James F. Cooper (New York: Henry G. Langley, 1844).

52. The letter, signed "S," appeared in the *New York Tribune*, 14 February 1843, p. 1. See also the January 26th and 28th issues of the *Tribune*.

53. Langley, *United States Navy*, p. 111, noted that this program was reinstated in 1855. By that time, of course, flogging was prohibited in the Navy.

Notes to Chapter 3

1. *Congressional Globe*, 30th Cong., 2nd sess., 20:488–489.

2. S.S.R., "Annual Reports of County Superintendents," *District School Journal* 5 (May 1844):53.

3. "Voices From Prison," *Prisoner's Friend* 1 (September 1848):36.

4. For a discussion of Hale's antislavery activities see Richard H. Sewell, *John Parker Hale and the Politics of Abolition* (Cambridge, Mass.: Harvard University Press, 1965).

5. "Thoughts on Common School Morals," *Common School Journal* 5 (May 1, 1843):143–144.

6. "Editorial Commentary," *Moral Advocate* 1 (March 1821):1–3; "Editorial Commentary," ibid., 1 (June 1822): 189–190; "Cock Fighting," ibid., 3 (May 1824):112; "The Dead Robin," ibid., 3 (July 1823):16.

7. J. H., "Intemperance," ibid., 2 (April 1823):157–159; "Fifty Years Ago," *Prisoner's Friend* 5 (July 1853):463; "Asylum for Inebriates," ibid. 8 (May 1856):261–264.

8. Jonathan Messerli, *Horace Mann: A Biography* (New York: Alfred A. Knopf, 1972), pp. 230, 212–213, 185–188 and passim, discusses Mann's temperance activities. Hale led the Congressional movement to abolish naval grog. For a discussion of this movement, see Harold Langley, *Social Reform in the United States Navy, 1798–1862* (Urbana, Chicago: University of Illinois Press, 1967), pp. 208–269.

9. Horace Mann, *Ninth Annual Report of the Massachusetts Board of Education Together with the Ninth Annual Report of the Secretary of the Board* (Boston: Dutton and Wentworth, State Printers, 1846), p. 97.

10. Mann's *Seventh Annual Report* to the Massachusetts Board of Education recounted the selfless actions of the inmates of the Rauke House for Orphans in Hamburg, Germany. This portion of Mann's *Report* was reprinted in the *Common School Journal* 6 (April 1, 1844):112.

11. Lyman Cobb, *The Evil Tendencies of Corporal Punishment as a Means of Moral Discipline in Families and Schools, Examined and Discussed* (New York: Mark H. Newman & Co., 1847), pp. 188–189.

12. Horace Mann, *Seventh Annual Report of the Massachusetts Board of Education, Together with the Seventh Annual Report of the Secretary of the Board* (Boston: Dutton and Wentworth, State Printers, 1844), p. 188.

13. Mann, "What God Does, And What He Leaves for Man to do, In the Work of Education" *Lectures on Education* (Boston: W. B. Fowle &. N. Capen, 1845), pp. 169–171; idem, "Means and Objects of Common School Education" ibid., p. 13; idem, *Ninth Annual Report*, esp. p. 68.

14. A. B. Muzzey, *The Fireside: An Aid to Parents*, 2d ed. (Boston: Crosby, Nichols &. Co., 1856), pp. 188 ff. For a recent discussion of the premium placed on self-discipline in antebellum childrearing literature, see Daniel T. Rodgers, "Socializing Middle-Class Children: Institutions, Fables, and Work Values in Nineteenth Century America," *Journal of Social History* 13 (Spring 1980): 354–367. See also David Brion Davis, ed., *Antebellum American Culture: An Interpretive Anthology* (Lexington, Mass.: D. C. Heath &. Co., 1979), pp. 1–83.

15. Lewis Perry, *Childhood, Marriage, and Reform: Henry Clarke Wright, 1797–1870* (Chicago: University of Chicago Press, 1980), esp. pp. 230–255.

16. Ronald G. Walters, *The Antislavery Appeal: American Abolitionism After 1830* (Baltimore: The John Hopkins University Press, 1976), pp. 70–87. For Weld's comments see p. 77. For a recent discussion of reformers' general concern with inner moral restraints, see idem, *American Reformers 1815–1860* (New York: Hill and Wang, 1978).

17. "Temperance Among Seamen," *Sailor's Magazine and Naval Journal* 5 (November 1832):65–67 (hereafter cited as *Sailor's Magazine*).

18. "Extract From Dr. Barton's 'Hints to Naval Officers," ibid., 3 (April 1831):247–248; "The Effects of Drunkenness on the Body," ibid., 3 (February 1831):179; "Intemperance, Pauperism and Crime," ibid., 3 (August 1831):375–377.

19. See the following articles: "Rum Rations and Flogging. A Sailor's Yarn or an Old Man-of-Warman's Story," ibid., 22 (January 1850):136–138; L.D.J., late of U.S.N., "Spirit Rations and Flogging," ibid., 22 (February 1850):177–178; "Grog and Flogging in the Navy," ibid., 21 (March 1849):205.

20. See Appendix C for a sampling of antebellum naval records on punishment.

21. See "Spirit Rations and Flogging," pp. 177–178; see also "The Lash," *Sailor's Magazine* 21 (September 1848): 20.

22. Cobb, *Corporal Punishment*, p. 70.

23. Gideon Haynes, *Pictures From Prison Life. An Historical Sketch of the Massachusetts State Prison with . . . Suggestions on Discipline* (Boston: Lee &. Shepard, 1869), p. 246.

24. "Spirit Rations and Flogging," pp. 177–178.

25. See, for example, "The Teacher, The School and Flogging," *District School Journal* 6 (November 1845):157–158; Mrs. J. Bakewell, *The Mother's Practical Guide in the Early Training of her Children; Containing Directions for Their Physical, Intellectual and Moral Education* (New York: Pub. by G. Lane and P. P. Sandford for the Methodist Episcopal Church, 1843), p.151.

26. John Griscom, *Memoirs of John Griscom; with an Account of New York High School, Society for the Prevention of Pauperism, House of Refuge and Other Institutions* (New York: Robert Carter & Bros., 1859), p. 41.

27. See the untitled excerpts from the *New York Daily Advertiser*, reprinted in the *Army and Navy Chronicle* 1 (September 17, 1835):295.

28. Robinson's comments are reprinted in the Prison Discipline Society of Boston, *Nineteenth Annual Report* (1844), p. 49. This latter report appears in volume 4 of the Society's *Twenty-nine Annual Reports of the Board of Managers, 1826–1854, with a Memoir of Louis Dwight*, 6 vols. (1855; reprint ed., Montclair, N.J.: Patterson Smith, 1972).

29. Cobb, *Corporal Punishment*, p.20.

30. John P. Lockwood, [Anonymous], *An Essay on Flogging in the Navy; Containing Strictures Upon Existing Naval Laws, and Suggesting Substitutes for the Discipline of the Lash* (New York: Pudney & Russell Printers, 1849), p. 50.

31. Haynes, *Pictures from Prison Life*, pp. 131 ff.

32. Richard Henry Dana, *Two Years Before the Mast: A Personal Narrative of Life at Sea* (Cleveland: The Fine Editions Press, 1946), p. 120.

33. Prison Discipline Society of Boston, *Second Annual Report* (1847), p. 16.

34. See Langley, *United States Navy*, pp. 172–174, for a discussion of buggery in the American Navy; see also Arthur N. Gilbert, "Buggery and the British Navy, 1700–1861," *Journal of Social History* 10 (Fall 1976):72–98.

35. Dana, *Two Years Before the Mast*, pp. 119–120.

36. Society for the Prevention of Pauperism, *Report on the Penitentiary System in the United States*, (1822; reprint ed., New York, Arno Press, 1974), pp. 80–82.

37. "The Penitentiary System," *Moral Advocate* 1 (February 1822):122.

38. Griscom's comments appear in Cobb, *Corporal Punishment*, p. 225.

39. "Education," *Moral Advocate* 2 (January 1823 Supplement):102.

40. "Parental Care, Christian Principle, &c," ibid., 2 (July 1822):7–11; see p. 7 for quote.

41. Harriet Beecher Stowe, *The Key to Uncle Tom's Cabin: Presenting the Original Facts and Documents Upon Which the Story Is Founded, Together with Corroborative Statements Verifying the Truth of the Work* (1854; reprint ed., New York: Arno Press, 1968), p. 249.

42. Stowe, *Uncle Tom's Cabin; or, Life Among the Lowly*, vol. 2 (Boston: Jewett, 1852), p. 180.

43. Ibid., pp. 181 and 164–165.

44. "The Penintentiary System," p. 122.

45. "Intemperance," *Moral Advocate* 2 (April 1823): 157–161.

46. Davis J. Rothman, *The Discovery of the Asylum: Social Order and Disorder in the New Republic* (Boston: Little, Brown and Company, 1971), esp. pp. 15–20.

47. John Robinson, "Of Children and Their Education," in Phillip J. Greven Jr., ed., *Child-Rearing Concepts, 1628–1861* (Itasca, Illinois: F. E. Peacock Pub., 1973), p. 13.

48. Daniel Defoe, *The Family Instructor in Three Parts, Part I* — *Relating to Fathers and Children*, 8th ed. (London: Printed for E. Mathews, 1720), p. 62.

49. The historical literature on childrearing provides a particularly good introduction to changing attitudes toward human nature during the post Revolutionary period. See, for example, Peter Gregg Slater, *Children in the New England Mind: In Death and in Life* (Hamden, Conn.: Archon Books, 1977); Daniel H. Calhoun, *The Intelligence of a People* (Princeton: Princeton University Press, 1973), pp. 134–205. For a discussion of how antebellum Americans perceived social deviants as malleable and therefore reformable people, see Rothman, *Asylum*, esp. pp. 56–78.

50. The chaplain's *Report* appears in the Prison Discipline Society of Boston, *Eleventh Annual Report* (1836), p. 45.

51. Cobb, *Corporal Punishment*, p. 21.

52. Walter Colton, *Deck and Port; or, Incidents of a Cruise in the United States Frigate Congress to California, with Sketches of Rio Janeiro, Valparaiso, Lima, Honolulu, and San Francisco* (New York: A. S. Barnes & Co., 1850), p. 221.

53. Samuel Read Hall, *Lectures to Female Teachers on School-Keeping* (Boston: Richardson, Lord & Holbrook, 1832), p. 83.

54. Lockwood, *An Essay on Flogging*, pp. 36 and 48.

55. See, for example, Prison Discipline Society of Boston, *Eighth Annual Report* (1833), pp. 35–38; *Seventeenth Annual Report* (1842), p. 49.

56. Cobb, *Corporal Punishment*, particularly stressed the efficacy of kindness in reforming "bad" boys. See, for example, pp. 98 and 100.

57. Edmonds' comments are reprinted in New York State Senate, *Report of the Committee on State Prisons, on petitions praying for a law abolishing the use of the whip in our penitentiaries*, Senate Document No. 120, vol. 4, 69th sess., April 11, 1846, p. 16.

58. Hall, *Lectures to Female Teachers*, pp. 58–59.

59. John Luckey, *Life in Sing Sing State Prison, as Seen in a Twelve Years' Chaplaincy* (New York: N. Tibbels, 1886), pp. 109–125.

60. Cobb, *Corporal Punishment*, pp. 27–28.

61. Charles S. Stewart, *A Visit to the South Seas, in the United States Ship Vincennes, During the Years 1829 and 1830; with Scenes in Brazil, Peru, Manila, the Cape of Good Hope, and St. Helena*, 2 vols. (New York: Sleight & Robinson, Printers, 1831), 1:30–31.

62. James Turner, *Reckoning with the Beast: Animals, Pain and Humanity in the Victorian Mind* (Baltimore: The John Hopkins University Press, 1980), esp. pp. 81–82. Martin Steven Pernick, "A Calculus of Suffering: Pain, Anesthesia, and Utilitarian Professionalism in Nineteenth Century American Medicine" (Ph.D. diss., Columbia University, 1979).

63. Turner, *Reckoning with the Beast*, esp. pp. 5–6; 16–17; 34–36; 139.

64. Cobb, *Corporal Punishment*, pp. 7–8; 87.

65. Ibid., pp. 195–197.

66. Frederick Robinson, "Treatment of Prisoners," *Prisoner's Friend* 2 (July 1850): 490.

67. Herman Melville, *White Jacket; or, the World in a Man-of-War* (Chicago: Northwestern University Press & The Newberry Library, 1970), p. 146.

68. Jackson Turner Main, "Government by the People—The American Revolution and the Democratization of the Legislature," *William & Mary Quarterly*, 3rd ser., 23 (July 1966):391–407, discusses the democratization in politics. See also Gordon Wood, *The Creation of the American Republic, 1776–1787* (Chapel Hill, N.C.: University of North Carolina Press, 1969), esp. pp. 344–390. For a discussion of the process of democratization in the antebellum period, see Arthur Schlesinger's classic and controversial study, *The Age of Jackson* (Boston: Little, Brown & Co., 1945).

69. John Murphy [An Observer], *An Inquiry into the Necessity and General Principles of Reorganization in the United States Navy; with an Examination of the True Sources of Subordination* (Baltimore: John Murphy, 1842), esp. pp. 6–9, 19.

70. "Does the Auburn System of Prison Discipline Depend on Stripes?," Prison Discipline Society of Boston, *Sixteenth Annual Report* (1841), p. 39.

71. Mann, *Ninth Annual Report*, p. 96.

72. For a discussion of how this view of freedom shaped different aspects of antebellum culture, especially politics, see Eric Foner, *Free Soil, Free Labor, Free Men: The Ideology of the Republican Party Before the Civil War* (New York: Oxford University Press, 1970).

73. "The Children of the Mobility Versus the Children of the Nobility," *Common School Journal* 4 (February 15, 1842):56.

74. See, for example, Jonathan A. Glickstein, "'Poverty is not Slavery': American Abolitionists and the Competitive Labor Market," in Lewis Perry and Michael Fellman, eds., *Antislavery Reconsidered: New Perspectives on the Abolitionists* (Baton Rouge: Louisiana State University Press, 1979), pp. 195–218; see also David Brion Davis, *The Problem of Slavery in the Age of Revolution, 1770–1823* (Ithaca, N.Y.: Cornell University Press, 1975), esp. pp. 265–266; 462–467.

75. See the following articles: "School Order," *Common School Journal* 5 (May 1, 1843):129–133; "The Teacher, The School, and Flogging," 157–158; "Motives to Obedience on the Part of Children," *District School Journal* 7 (June 1846):57.

76. Dana, *Two Years Before the Mast*, pp. 121 & 145.

77. Horace Mann, *Tenth Annual Report of the Massachusetts Board of Education, Together with the Tenth Annual Report of the Secretary of the Board* (Boston: Dutton and Wentworth, State Printers, 1847), p. 83.

78. "Excessive Punishment," *American Annals of Education* 4 (January 1834):44–45.

79. Pernick, "A Calculus of Suffering," pp. 217–221.

80. Mann's comments appear in ibid., p. 220, fn. 149. For original citation see Mann, "On School Punishments," *Lectures on Education*, p. 304.

81. Ibid., pp. 307–308.

82. Dorothea Lynde Dix, *Remarks on Prisons and Prison Discipline in the United States* (1845; reprint ed., Montclair, N.J.: Patterson Smith, 1967), p. 16.

83. Dana, *Two Years Before the Mast*, p. 405.

84. Cobb, *Corporal Punishment*, p. 11; Horace Mann, *Reply to the "Remarks" of Thirty-one Boston Schoolmasters on the Seventh Annual Report of the Secretary of the Massachusetts Board of Education* (Boston: W. B. Fowle & N. Capen, 1844), p. 164.

85. For a discussion of antebellum attitudes toward female criminals, many of whom were incarcerated for prostitution, see W. David Lewis, *From Newgate to Dannemora: The Rise of the Penitentiary in New York, 1796–1848* (Ithaca: Cornell University Press, 1965), pp. 157–177; Estelle B. Freedman, *Their Sisters' Keepers: Women's Prison Reform in America, 1830–1930* (Ann Arbor: University of Michigan Press, 1981), esp. pp. 15–21.

86. New York State Senate, "Female Prison," *Annual Report of the Inspectors of the Mount-Pleasant State Prison*, Senate Document No. 20, vol. 1, 67th sess., January 12, 1844, p. 29.

87. Orlando F. Lewis, *The Development of American Prisons and Prison Customs, 1776–1845. With Special Reference to Early Institutions in the State of New York* (Albany: J. B. Lyon Co., 1922), p. 263, reprints Barrett's remarks.

88. John W. Edmonds, *A Letter from John W. Edmonds, one of the inspectors of the State Prison at Sing Sing to General Aaron Ward in regard to the removal of Captain Elam Lynds as principal keeper of that prison* (New York: W. G. Boggs, 1844), pp. 25–26. Edmonds could not have legally prescribed whipping since an 1819 New York State law prohibited the use of the lash on women convicts. See *Laws of the State of New York*, 42nd sess. (1819), p. 87. Lewis, *From Newgate to Dannemora*, p. 95, brought this citation to my attention.

Notes to Chapter 4

1. Jane Grey Swisshelm, *Half a Century*, 2nd ed. (Chicago: Jansen, McClurg & Co., 1970), pp. 51–60.

2. John Rankin, *Letters on American Slavery, Addressed to Mr. Thomas Rankin, Merchant at Middlebrook, Augusta, Co., Virginia* (1837; reprint ed., Westport, Conn.: Negro University Press, 1970), p. 59.

3. Theodore Weld, *American Slavery As It Is*, eds., Richard D. Curry and Joanna Dunlap Cowden (Itasca, Ill.: F. E. Peacock Pub., Inc., 1972), p. 38.

4. Arthur W. Calhoun, *A Social History of the American Family*, 3 vols. (1918; reprint ed., New York: Barnes & Noble, Inc., 1960), 2:139–140, reprints this quote. For original citation see Reverend Fred A. Ross, *Slavery Ordained of God* (Philadelphia: J. B. Lippincott & Co., 1857), p. 53.

5. *New York Times*, 15 February 1863, p. 6.

6. Ibid., 13 July 1863, p. 2.

7. Ibid., 25 November 1866, p. 3.

8. For Anthony's involvement in this case of marital abuse, see Ida Husted Harper, *The Life and Work of Susan B. Anthony*, 3 vols. (Indianapolis: The Hollenbeck Press, 1898), 1:200–205.

9. Theodore Woolsey, *Divorce and Divorce Legislation, Especially in the United States*, 2nd ed. rev. (New York: Charles Scribner's & Sons, 1882), pp. 230–240, especially p. 234 for statistics.

10. Lawrence Stone, *The Family, Sex and Marriage in England, 1500–1800* (New York: Harper & Row, 1977), pp. 197–198, discusses these homilies.

11. Benjamin Wadsworth, *The Well Ordered Family; or, Relative Duties Being the Substance of Several Sermons—Duties of Husbands and Wives; Duties of Parents and Children; Duties of Masters and Servants* (Boston: B. Greven, 1712), pp. 26–28; 34–35.

12. Sir. William Blackstone, *Commentaries on the Laws of England in Four Books*, 12th ed. (London: A. Strahan & W. Woodhull, 1793)1:442.

13. James Kent, *Commentaries on American Law*, 4 vols., 11th ed., ed. George F. Comstock (Boston: Little, Brown and Co., 1866)2:180.

14. Blackstone, *Commentaries*, 1:444–445.

15. Various legal scholars have stressed this point. See, for example, Richard B. Morris, *Studies in the History of American Law With Special Reference to the Seventeenth and Eighteenth Centuries* (New York: Columbia University Press, 1930) esp. pp. 126–201; James Schouler, *Law of Domestic Relations Embracing Husband and Wife, Parent and Child, Guardian and Ward, Infancy and Master and Servant* (Boston: Little, Brown & Co., 1905), pp. 54–56; Tapping Reeve, *The Law of Baron and Femme, of Parent and Child, Guardian and Ward, Master and Servant and of the Powers of the Courts of Chancery; . . . with Notes and References to English and American Cases*, 3rd ed. (Albany: William Gould & Son, 1874), pp. 141–142.

16. Henry Harrison Sprague, *Women under the Law of Massachusetts, Their Rights, Privileges, and Disabilities* (Boston: W. B. Clarke & Carruth, 1884), pp. 12–13.

17.Lyle Koehler, *A Search for Power: The "Weaker Sex" in Seventeenth Century New England* (Urbana, Ill.: University of Illinois Press, 1980), pp. 140–142.

18. Nelson Manfred Blake, *The Road to Reno: A History of Divorce in the United States* (New York: Macmillan Co., 1962), esp. pp. 48–63.

19. Joel Prentiss Bishop, *Commentaries on the Law of Marriage and Divorce, of Separations without Divorce, and of the Evidence of Marriage in all Issues; Embracing also Pleading, Practice, and Evidence in Divorce Causes, with Forms*, vol. 1, 4th ed. (Boston: Little, Brown, & Co., 1864), p. 586.

20. Ibid., pp. 589–590, reprints Stowell's comments. For the original citation see Evans v. Evans, 1 Hag. Con. 35; 4 Eng. Ec. 310–312.

21. For a discussion of the expanding legal definition of marital cruelty, see the following works: H. Campbell Black, "Cruelty as a Ground for Divorce," *The Central Law Journal* 20 (1885):284–288; James C. Courtney, "What is Legal

Cruelty," ibid. 37 (1893):66–70. See also John M. Biggs, *The Concept of Matrimonial Cruelty* (London: University of London, The Athlone Press, 1962).

22. Barrere v. Barrere, 4 Johns. Ch. 189. See also Bishop, *Marriage and Divorce*, p. 613; and Finley v. Finley, 9 Dana 53.

23. Ibid., pp. 634–635.

24. For Collins' anecdote see Elizabeth Cady Stanton, Susan B. Anthony, and Matilda Joslyn Gage, eds., *History of Woman Suffrage*, 6 vols., 2d ed. (Rochester, New York: Charles Mann, 1889), 2:88–89.

25. Ibid.

26. For a discussion of radical feminist efforts against wife beating in the post-Civil War period, see Elizabeth Pleck, "Feminist Responses to 'Crimes Against Women', 1868–1896," *Signs: Journal of Women in Culture and Society* 8 (Spring 1983):451–470.

27. *Address of Elizabeth Cady Stanton, on the Divorce Bill, before the Judiciary Committee of the New York Senate, in the Assembly Chamber, Feb. 8, 1861* (Albany: Weed, Parsons & Co., 1861), esp. pp. 10–11.

28. Jay Fliegelman, *Prodigals and Pilgrims: The American Revolution against Patriarchal Authority, 1750–1800* (Cambridge, Mass.: Cambridge University Press, 1982), esp. pp. 123–154.

29. Lonna Myers Malmsheimer, "New England Funeral Sermons and Changing Attitudes toward Women, 1672–1792" (Ph.D. diss., University of Minnesota, 1973), esp. chapter 4, "Daughters of Zion," pp. 133 ff.

30. Daniel Scott Smith, "Parental Power and Marriage Patterns: Analysis of Historical Trends in Hingham, Massachusetts," *Journal of Marriage and Family* 35 (1973):419–428.

31. Herman R. Lantz et al., "Pre-Industrial Patterns in the Colonial Family in America: A Content Analysis of Colonial Magazines," *American Sociological Review* 33 (1968):413–426.

32. Catherine E. Beecher, *A Treatise on Domestic Economy, for the Use of Young Ladies at Home and at School*, rev. 2d ed. (Boston: Thomas H. Webb & Co., 1842), p. 27.

33. William A. Alcott, *The Young Wife; or, Duties of Women in the Marriage Relation* (1837; reprint ed., New York: Arno Press & The New York Times, 1972), pp. 25–32.

34. Catherine E. Beecher, *The True Remedy for the Wrongs of Women* (Boston: Phillips & Sampson, 1851), p. 230.

35. Alcott, *The Young Wife*, esp. pp. 22, 25–26; idem, *The Young Husband; or, Duties of Man in the Marriage Relation* (1839; reprint ed., New York: Arno Press & The New York Times, 1972), pp. 25–26.

36. Ibid., p. 234.

37. Ibid. pp. 24–26. See also Michael Gordon, "The Ideal Husband as Depicted in Nineteenth Century Marriage Manuals," *Family Coordinator* 18, No. 3 (July 1969):226–231.

38. Ibid., p. 230.

39. Ibid., pp. 346–349.

40. Ibid., pp.342–343.

41. Ibid., pp. 273–275.

42. Ibid., p. 263.

43. Lyman Cobb, *The Evil Tendencies of Corporal Punishment as a Means of Moral Discipline in Families and Schools, Examined and Discussed* (New York: Mark H. Newman & Co., 1847), p. 81.

44. Ibid., p. 64.

45. Timothy Shay Arthur, *Six Nights with the Washingtonians; and Other Temperance Tales* (Philadelphia: T. B. Peterson & Brothers, 1871). See esp. "The Drunkard's Wife," pp. 146–184; "The Reclaimed," pp. 68–81.

46. Stanton, *Address*, esp. p. 8.

47. Ibid., pp. 7–9.

48. Greeley's opposition to divorce reform is also apparent in a series of debates that he had with socialist Robert Owen about this matter. These debates were published in the *New York Tribune* during March and April 1860. See especially Greeley's *Tribune* editorials in the March 1, March 6, and March 17 issues.

49. Thomas and Mary Gove Nichols, *Marriage: Its History, Character and Results; Its Sanctities, and Its Profanities; Its Science and Its Facts Demonstrating Its Influence, as a Civilized Institution, on the Happiness of the Individual, and the Progress of the Race* (New York: T. L. Nichols, 1854), p. 85.

50. According to contemporary sociologists, a view of the family as a private, peaceful haven continues to blunt public awareness of wife and child abuse. See, for example, Richard J. Gelles, *The Violent Home: A Study of Physical Aggression between Husbands and Wives* (Beverly Hills, Calif.: Sage Publications, Inc., 1972), pp. 13 & 20; Murray A. Straus, Richard J. Gelles, and Suzanne K. Steinmetz, *Behind Closed Doors: Violence in the American Family* (New York: Anchor Press, 1980), p. 31.

51. Ian Gibson, *The English Vice: Beating, Sex, and Shame in Victorian England and After* (London: Duckworth Press & Co., 1978); Steven Marcus, *The Other Victorians: A Study of Sexuality and Pornography in Mid-Nineteenth-Century England* (New York: Basic Books, Inc., 1966), esp. pp. 252–265.

Notes to Chapter 5

1. These comments appear in the *New York Tribune* 13 April 1850, p. 1.

2. Solomon Hewes Sanborn, *An Exposition of Official Tyranny in the United States Navy* (New York: n.p., 1841), esp. pp. 13–14, 9–10.

3. William Meacham Murrell, *Cruise of the Frigate Columbia Around the World, Under the Command of Commodore George Read in 1838, 1839, and 1840* (Boston: Benjamin B. Mussey, 1840), p. 176.

4. Levi S. Burr, *A Voice From Sing Sing; Giving a General Description of the State Prison . . . a Synopsis of the Horrid Treatment of the Convicts in that Prison* (Albany: n. p., 1833), p. 17.

5. W. A. Coffey, *Inside Out; or, an Interior View of the New York State Prison, Together with Biographical Sketches of the Lives of Several of the Convicts* (New York: James Costigan, 1823), see esp. introduction and p. 103.

6. Burr, *A Voice From Sing Sing*, pp. 3–4.

7. A particularly detailed survey of convicts' backgrounds appears in New York State Senate, *Annual Report of the Inspectors of the State Prison at Auburn*, "Abstract of Brief Biographical Sketches," Senate Document No. 15, vol. 1, 54th sess., January 24, 1831, pp. 35–62.

8. Horace Lane, *The Wandering Boy, Careless Sailor, and Result of Inconsideration. A True Narrative* (Skaneateles, N.Y.: Luther A. Pratt, 1839), esp. pp. 7–13.

9. Ibid., p. 10.

10. For a discussion of Lane's restlessness as an apprentice and his efforts to escape to the sea, see ibid., pp. 10–17.

11. Ibid., pp. 27–29, discusses Lane's introduction to taverns and dance halls.

12. Ibid., pp. 119–120.

13. Ibid., pp. 190–192.

14. Ibid., pp. 193–195.

15. James Holly Garrison, *Behold Me Once More: The Confessions of James Holly Garrison*, ed. Walter McIntosh Merrill (Boston: Houghton Mifflin Co., 1954), esp. pp. 90–91; 93–94. See also Garrison's unpublished diary, MSS, New York Public Library.

16. William McNally, *Evils and Abuses in the Naval and Merchant Service Exposed; with Proposals for Their Remedy and Redress* (Boston: Cassady & March, 1839), pp. 35–42, for comments on grog.

17. Lane, *The Wandering Boy*, pp. 36–37.

18. Richard Henry Dana, *Two Years Before the Mast: A Personal Narrative of Life at Sea* (Cleveland: The Fine Editions Press, 1946), p. 414.

19. Ibid., p. 402.

20. Jacob A. Hazen, *Five Years Before the Mast; or, Life in the Forecastle Aboard of a Whaler and Man-of-War* (Chicago: Belford, Clarke & Co., 1888), pp. 212–217.

21. Nathaniel Ames, *Nautical Reminiscences* (Providence, R.I.: Wm. Marshall & Co., 1832), pp. 47–48. For biographical information on Ames, see pp. 7–8.

22. John Reynolds, *Recollections of Windsor Prison: Containing Sketches of Its History and Discipline with Appropriate Strictures, and Moral and Religious Reflections*, 3rd ed. (Boston: A. Wright, 1839), esp. pp. 16–19; 178–206.

23. Ibid., p. 19.

24. Burr, *A Voice From Sing Sing*, p. 33.

25. Charles Nordhoff, *Man-Of-War Life: A Boy's Experience in the United States Navy, During a Voyage Around the World in a Ship of the Line* (New York: Dodd, Mead & Co., 1895), p. 140.

26. Hazen, *Five Years Before the Mast*, p. 223.

27. Herman Melville, *White Jacket; or, the World in a Man-of-War* (Chicago: Northwestern University Press & The Newberry Library, 1970), pp. 137–138.

28. Hazen, *Five Years Before the Mast*, p. 222.

29. Ibid., pp. 219 and 164.

30. Dana, *Two Years Before the Mast*, pp. 117–120.

31. James R. Brice, *Secrets of the Mount Pleasant State Prison, Revealed and Exposed ... an Account of the Inhumane Treatment of Prisoners ... with Other Curious Matters before Unknown to the Public* (Albany: The Author, 1839), p. 69.

32. Murrell, *Cruise of the Frigate Columbia*, p. 35.

33. Coffey, *Inside Out*, p. 74.

34. Ibid., p. 62.

35. Ibid., p. 78.

36. Brice, *Secrets of the Mount Pleasant State Prison*, esp. pp. 46 and 49.

37. Tiphys Aegyptus, *The Navy's Friend; or, Reminiscences of the Navy; Containing Memoirs of a Cruise in the U. S. Schooner Enterprise* (Baltimore: Printed by the Author, 1843), esp. pp. 16–19; 29.

38. Ames, *Nautical Reminiscences*, pp. 123–125.

39. See pp. 00 and 00 in Chapters three and one respectively.

40. Brice, *Secrets of the Mount Pleasant State Prison*, pp. 41–42.

41. Garrison, *Behold Me Once More*, p. 85.

42. Coffey, *Inside Out*, p. 42.

43. Ibid., p. 44.

44. Ibid., p. 77.

45. Sanborn, *An Exposition of Official Tyranny in the United States Navy*, p. 22.

46. Reynolds, *Recollections of Windsor Prison*, pp. 18–19.

47. Burr, *A Voice From Sing Sing*, p. 16.

48. James Durand, *An Able Seaman of 1812: His Adventures on "Old Ironsides" and as an Impressed Sailor in the British Navy*, ed. George S. Brooks (New Haven: Yale University Press, 1926), p. 18.

49. Nordhoff, *Man-Of-War Life*, p. 286.

50. Roland Freeman Gould, *The Life of Gould, An Ex-Man-Of-War's Man ... Including the Three Year's Cruise of the Line of Battle Ship Ohio, on the Mediterranean Station, Under ... Commodore Hull* (Claremont, N.H.: Claremont Manufacturing Co., 1867), p. 191.

51. Durand, *An Able Seaman of 1812*, pp. 32–34.

52. Hazen, *Five Years Before the Mast*, pp. 110–121. This incident occurred aboard a whaling ship and caused the captain to rescind an earlier order which permitted the first mate to arbitrarily flog men. It is unlikely that the

captain of a man-of-war would have tolerated his crew's rebellion, much less capitulated to their demand for less punishment.

53. Dana, *Two Years Before the Mast*, p. 119.

54. Dana, *Cruelty to Seamen: Being the Case of Nichols and Couch* (Berkeley: Privately printed, 1937) esp. pp. 5, 9–10.

55. Dana, *Two Years Before the Mast*, pp. 405 and 399.

56. The following works, all written by former sailors, were particularly adamant about abolishing flogging: Sanborn, *An Exposition of Official Tyranny in the United States Navy*, esp. preface; McNally, *Evils and Abuses in the Naval and Merchant Service Exposed*, esp. p. 128; and Melville, *White Jacket*, esp. p. 146.

57. See Prison Discipline Society of Boston, *Twenty-First Annual Report* (1846), p. 24, for Johnson's May 26, 1846 letter to Dwight. This report appears in volume 5 of the Society's *The Twenty-nine Annual Reports of the Board of Managers, 1826–1854, with a Memoir of Louis Dwight*, 6 vols. (1855; reprint ed., Montclair, N.J.: Patterson Smith, 1972).

58. This lecture was published as *Obstacles to the Greater Success of Common Schools: An Address Delivered before the American Institute of Instruction, at Portland, Me., August 30, 1844* (Boston: William Ticknor & Co., 1844); see esp. pp. 30–32.

59. Secretary of the Navy William B. Preston, *Corporal Punishment and the Spirit Ration, Reports of Officers*. Circular, January 29, 1850. *NJ-Discipline*, Record Group 45, *National Archives*, Washington, D.C. Out of the eighty-six replies, only eight were against corporal punishment and only two indicated any desire to modify discipline regulations.

60. William A. Alcott, *The Young Husband; or, Duties of Man in the Marriage Relation* (1839; reprint ed., New York: Arno Press & The New York Times, 1972), p. 343.

Notes to Chapter 6

1. Committee of the Association of Masters of the Boston Public Schools, *Remarks on the Seventh Annual Report of the Honorable Horace Mann, Secretary of the Massachusetts Board of Education*, (Boston: Charles C. Little & James Brown, 1844), p. 138.

2. See, for example, the remarks of North Carolina Senator George Badger in the *Congressional Globe*, 30th Cong., 2nd sess., 20:506 (February 12, 1849).

3. See Appendix B for biographical information on the "Thirty-One." The *Boston Evening Transcript* in its June 26, 1888 obituary of Bates, Jr. noted that he was the acknowledged leader of the "Thirty-One."

4. The recommendations of this Committee are detailed in "Bostonian," *The Scholiast Schooled: An Examination of the Reports of the Annual Visiting*

Committees of the Public Schools of the City of Boston, 1845. By "Scholiast" (Cambridge: Metcalf & Co., 1846), p. 56 ff.

5. Association, *Remarks*, p.8.

6. Ibid.

7. Ibid., p. 12.

8. The following works provide a useful introduction to the controversy over school centralization in antebellum Massachusetts: George H. Martin, *The Evolution of the Massachusetts Public School System: A Historical Sketch* (New York: D. Appleton & Co., 1901), esp. pp. 151–153; 177; 183; Michael B. Katz, *Class, Bureaucracy, and Schools: The Illusion of Educational Change in America* (New York: Praeger Pubs., 1971), esp. pp. 56–104; Stanley K. Schultz *The Culture Factory: Boston Public Schools 1789–1860* (New York: Oxford University Press, 1973), esp. pp. 132–153. See also the *Transactions of the Massachusetts Teachers' Federation, 1845–47* (Boston: Samuel Coolidge, 1852).

9. Association, *Remarks*, p. 16.

10. "Bostonian," *The Scholiast Schooled*, p. 4.

11. Ibid., p. 9.

12. "Bates, Joshua," *Appleton's Encyclopedia of American Biography* 1:193–194. See Appendix B for biographical information on Bates, Jr.

13. "Withington, Leonard," ibid. 6:586.

14. Raymond B. Culver, *Horace Mann and Religion in the Massachusetts Public Schools*, (New Haven: Yale University Press, 1929), p. 205, notes Smith's conversion to Calvinism.

15. George Barrell Emerson, *Reminiscences of an Old Teacher* (Boston: Alfred Mudge & Son, 1878), p. 88. See also "Emerson, George Barrell," *DAB*, vol. 3, Part II, pp. 127–128. Emerson defended Mann in *Observations on a Pamphlet Entitled "Remarks on the Seventh Annual Report of the Honorable Horace Mann, Secretary of the Massachusetts Board of Education"* (Boston: S. N. Dickinson, Printers, 1844).

16. For a discussion of Howe's support of Mann, see Harold Schwartz, *Samuel Gridley Howe: Social Reformer, 1801–1876* (Cambridge, Mass.: Harvard University Press, 1956), esp. pp. 120–136.

17. For a review of the controversy between Mann and orthodox Calvinists, see Culver, *Horace Mann and Religion*, esp. pp. 55–82, 181–213.

18. Matthew Hale Smith, *The Bible, The Rod, and Religion in Common Schools. The Ark of God on a New Cart: A Sermon by the Reverend Matthew Hale Smith* (Boston: Redding & Co., 1847), p. 11. See also Smith's letter to Mann, dated December 23, 1846, reprinted in idem, *Correspondence between the Hon. Horace Mann and Reverend Matthew Hale Smith, Occasioned by the Sermon Entitled "The Ark of God on a New Cart"* (Boston: n.p., 1846), esp. pp. 36–38, 48.

19. Smith to Mann, 27 October 1846, reprinted in ibid., p. 42; Smith, *The Bible, The Rod, and Religion* p. 6.

20. Mann to Smith, 30 January 1847, reprinted in Matthew Hale Smith, *Sequel to the So Called Correspondence between the Reverend M. H. Smith*

and Horace Mann, Surreptitiously Published by Mr. Smith, Containing a Letter from Mr. Mann, Suppressed by Mr. Smith, with the Reply Therein Promised (Boston: W. B. Fowle, 1847), p. 31.

21. Ibid., esp. pp. 27–28; 47–48.

22. Mark Anthony De Wolfe Howe [Scholiast], Review of the Reports of the Annual Visiting Committees of the Public Schools of the City of Boston (Boston: Charles Stimpson, 1846), p. 14. See also Association, Remarks, p. 13.

23. Leonard Withington, Penitential Tears: A Cry from the Dust, by "The 31," Prostrated and Pulverized by the Hand of Horace Mann, Secretary of the Massachusetts Board of Education (Boston: C. Stimpson, 18?) p. 53.

24. Committee of the Association of Masters of the Boston Public Schools, Rejoinder to the "Reply" of the Honorable Horace Mann, Secretary of the Massachusetts Board of Education, to the "Remarks" of the Association of Boston Masters Upon His Seventh Annual Report (Boston: Charles C. Little & James Brown, 1845), pp. 54–55; idem, Remarks, pp. 120, 129–131.

25. Association, Remarks, p. 108.

26. Smith, The Bible, The Rod, and Religion, esp. pp. 5–9.

27. Ibid.; see also the Association, Remarks, p. 35; idem, Rejoinder, p. 49.

28. Smith, The Bible, The Rod, and Religion, pp. 9–10.

29. For a comprehensive analysis of the building sectional tensions over slavery, see David M. Potter's classic study The Impending Crisis 1848–1861 (New York: Harper & Row, 1976), esp. pp. 67–68 for Delano's remarks.

30. See "Hale, John Parker," DAB, vol. 4, Part II, pp. 105–107; Richard H. Sewell, John Parker Hale and the Politics of Abolition (Cambridge, Mass.: Harvard University Press, 1965), esp. pp. 105ff. Eric Foner, Free Soil, Free Labor, Free Men: The Ideology of the Republican Party Before the Civil War (New York: Oxford University Press, 1970), pp. 82, 104, 149, 228, 239. On Hale's abolitionist activities in Congress, see also the Cong. Globe, 30th Cong., 1st sess., 18:62–63. During this session of Congress Hale offered antislavery memorials calling for an immediate end of the war with Mexico and an end to the gag rule.

31. For biographical and political data on these men, see the Biographical Directory of the American Congress 1774–1791 (Washington, D. C., 1971). For data on Chase, see ibid., pp. 728–729; for Hamlin, see ibid., p. 1059; for Niles, see ibid., p. 1473. See also Foner, Free Soil, Free Labor, Free Men, pp. 73–185.

32. Hale in particular denounced corporal punishment in these terms. See the Cong. Globe, 30th Cong., 2nd sess., 20:489 (February 9, 1849); ibid., 30th Cong., 2nd sess., 20:507 (February 12, 1849); ibid., 31st Cong., 1st sess., 21, Part 2:2058 (September 28, 1850).

33. Foner, Free Soil, Free Labor, Free Men, pp. 11–39.

34. Foner stresses this commitment to internalized self-restraints in "The Causes of the American Civil War: Recent Interpretations and New Directions." This essay was recently reprinted in Foner's Politics and Ideology in the Age of the Civil War (New York: Oxford University Press, 1980), pp. 15–33. For quote see p. 25.

35. For biographical data on Yulee, see the *Biographical Directory of the American Congress*, p. 1971; for data on Badger, see ibid., p. 537; for data on Venable, see ibid., p. 1857.

36 *Cong. Globe*, 31st Cong., 1st sess., 21, Part 2:1907 (September 21, 1850).

37. Ibid., 32nd Cong., 1st sess., 24, Part 2:1016 (April 8, 1852).

38. Ibid., 30th Cong., 2nd sess., 20:510 (February 12, 1849).

39. Ibid., 32nd Cong., 1st sess., 24, Part 1:222–223 (January 7, 1852).

40. Ibid., 30th Cong., 2nd sess., 20:511 (February 12, 1849).

41. Ibid., 31st Cong., 1st sess., 21, Part 2:1907 (September 21, 1850).

42. Ibid., 32nd Cong., 1st sess., 24, Part 2:915–916 (March 29, 1852).

43. Ibid., p. 916.

44. Ibid., p. 919.

45. For Badger's remarks, see ibid., 30th Cong., 2nd sess., 20:509 (February 12, 1849). Yulee expressed a similar concern with tradition when he criticized disciplinary reform as an unwarranted "radical" change from the past. See ibid., p. 510.

46. For Butler's comments, see ibid., p. 511.

47. Ibid., 31st Cong., 1st sess., 21, Part 2:2059 (September 28, 1850).

48. E. Anthony Rotundo, "Manhood in America: The Northern Middle Class, 1770–1920." (Ph.D. diss., Brandeis University, 1982), provides an excellent introduction to this topic.

49. Andrew Jackson illustrated "manly" stoicism to pain when he refused to flinch after a bullet struck him during his famous duel with Charles Dickinson. For an account of this duel and Jackson's reputation as a "man of iron," see John William Ward, *Andrew Jackson: Symbol For An Age* (New York: Oxford University Press, 1962), pp. 153–165, esp. pp. 164–165. See also Martin Steven Pernick, "A Calculus of Suffering: Pain, Anesthesia, and Utilitarian Professionalism in Nineteenth Century American Medicine" (Ph.D. diss., Columbia University, 1979), pp. 275–276, for a brief discussion of men's alleged insensitivity to pain. Ibid., pp. 302–310, discusses the crucial nineteenth-century distinction between "'insensitivity'— the inability to feel pain, and 'endurance'— the ability to bear it." My research suggests that antebellum Americans believed that "manly" men felt pain but that they should and did endure it.

50. Ronald G. Walters, ed., *Primers For Prudery: Sexual Advice to Victorian America* (Englewood Cliffs, N.J.: Prentice-Hall, 1974), offers a good sampling of this literature.

51. David Grimsted, ed., *Notions of The Americans, 1820–1860* (New York: George Braziller, 1970), pp. 148–149, reprints this complete broadside.

52. Bertram Wyatt-Brown, *Southern Honor: Ethics and Behavior in the Old South* (New York: Oxford University Press, 1982), esp. pp. 154–159 and 164–170.

53. *Cong. Globe*, 31st Cong., 1st sess., 21, Part 2:2059 (September 28, 1850).

54. Ibid., 32nd Cong., 1st sess., 24, Part 1:283 (January 15, 1852).

55. Ibid., 30th Cong., 2nd sess., 20:508 (February 12, 1849).

56. Recall, for example, seaman-author Charles Nordhoff's view that flogging scourged the manhood out of his fellow seamen. See chap. 5, p. 000.

57. *Cong. Globe*, 32nd Cong., 1st sess., 24, Part 1:220 (January 7, 1852).

58. "Woman," *Moral Advocate* 2 (February 1823): 121–122; "Address to Female Readers," ibid., 2 (November 1822):73–74.

59. Horace Mann, *Reply to the "Remarks" of Thirty-one Boston Schoolmasters on the Seventh Annual Report of the Secretary of the Massachusetts Board of Education* (Boston: W. B. Fowle & N. Capen, 1844), pp. 128 & 130.

60. *Cong. Globe*, 30th Cong., 2nd sess., 20:507 & 512 (February 12, 1849).

61. Mann, *Reply to the "Remarks,"* p. 121.

62. *Cong. Globe*, 30th Cong., 2nd sess., 20:511 (February 12, 1849).

63. Lyman Cobb, *The Evil Tendencies of Corporal Punishment as a Means of Moral Discipline in Families and Schools, Examined and Discussed* (New York: Mark H. Newman & Co., 1847), p. 253, reprinted the comments of this convention.

64. Ibid.

65. This testimonial appears in Horace Mann, *Eighth Annual Report of the Massachusetts Board of Education, Together with the Eighth Annual Report of the Secretary of the Board* (Boston: Dutton and Wentworth, State Printers, 1845), p. 29.

66. "Mr. Mann and the Teachers of the Boston Schools," *North American Review* 126 (January 1845):224–245.

67. For a review of the controversy between Mann and the Association, see the *Boston Post*, 11 December 1844, p. 1; see also "Mr. Mann's Report on Education Abroad," *Boston Daily Advertiser*, 12 March 1844, p. 2.

68. See letters to the editor of the *Boston Atlas*, January 7, 1845, reprinted in Horace Mann, *Answer to the "Rejoinder" of Twenty-Nine Boston Schoolmasters, Part of the Thirty-one who Published "Remarks" on the Seventh Annual Report of the Secretary of the Massachusetts Board of Education* (Boston: William B. Fowle & Nahum Capen, 1845), pp. 110 & 113.

69. These letters are reprinted in ibid., pp. 111 & 113. See also the *Boston Olive Branch*, May 26, 1845; *Boston Courier*, May 10, 1845.

70. Walt Whitman, "The Whip in Schools," in David B. Tyack, ed., *Turning Points in American Educational History* (Lexington, Mass.: Xerox College Pub., 1967), pp. 165–167; see also the *Brooklyn Evening Star*, October 22, 1845; *Brooklyn Daily Eagle*, February 4, 1847.

71. For a discussion of the 1845 Boston School Committee elections, see B. A. Hinsdale, *Horace Mann and the Common School Revival in the United States* (New York: Charles Scribner's Sons, 1900), p. 202.

72. Culver, *Horace Mann and Religion*, p. 201; pp. 287–289 (Appendix C) reprints a public letter signed by thirty-four leading Bostonians pledging their support to Mann.

73. "Senatorial Science," *New York Tribune*, April 22, 1850, p. 1.

74. See note 27 in chapter one.

75. For the resolution from the Indiana legislature, see *Senate Journal*, 31st Cong., 1st sess. (Serial 548), pp. 227–228; for the resolution from the Rhode Island legislature, see *Senate Miscellaneous Documents*, 30th Cong., 2nd sess. (Serial 533), Doc. 63 (March 1849).

76. Hale's petitions are referred to in the *Cong. Globe*, 30th Cong., 2nd sess., 20:488 (February 9, 1849); for Seward's petitions, see *Senate Journal*, 31st Cong., 1st sess. (Serial 548), p. 401.

77. *Cong. Globe*, 30th Cong., 2nd sess., 20:509 (February 12, 1849); see also p. 512, where Hale notes that the "age of the cat-o'-nine tails is past," and that the Senate cannot shelter this "relic of barbarism" from "the execrations of an outraged humanity."

78. Ibid., pp. 510–511.

79. Ibid., p. 507.

80. Ibid., 32nd Cong., 1st sess., 24, Part 2:919 (March 29, 1852).

81. The following works explore antebellum Southern attitudes toward violence and punishment: Wyatt-Brown, *Southern Honor*; Dickson D. Bruce, Jr., *Violence and Culture in the Antebellum South* (Austin: University of Texas Press, 1979); Michael Stephen Hindus, *Prison and Plantation: Crime, Justice, and Authority in Massachusetts and South Carolina, 1767–1878* (Chapel Hill: University of North Carolina Press, 1980).

82. Association, *Rejoinder to the "Reply,"* p. 43.

83. Withington, *Penitential Tears*, preface and p. 7.

84. The resolution in support of corporal punishment occurred during the opening meeting of the Massachusetts Teachers Federation. See *Transactions of the Massachusetts Teachers Federation, 1845–47* (Boston: Samuel Coolidge, 1852), 1:22.

85. Reverend John P. Cowles, "First Principles of School Government," ibid., pp. 67–93.

86. "The Influences of the Teacher's Example," *The Massachusetts Teacher*, April 1849, pp. 109–111; for other examples urging moral suasion, see: Mrs. Rachel C. Mather, "The True Mission of the Teacher," ibid., April 1856, pp. 151–152; "Prize Essay on School Punishment for the Norfolk County Teacher's Association," ibid., March 1852, p. 72.

Notes to Chapter 7

1. This circular was reprinted in *Senate Documents*, 22nd Cong., 1st sess., Appendix, p. 265. See also Leo F. S. Horan, "Flogging in the United States Navy; Unfamiliar Facts Regarding Its Origins and Abolition," *United States Naval Institute Proceedings* 76 (1950):969–975, esp. p. 972.

2. Ibid.

3. For these records see *Reports of the Secretary of the Navy, Communicating copies of returns of punishment in the navy, in compliance with a res-*

olution of the Senate. These reports are found in: 30th Cong., 1st sess. (Sen.) Exec. No. 69; 30th Cong., 2nd sess. (House of Rep.) Exec. Doc. No. 51; 30th Cong., 2nd sess. (Sen.) Exec. Doc. No. 23; 31st Cong., 2nd sess. (House of Rep.) Exec. Doc. No. 26.

4. *Congressional Globe,* 31st Cong., 1st sess., 21, Part 2: 2058 (September 28, 1850).

5. Ibid., 30th Cong., 2nd sess., 20:481 (February 9, 1849).

6. Ibid., 31st Cong., 1st sess., 21, Part 2: 2058 (September 28, 1850).

7. Ibid., 30th Cong., 2nd sess., 20:489 (February 9, 1849).

8. For voting tabulation, see ibid., 31st Cong., 1st sess., 21, Part 2:2061.

9. For a description of these punishments see "Notes and Commentaries on a Voyage to China," *Southern Literary Messenger* 18 (April 1852):190–208; Frederick J. Bell, Lieut., U.S. Navy, *Room to Swing a Cat: Being Some Tales of the Old Navy* (New York: Longmans, Green & Co., 1938), p. 171. Florida Senator Stephen Mallory noted the increased use of punishments like "bucking" after the Congressional prohibition on flogging. His comments are found in *Reports of the Committee of the Senate,* 33rd Cong., 1st sess. (Serial 707).

10. Commander F. Engle to Secretary William A. Graham, July 18, 1851, *Report of the Secretary of the Navy, Communicating . . . on the subject of Corporal Punishment in the Navy, and a revision of the regulations for the better government of the Navy,* 32nd Cong., 1st sess. (Sen.) Exec. Doc. No. 10. See pp. 7–8 for Engle's comments.

11. Commander William Salter to Secretary Graham, July 21, 1851, ibid., pp. 5–6.

12. *Cong. Globe,* 32nd Cong., 1st sess., 24, Part 1:282–283 (January 15, 1852).

13. U. S. *Statutes at Large,* vol. 10, chap. 13, pp. 627–628, "An Act to Provide a More Efficient Discipline for the Navy," March 2, 1855.

14. For the statistics on Clinton State Prison, see *Third Report of the Prison Association of New York for 1846. Including the Constitution and By-Laws, Act of Incorporation and a List of Officers and Members. In 2 Parts* (New York: Pub. by the Association, 1847), p. 38.

15. See footnote 42, chapter 2.

16. New York Prison Association, *Third Report,* p. 38.

17. "Lynds, Elam," *DAB,* vol. 6, Part I:527.

18. *Fourth Report of the Prison Association of New York for 1847 and 1848. Including a List of the Officers and Members,* 2nd ed. (Albany: Weed, Parsons & Co., Public Printers, 1849), p. 15.

19. New York Prison Association, *Third Report,* p. 38.

20. New York State Assembly, *Report of the Board of Inspectors of the State Prison at Auburn, in Answer to the resolutions of the Assembly of January 30, 1846,* Assembly Document No. 83, vol. 3, 69th sess., February 9, 1846, esp. p. 34.

21. "An Act for the better regulation of the county and state prisons of the state, and consolidating and amending the existing laws in relation thereto,"

ch. 460, sec. 108, in *Laws of the State of New York, Passed at the Seventieth Session of the Legislature . . . 1847*, vol. 2 (Albany: Charles Van Benthuysen, 1847), p. 620.

22. This *Report* is found in New York State Assembly, Assembly Document No. 143, vol. 4, 77th sess., April 1854, pp. 47–48.

23. *The Annual Reports of the Board of Inspectors of the Massachusetts State Prison* (Boston, 1828–1860), provide a wealth of information on Massachusetts' antebellum prison system. The 1849 *Annual Report*, p. 4, stressed that solitary confinement was now the only way to punish convicts in Massachusetts.

24. Robinson's 1849 *Annual Report* expressed confidence that prisons could be governed without the use of any corporal punishment. His comments are reprinted in *Fifth Report of the Prison Association of New York for 1849. Including a List of the Officers and Members* (Albany: Weed, Parsons & Co., Public Printers, 1850), pp. 150–153.

25. 1849 *Annual Report of the Board of Inspectors of the Massachusetts State Prison*, p. 6. Their comments are also reprinted in ibid., p. 148.

26. Ibid., pp. 149–150.

27. Ibid., esp. pp. 150 and 148.

28. The *Prisoner's Friend* blamed these factors for the increased crime rate. See "The Massachusetts States Prison, 1849," ibid. 2 (April 1850):374.

29. Michael Stephen Hindus, *Prison and Plantation: Crime, Justice, and Authority in Massachusetts and South Carolina, 1767–1878* (Chapel Hill: University of North Carolina Press, 1980), esp. pp. 71–75.

30. The 1850 *Annual Report of the Board of Inspectors of the Massachusetts State Prison*, p. 9, approvingly noted passage of this May 3, 1850 Act.

31. New York Prison Association, *Fifth Report*, pp. 165–168, reprinted statistics on the punishments administered in Maine's State Prison.

32. Carl Degler, *At Odds: Women and the Family in America from the Revolution to the Present* (New York: Oxford University Press, 1980), pp. 86–110; Elizabeth Pleck, "Trouble the Spirit: Patterns of Childhood Punishment in American Families, 1780–1900." Paper presented at the Fourth Berkshire Conference on the History of Women, Mount Holyoke, Massachusetts, August 1978; Barbara Finkelstein, "Governing the Young: Teacher Behavior in American Primary Schools, 1820–1880. A Documentary History" (Ed.D. diss., Department of Education, Teacher's College, Columbia University, 1970). These scholars utilized impressionistic evidence, particularly the diaries, memoirs, and personal correspondence of teachers, parents, and children to document the shift away from corporal punishment.

33. Lyman Cobb, *The Evil Tendencies of Corporal Punishment as a Means of Moral Discipline in Families and Schools, Examined and Discussed* (New York: Mark H. Newman & Co., 1847), pp. 253–254, excerpts the comments from the Public School Society of New York City on this bylaw.

34. Ibid., p. 254.

35. Horace Mann, *Answer to the "Rejoinder" of Twenty-nine Boston School-masters, Part of the Thirty-one Who Published "Remarks" on the Seventh Annual Report of the Secretary of the Massachusetts Board of Education.* (Boston: William B. Fowle & Nahum Capen, 1845), p. 81.

36. Mann, *Tenth Annual Report of the Massachusetts Board of Education, Together with the Tenth Annual Report of the Secretary of the Board* (Boston: Dutton and Wentworth, State Printers, 1847), pp. 81–84.

37. *Cong. Globe*, 32nd Cong., 1st sess., 24, Part 1:219–220 (January 7, 1852).

38. Ibid.

39. My discussion of the literature on the psychology of punishment relies on the following works: Justin Aronfreed, *Conduct and Conscience: The Socialization of Internalized Overt Behavior* (New York: Academic Press, 1968), esp. chapers 1 and 2; Lawrence Kohlberg, "Development of Moral Character and Moral Ideology," in *Review of Child Development Research*, eds. M. L. Hoffman and L. W. Hoffman (New York: Russell Sage Foundation, 1964), pp. 383–432; Martin L. Hoffman, "Childrearing Practices and Moral Development: Generalizations from Empirical Research," *Child Development* 34 (1963):295–318; R. H. Walters and Joan Grusec, *Punishment* (San Francisco: W. Freeman Press, 1977); R. D. Parke, "Effectiveness of Punishment as an Interaction of Intensity, Timing, Agent Nurturance, and Cognitive Structuring," *Child Development* 40 (1969):213–235; M. L. Hoffman, et al., "Parental Discipline and the Child's Moral Development," *Journal of Personality and Social Psychology* 5 (1967):45–57; R. D. Parke, "Rules, Roles and Resistance to Deviation: Recent Advances in Punishment, Discipline and Self-Control," in *Minnesota Symposia On Child Psychology* 8, ed. Anne D. Pick (Minneapolis: University of Minnesota Press, 1974), pp. 111–144; Roger V. Burton, "Honesty and Dishonesty," in *Moral Development and Behavior*, ed. Thomas Lickona (New York: Holt, Rinehart, and Winston, 1976), pp. 175–197. I am grateful to Professor Roger Burton at the State University of New York in Buffalo for bringing these citations to my attention.

40. T. H. Gallaudet, "Recollection of the Deaf and Dumb," *American Annals of Education* 8 (January 1838):3–11.

41. John Griscom, "On School Discipline," *American Annals of Education* 2 (October 1832):488–492.

42. Jacob Abbott, "Description of the Mount Vernon School in 1832, Addressed to a New Scholar," *American Annals of Education* 3 (May 1833):224–227.

43. Cobb, *Corporal Punishment*, esp. pp. 104–105.

44. See, for example, Mann's *Fifth Annual Report of the Massachusetts Board of Education, Together with the Fifth Annual Report of the Secretary of the Board* (Boston: Dutton and Wentworth, State Printers, 1842), p. 58; Samuel Read Hall, *Lectures on School Keeping* (Boston: Richardson, Lord & Holbrook, 1829), p. 71; Mrs. J. Bakewell, *The Mother's Practical Guide in the Early Training of her Children; Containing Directions for Their Physical, Intellectual and Moral*

Education (New York: Pub. by G. Lane and P. P. Sandford for the Methodist Episcopal Church, 1843), pp. 158–164.

45. See p. 00 of chapter 3.

46. Chaplain McLaughlin's comments are found in the December 1830 issue of the *Sailor's Magazine*. They were reprinted in Clifford M. Drury, *United States Navy Chaplains 1778–1945*, vol. 1 (Washington, D.C.: Government Printing Office, 1949), p. 54.

47. Rockwell's comments are cited in ibid., p. 40. Seamen-authors also viewed education as a crucial way to reform seamen. See, for example, William McNally, *Evils and Abuses in the Naval and Merchant Service Exposed; with Proposals for Their Remedy and Redress* (Boston: Cassady & March, 1839), p. 156.

48. Luckey's comments are reported in the Prison Discipline Society of Boston, *Twentieth Annual Report* (1845), p. 87. This latter report appears in the 4th volume of the Society's *The Twenty-nine Annual Reports of the Board of Managers, 1826–1854, with a Memoir of Louis Dwight*, 6 vols. (1855; reprint ed., Montclair, N.J.: Patterson Smith, 1972).

49. Gideon Haynes, *Pictures From Prison Life. An Historical Sketch of the Massachusetts State Prison with . . . Suggestions on Discipline* (Boston: Lee & Shepard, 1869), p. 241.

50. *Cong. Globe*, 32nd Cong., 1st sess., 24:451 (February 5, 1852).

51. Society for the Prevention of Pauperism, *Report on the Penitentiary System in the United States* (1822; reprint ed., New York: Arno Press, 1974), pp. 53–54.

52. Catherine Sedgwick, *Home* (Boston: James Monroe & Co., 1835), pp. 14–27.

53. *Report on the Penitentiary System*, p. 53.

54. Elizabeth Peabody, *Record of a School* (1836; reprint ed., New York: Arno Press & The New York Times, 1969), p. 124.

55. Ibid., p. 24.

56. Ibid., p. 108.

57. "French Society for Elementary Instruction" *American Journal of Education* 3 (March 1828):173.

58. For a review of Levy's disciplinary procedures while captain of the *U.S.S. Vandalia*, see Abram Kanof, "Uriah Phillips Levy: The Story of a Pugnacious Commodore," *Publications of the American Historical Jewish Society*, Part I, 39 (September 1949):1–66.

59. The *Norfolk Herald's* editorial was reprinted in several places. See, for example, the January 18, 1840 issue of the *New York Evening Star* and the *Army and Navy Chronicle* 10 (January 1840):54.

60. For Hooe's charges, see "Record of the Proceedings in the Case of Commander Uriah P. Levy, Upon Charges Preferred upon information of Lieutenant George Mason Hooe," *Uriah P. Levy Manuscripts*, Library of Congress.

61. Ibid., p. 21; after reconsidering its verdict, the Court upheld its initial decision, pp. 78–79.

62. Ibid., p. 24. President Tyler subsequently remanded Levy's sentence, noting that it was too harsh.

63. Kanof, "Uriah Phillips Levy," p. 8. While reviewing his naval career in 1857 Levy noted the anti-Semitism and personal hostility of his fellow officers. See "Defense of Captain Uriah P. Levy, United States Navy, Before a Court of Inquiry, Convened at Washington, D.C. in November 1857," *Uriah P. Levy Manuscripts*, Library of Congress, esp. pp. 54ff.

64. See, for example, Captain J. H. Aulick to Naval Secretary Preston, February 7, 1850, U.S. Navy Department Archives, Record Group 45, National Archives, Washington, D. C. *Corporal Punishment and the Spirit Rations, Reports of Officers. Circular, January 29, 1850*, No. 22, pp. 94–96. Commodore S. Barron to Secretary Preston, February 5, 1850, ibid., No. 49, pp. 179–180.

65. Captain J. H. Aulick's *Report* was particularly critical of solitary confinement. See also Commodore Matthew C. Perry to Secretary Preston, February 4, 1850, ibid., No. 12, pp. 61–70; Commodore Charles Stewart to Secretary Preston, March 11, 1850, ibid., No. 1, pp. 6–17; Commodore J. Downes to Secretary Preston, February 4, 1850, ibid., No. 4, pp. 26–27.

66. John L. Thomas, "Romantic Reform in America, 1815–1865," in David Brion Davis, ed., *Ante-Bellum Reform* (New York: Harper & Row, 1967), pp. 153–176.

Selected Bibliography

For the convenience of the reader this bibliography is divided into four major divisions: General Works on Punishment, Pain, and Violence; Children and Women; Seamen; and Prisoners.

General Works on Punishment, Pain, and Violence

Andrews, William. *Old-Time Punishments*. 1890. Reprint. Detroit: Single Tree Press, 1970.

Aronfreed, Justin. *Conduct and Conscience: The Socialization of Internalized Overt Behavior*. New York: Academic Press, 1968.

Barnes, Harry Elmer. *The Story of Punishment: A Record of Man's Inhumanity to Man*. 2d ed. rev. Montclair, N.J.: Patterson Smith, 1972.

Berkson, Larry Charles. *The Concept of Cruel and Unusual Punishment*. Lexington, Mass.: Lexington Books, 1975.

Brown, Richard Maxwell. *Strain of Violence: Historical Studies of American Violence and Vigilantism*. New York: Oxford University Press, 1975.

Bruce, Jr., Dickson, D. *Violence and Culture in the Antebellum South*. Austin: University of Texas Press, 1979.

Davis, David Brion. "The Movement to Abolish Capital Punishment in America, 1787–1861." *American Historical Review* 63 (October 1957):23–46.

Earle, Alice Morse. *Curious Punishments of Bygone Days*. 1896. Reprint. Detroit: Single Tree Press, 1968.

Foucault, Michel. *Discipline and Punish: The Birth of the Prison*. Translated by Alan Sheridan. New York: Pantheon Books, 1977.

Gibson, Ian. *The English Vice: Beating, Sex, and Shame in Victorian England and After*. London: Duckworth Press & Co., 1978.

Gurr, Ted Robert, and Graham, Hugh Davis, eds. *The History of Violence in America: Historical and Comparative Perspectives.* New York: Frederick A. Praeger Pubs., 1969.

Hyman, Irwin A., and Wise, James H., eds. *Corporal Punishment in American Education: Readings in History, Practice, and Alternatives.* Philadelphia: Temple University Press, 1979.

Lickona, Thomas, ed. *Moral Development and Behavior.* New York: Holt, Rinehart, and Winston, 1976.

Pernick, Martin Steven. "A Calculus of Suffering: Pain, Anesthesia, and Utilitarian Professionalism in Nineteenth Century American Medicine." Ph.D. dissertation, Columbia University, 1979.

Rothman, David J. *Conscience and Convenience: The Asylum and its Alternatives in Progressive America.* Boston: Little, Brown and Company, 1980.

———. *The Discovery of the Asylum: Social Order and Disorder in the New Republic.* Boston: Little, Brown and Company, 1971.

Rusche, Georg, and Kirchheimer, Otto. *Punishment and Social Structure.* New York: Columbia University Press, 1939.

Sloan, Irving J. *Our Violent Past: An American Chronicle.* New York: Random House, 1970.

Turner, James. *Reckoning with the Beast: Animals, Pain and Humanity in the Victorian Mind.* Baltimore: The John Hopkins University Press, 1980.

Walters, R. H., and Grusec, Joan. *Punishment.* San Francisco: W. Freeman Press, 1977.

Wyatt-Brown, Bertram. *Southern Honor: Ethics and Behavior in the Old South.* New York: Oxford University Press, 1982.

Children and Women

A. Manuscript Collections

Massachusetts Historical Society, Boston, Mass. Horace Mann Papers.

B. Periodicals and Newspapers

American Annals of Education, January 1826–December 1829, January–July 1830, January 1832–December 1839.

American Journal of Education, January 1826–December 1829.

Boston Daily Advertiser, 1844–1847.

Boston Post, 1844–1847.

Common School Assistant, January 1836–April 1840.

Common School Journal, November 1838–October 1847.

District School Journal of the State of New York, March 1840–April 1852.

Ladies Magazine, 1828–36.

The Lily. A Ladies Magazine Devoted to Temperance and Literature, 1849–53.

The Massachusetts Teacher, 1849, 1852–61, 1863–70.
New York Times, 1858–68.
North American Review, 1844–1847.

C. Books, Pamphlets, Articles, and Dissertations

Abbott, Jacob. *Gentle Measures in the Management and Training of the Young; or, the Principles on which a Firm Parental Authority May be Established and Maintained, without Violence or Anger and the Right Development of the Moral and Mental Capacities be Promoted by Methods in Harmony with the Structure and the Characteristics of the Juvenile Mind.* New York: Harper & Bros., 1871.

Abbott, John S. C. *The Mother at Home; or the Principle of Maternal Duty.* Boston: Crocker and Brewster, 1834.

Alcott, William A. *The Young Husband; or, Duties of Man in the Marriage Relation.* 1839. Reprint. New York: Arno Press & The New York Times, 1972.

————. *The Young Wife; or, Duties of Woman in the Marriage Relation.* 1837. Reprint. New York: Arno Press & The New York Times, 1972.

American Institute of Instruction. *Lectures and Journal of Proceedings of the American Institute of Instruction.* Boston: Ticknor, Reed & Fields, 1830–52, 1864–68.

Arthur, Timothy Shay [Mary Elmwood]. *Hints and Helps for the Home Circle; or, the Mother's Friend.* New York: John Allen, 1844.

————. *The Iron Rule; or, Tyranny in the Household.* Philadelphia: T. B. Peterson, 1853.

————. *Married Life: Its Shadows and Sunshine.* Philadelphia: Lippincott, Grambo & Co., 1852.

————. *The Mother.* New York: E. Ferrett & Co., 1846.

————. *The Orphan Children: A Tale of Cruelty and Oppression.* Philadelphia: T. B. Peterson, 1850.

————. *Six Nights with the Washingtonians; and Other Temperance Tales.* Philadelphia: T. B. Peterson & Brothers, 1871.

————. *Stories for Parents.* Philadelphia: Lippincott, Grambo & Co., 1851.

Bakewell, Mrs. J. *The Mother's Practical Guide in the Early Training of her Children; Containing Directions for Their Physical, Intellectual and Moral Education.* New York: Pub. by G. Lane and P. P. Sandford for the Methodist Episcopal Church, 1843.

Barnard, Henry, ed. *Memoirs of Teachers, Educators, and Promoters and Benefactors of Education, Literature, Science.* 1861. Reprint. New York: Arno Press & The New York Times, 1969.

Beecher, Catherine E. *A Treatise on Domestic Economy for the Use of Young Ladies at Home and at School.* Rev. 2d ed. Boston: Thomas H. Webb & Co., 1842.

Behlmer, George K. *Child Abuse and Moral Reform in England, 1870–1908.* Stanford, Calif.: Stanford University Press, 1982.

Biggs, John M. *The Concept of Matrimonial Cruelty.* London: University of London, The Athlone Press, 1962.

Bishop, Joel Prentiss. *Commentaries on the Law of Marriage and Divorce, of Separations without Divorce, and of the Evidence of Marriage in all Issues; Embracing also Pleading, Practice, and Evidence in Divorce Causes, with Forms.* vol. 1, 4th ed. Boston: Little, Brown, & Co., 1864.

Blake, Nelson Manfred. *The Road to Reno: A History of Divorce in the United States.* New York: Macmillan Co., 1962.

Boston School Committee. *Annual Reports of the Boston School Committee of the City of Boston.* Boston: City Printers, 1857–74.

———. *Report of the Committee on Corporal Punishment in the Public Schools.* Boston: City Printers, 1864.

———. *Report of the Committee on the Rules and Regulations on Corporal Punishment in the Public Schools.* Boston: Rockwell & Churchill, City Printers, 1873.

———. *Report on Corporal Punishment in the Public Schools of the City of Boston.* Boston: Alfred Rudge & Son, Printers, 1867.

"Bostonian." *The Scholiast Schooled: An Examination of the Reports of the Annual Visiting Committees of the Public Schools of the City of Boston, 1845. By "Scholiast."* Cambridge: Metcalf & Co., 1846.

Brayley, Arthur W. *Schools and Schoolboys of Old Boston.* Boston: Louis P. Hager, 1894.

Breines, Wini, and Gordon, Linda. "The New Scholarship on Family Violence," *Signs: Journal of Women in Culture and Society* 8 (Spring 1983):490–531.

Burke, Dennis P. "A Study of Court Cases Resulting from Corporal Punishment in the Public Schools." Ph.D. dissertation, Department of Education, University of Pittsburgh, 1958.

Burton, Warren. *The District School as It Was by One Who Went to It.* Edited by Clifton Johnson. Boston: Lee & Shepard, 1897.

Calhoun, Arthur W. *A Social History of the American Family.* 3 vols. 1918. Reprint. New York: Barnes & Noble, Inc., 1960.

Calhoun, Daniel C. *The Intelligence of a People.* Princeton: Princeton University Press, 1973.

Cambridge (Massachusetts) School Committee. *Address to the People of Cambridge from the School Committee Concerning a Recent Case of Corporal Punishment in the Allston Grammar School.* Cambridge: John Wilson & Son, 1866.

———. *Annual Reports of the School Committee of the City of Cambridge.* Cambridge: City Printers, 1842–1868.

Cobb, Lyman. *The Evil Tendencies of Corporal Punishment as a Means of Moral Discipline in Families and Schools, Examined and Discussed.* New York: Mark H. Newman & Co., 1847.

Cohen, Sol, ed. *Education in the United States. A Documentary.* 5 vols. New York: Random House, 1974.

Committee of the Association of Masters of the Boston Public Schools. *Re-joinder to the "Reply" of the Honorable Horace Mann, Secretary of the Massachusetts Board of Education, to the "Remarks" of the Association of Boston Masters upon His Seventh Annual Report.* Boston: Charles C. Little & James Brown, 1845.

_____. *Remarks on the Seventh Annual Report of the Honorable Horace Mann, Secretary of the Massachusetts Board of Education.* Boston: Charles C. Little & James Brown, 1844.

Cott, Nancy F. *The Bonds of Womanhood: "Woman's Sphere" in New England, 1780–1835.* New Haven: Yale University Press, 1977.

_____. "Divorce and the Changing Status of Women in Eighteenth Century Massachusetts," *William & Mary Quarterly* 33 (October 1976):586–614.

_____. "Notes Toward an Interpretation of Antebellum Childrearing." *The Psychohistory Review* 6, No. 4 (Spring 1978), pp. 4–20.

Cremin, Lawrence. *The American Common School: An Historic Conception.* New York: Bureau of Pub. Teachers College, Columbia University, 1951.

_____. *American Education: The Colonial Experience 1607–1783.* New York: Harper & Row, Pub., 1970.

_____. *American Education: The National Experience, 1783–1876.* New York: Harper & Row, 1980.

Culver, Raymond B. *Horace Mann and Religion in the Massachusetts Public Schools.* New Haven: Yale University Press, 1929.

de Mause, Lloyd, ed., *The History of Childhood.* New York: Psychohistory Press, 1974.

Degler, Carl N. *At Odds: Women and the Family in America from the Revolution to the Present.* New York: Oxford University Press, 1980.

Dobash, R. Emerson, and Dobash, Russell. *Violence against Wives: A Case against the Patriarchy.* New York: Free Press, 1979.

Douglas, Ann. *The Feminization of American Culture.* New York: Alfred A. Knopf, 1977.

Emerson, George Barrell. *Observations on a Pamphlet, Entitled "Remarks on the Seventh Annual Report of the Honorable Horace Mann, Secretary of the Massachusetts Board of Education."* Boston: S. N. Dickinson, Printers, 1844.

_____. *Reminiscences of an Old Teacher.* Boston: Alfred Mudge & Son, 1878.

Epstein, Barbara Leslie. *The Politics of Domesticity: Women, Evangelism, and Temperance in Nineteenth-Century America.* Middletown, Conn.: Wesleyan University Press, 1981.

Faulkner, Theodore Alvin. "The History of Legal Action in Corporal Punishment Cases in New York State 1812–1965. An Investigation of Judicial Decisions Arising from Punishment of Pupils by Teachers in Public and Private Schools of New York State." Ed.D. dissertation, New York University, 1967.

Finkelstein, Barbara. "Governing the Young: Teacher Behavior in American Primary Schools, 1820–1880. A Documentary History." Ed.D. dissertation, Department of Education, Teachers College, Columbia University, 1970.

_____. ed. *Regulated Children/Liberated Children: Education in Psychohistorical Perspective.* New York: Psychohistory Press, 1979.

Fleming, Sandford. *Children and Puritanism: The Place of Children in the Life and Thought of the New England Churches 1620–1847.* 1933. Reprint. New York: Arno Press & The New York Times, 1969.

Fliegelman, Jay. *Prodigals and Pilgrims: The American Revolution against Patriarchal Authority, 1750–1800.* Cambridge, Mass.: Cambridge University Press, 1982.

Gelles, Richard J. *The Violent Home: A Study of Physical Aggression between Husbands and Wives.* Beverly Hills, Calif.: Sage Publications, Inc., 1972.

Gil, David G. *Violence against Children: Physical Child Abuse in the United States.* Cambridge, Mass.: Harvard University Press, 1970.

Goodrich, S. F. *Fireside Education.* London: William Smith, 1839.

Goodsell, Willystine. *A History of Marriage and the Family.* New York: Macmillan Co., 1934.

Gordon, Michael. "The Ideal Husband as Depicted in Nineteenth Century Marriage Manuals," *Family Coordinator* 18, No. 3 (July 1969), pp. 226–231.

Greven, Philip J. Jr., ed. *Child-Rearing Concepts, 1628–1861.* Itasca, Illinois: F. E. Peacock Pub., 1973.

_____. *The Protestant Temperament: Patterns of Child-Rearing, Religious Experience and the Self in Early America.* New York: Alfred A. Knopf, 1977.

Griscom, John. *Memoirs of John Griscom; with an Account of New York High School, Society for the Prevention of Pauperism, House of Refuge and other Institutions.* New York: Robert Carter & Bros., 1859.

Hall, Samuel Read. *Lectures on School-Keeping.* Boston: Richardson, Lord & Holbrook, 1829.

_____. *Lectures to Female Teachers on School-Keeping.* Boston: Richardson, Lord & Holbrook, 1832.

Harper, Ida Husted. *The Life and Work of Susan B. Anthony.* 3 vols. Indianapolis: The Hollenbeck Press, 1898.

Hiner, N. Ray. "Children's Rights, Corporal Punishment, and Child Abuse: Changing American Attitudes, 1870–1920," *Bulletin of the Menninger Clinic* 43 (May 1979):233–248.

Hinsdale, B. A. *Horace Mann and the Common School Revival in the United States.* New York: Charles Scribner's Sons, 1900.

Hirschberger, Emma Jane. "A Study of the Development of the *In Loco Parentis* Doctrine: Its Application and Emerging Trends." Ph.D. dissertation, University of Pittsburgh, 1971.

Hoare, Louisa Gurney. *Hints for the Improvement of Early Education and Nursery Discipline.* Salem, Mass.: James R. Buffum, 1826.

Holbrook, Alfred. *Reminiscences of the Happy Life of a Teacher.* Cincinnati: Elm
   St. Pub. Co., 1885.
Howe, Mark Anthony De Wolfe [Scholiast]. *Review of the Reports of the Annual
   Visiting Committees, of the Public Schools of the City of Boston.* Boston:
   Charles Stimpson, 1846.
"In-mate of the Alms-House." *Autobiography of a Reformed Drunkard; or, Let-
   ters and Recollections.* Philadelphia: Griffith & Simon, 1845.
Jaquith, Moses. *An Appeal to the Public in a Case of Cruelty, Inflicted on a Child
   of Mr. Jaquith at the Mayhew School . . . by William Clough . . . Together
   with Other Matters.* Boston: privately printed, 1832.
Kaestle, Carl. *The Evolution of an Urban School System: New York City, 1750–
   1850.* Cambridge, Mass.: Harvard University Press, 1973.
_____. *Pillars of the Republic: Common Schools and American Society, 1780–
   1860.* New York: Hill & Wang, 1983.
_____. "Social Change, Discipline, and the Common School in Early Nine-
   teenth-Century America," *Journal of Interdisciplinary History* 9 (Summer
   1978):1–17.
Katz, Michael B. *Class, Bureaucracy, and Schools: The Illusion of Educational
   Change in America.* New York: Praeger Pubs., 1971.
_____. *The Irony of Early School Reform: Educational Innovation in Mid Nine-
   teenth Century Massachusetts.* Cambridge, Mass.: Harvard University
   Press, 1968.
Koehler, Lyle. *A Search for Power: The "Weaker Sex" in Seventeenth Century
   New England.* Urbana, Ill.: University of Illinois Press, 1980.
Kuhn, Anne L. *The Mother's Role in Childhood Education: New England Con-
   cepts, 1830–60.* New Haven: Yale University Press, 1947.
Lazerson, Marvin. *Origins of the Urban School: Public Education in Massachu-
   setts, 1870–1915.* Cambridge, Mass.: Harvard University Press, 1971.
Mann, Horace. *Annual Reports on Education.* Boston: Horace B. Fuller, 1868.
_____. *Answer to the "Rejoinder of Twenty-nine Boston Schoolmasters, Part
   of the Thirty-one Who Published "Remarks" on the Seventh Annual Re-
   port of the Secretary of the Massachusetts Board of Education.* Boston:
   William B. Fowle & Nahum Capen, 1845.
_____. *Lectures on Education.* Boston: W. B. Fowle & N. Capen, 1845.
_____. *Reply to the "Remarks" of Thirty-one Boston Schoolmasters on the
   Seventh Annual Report of the Secretary of the Massachusetts Board of
   Education.* Boston: W. B. Fowle & N. Capen, 1844.
Mann, Mary. *Life and Works of Horace Mann.* 5 vols. Boston: Lee and Shepard,
   1891.
Martin, George H. *The Evolution of the Massachusetts Public School System:
   A Historical Sketch.* New York: D. Appleton & Co., 1901.
Mattingly, Paul H. *The Classless Profession: American Schoolmen in the Nine-
   teenth Century.* New York: New York University Press, 1975.
Messerli, Jonathan. *Horace Mann: A Biography.* New York: Alfred A. Knopf, 1972.

Morgan, Edmund S. *The Puritan Family: Religion and Domestic Relations in Seventeenth Century New England.* New ed., rev. and enl. New York: Harper & Row, 1966.

Muzzey. A. B. *The Fireside: An Aid to Parents.* 2d ed. Boston: Crosby, Nichols & Co., 1856.

New York City Board of Education. *Annual Reports and Extracts from Teachers' Reports . . . and Annual Reports of City and Assistant Superintendents.* New York: William C. Bryant & Co., Printers, 1849–70.

————. *Reports on Corporal Punishment, Report of Commissioner Jarvis, October 5, 1870. Report of Commissioner Halsted, November 5, 1873. Report of Commissioner West, June 6, 1877. Report of Commissioner Walker, June 6, 1877.* New York: Printed by the Board of Education, 1877.

Nichols, Thomas L. and Nichols, Mary Gove. *Marriage: Its History, Character and Results; Its Sanctities, and Its Profanities; Its Science and Its Facts Demonstrating Its Influence, as a Civilized Institution, on the Happiness of the Individual, and the Progress of the Race.* New York: T. L. Nichols, 1854.

Northend, Charles. *Obstacles to the Greater Success of the Common Schools: An Address Delivered before the American Institute of Instruction, at Portland, Me., August 30, 1844.* Boston: William Ticknor & Co., 1844.

Orcutt, Hiram. *Hints to Common School Teachers, Parents, and Pupils; or, Gleanings from School-Life Experience.* Boston: George A. Tuttle & Co., 1859.

————. *Reminiscences of School Life; An Autobiography.* Cambridge: University Press, 1898.

Ordway, John P. & Gaylord, Noah M. *Minority Report on the Abolition of Corporal Punishment in the Public Schools* (House No. 335). Boston: Wright and Potter, 1868.

Peabody, Elizabeth. *Record of a School.* 1836. Reprint. New York: Arno Press & The New York Times. 1969.

Permanent Temperance Documents of the American Temperance Society. 1835. Reprint. New York: Arno Press, 1972.

Pleck, Elizabeth. "Feminist Responses to 'Crimes against Women,' 1868–1896," *Signs: Journal of Women in Culture and Society* 8 (Spring 1983):451–470.

————. "Trouble the Spirit: Patterns of Childhood Punishment in American Families, 1780–1900." Paper presented at the Fourth Berkshire Conference on the History of Women, Mount Holyoke, Massachusetts, August 1978.

————. "Wife-Beating in Nineteenth Century America," *Victimology* 4 (Fall 1979):60–74.

Potter, Alonzo and Emerson, George B. *The School and the Schoolmaster. A Manual for the Use of Teachers, Employers, Trustees, Inspectors, etc. etc. of Common Schools. In Two Parts.* Boston: W. B. Fowle & N. Capen, 1843.

Raichle, Donald. "School Discipline and Corporal Punishment: An American Retrospect," *Interchange* 8 (1977–78):71–83.

Reeve, Tapping. *The Law of Baron and Femme, of Parent and Child, Guardian and Ward, Master and Servant and of the Powers of the Courts of Chancery; . . . with Notes and References to English and American Cases.* 3rd ed. Albany: William Gould & Son, 1874.

Rodgers, Daniel T. "Socializing Middle-Class Children: Institutions, Fables, and Work Values in Nineteenth-Century America," *Journal of Social History* 13 (Spring 1980):354–367.

Rotundo, E. Anthony. "Manhood in America: The Northern Middle Class, 1770–1920." Ph.D. dissertation, Brandeis University, 1982.

Ryan, Mary P. *Cradle of the Middle Class: The Family in Oneida County, New York 1790–1865.* Cambridge, Mass.: Cambridge University Press, 1981.

Schouler, James. *Law of Domestic Relations Embracing Husband and Wife, Parent and Child, Guardian and Ward, Infancy and Master and Servant.* Boston: Little, Brown & Co., 1905.

Schultz, Stanley K., *The Culture Factory: Boston Public Schools 1789–1860.* New York: Oxford University Press, 1973.

Sedgwick, Catherine. *Home.* Boston: James Monroe & Co., 1835.

Sigourney, Lydia H. *Letters to Mothers.* 6th ed. New York: Harper & Bros., 1848.

Sklar, Kathryn, Kish. *Catherine Beecher: A Study in American Domesticity.* New York: W. W. Norton & Co., 1973.

Slater, Peter Gregg. *Children in the New England Mind: In Death and in Life.* Hamden, Conn.: Archon Books, 1977.

Smith, Rev. Matthew Hale. *The Bible, the Rod, and Religion in Common Schools. The Ark of God on a New Cart: A Sermon by the Reverend Matthew Hale Smith.* Boston: Redding & Co., 1847.

_____. *Correspondence between the Honorable Horace Mann and Reverend Matthew Hale Smith, Occasioned by the Sermon Entitled "The Ark of God on a New Cart."* Boston: n.p., 1846.

_____. *Sequel to the So Called Correspondence between the Reverend M. H. Smith and Horace Mann, Surreptitiously Published by Mr. Smith, Containing a Letter from Mr. Mann, Suppressed by Mr. Smith, with the Reply Therein Promised.* Boston: W. B. Fowle, 1847.

Sprague, Henry Harrison. *Women under the Law of Massachusetts, Their Rights, Privileges, and Disabilities.* Boston: W. B. Clarke & Carruth, 1884.

Stanton, Elizabeth Cady. *Address of Elizabeth Cady Stanton on the Divorce Bill Before the Judiciary Committee of the New York Senate, in the Assembly Chamber, February 8, 1861.* Albany: Weed, Parsons & Co., 1861.

_____. *Eighty Years and More: Reminiscences of Elizabeth Cady Stanton.* 1898. Reprint. New York: Schocken Books, 1971.

Stanton, Elizabeth Cady; Anthony, Susan B.; and Josclyn, Mathilda, eds., *History of Woman's Suffrage.* 6 vols., 2d ed. Rochester, New York: Charles Mann, 1889.

Steinmetz, Suzanne K., and Straus, Murray A., eds., *Violence in the Family*. New York: Harper & Row, 1974.

Stone, Lawrence. *The Family, Sex and Marriage in England, 1500–1800*. New York: Harper & Row, 1977.

Straus, Murray A.; Gelles, Richard J.; and Steinmetz, Suzanne K. *Behind Closed Doors: Violence in the American Family*. New York: Anchor Press, 1980.

Tomes, Nancy. "A 'Torrent of Abuse': Crimes of Violence between Working-Class Men and Women in London, 1840–1875," *Journal of Social History* 11 (Spring 1978):328–345.

Transactions of the Massachusetts Teachers' Federation, I (1845-47). Boston: Samuel Coolidge, 1852.

Tyack, David B., and Hansot, Elizabeth. *Managers of Virtue: Public School Leadership in America 1820–1980*. New York: Basic Books, Inc., 1982.

Tyack, David B. *The One Best System: A History of American Urban Education*. Cambridge, Mass.: Harvard University Press, 1974.

_____. ed. *Turning Points in American Educational History*. Lexington, Mass.: Xerox College Pub., 1967.

Wishy, Bernard. *The Child and the Republic: The Dawn of Modern American Child Nurture*. Philadelphia: University of Pennsylvania Press, 1968.

Withington, Leonard. *Penitential Tears: A Cry from the Dust, by "The 31," Prostrated and Pulverized by the Hand of Horace Mann, Secretary of the Massachusetts Board of Education*. Boston: C. Stimpson, 18 ?

Wyman, Morrill. *Progress in School Discipline–Corporal Punishment in the Public Schools, Addressed to the Citizens of Cambridge (contains the substance of two addresses—delivered the one, at a meeting of the citizens of Cambridge, in November, 1866 and the other, before the American Institute of Instruction, in Boston—August, 1867)*. Cambridge: John Wilson & Son, 1867.

Seamen

A. Manuscript Collections

Library of Congress, Washington, D. C. Uriah P. Levy Papers

New York Public Library, New York City. Diary of James Holly Garrison.

B. Archives

U. S. Navy Department Archives, Record Group 45, National Archives, Washington, D.C.: *Corporal Punishment and the Spirit Ration, Reports of Officers. Circular, January 29, 1850*.

_____. Subject File: NJ-Discipline.

C. Official Publications

U. S. Congress. *Annual Reports of the Secretary of the Navy, 1826–60*.

_____. *Congressional Globe, 1833–61*.

_____. *House Executive Documents*.

_____. *House Journals,* 1840–50.

_____. *House Reports.*

_____. *Senate Documents.*

_____. *Senate Executive Documents.*

_____. *Senate Journals,* 1840–50.

_____. *Senate Miscellaneous Documents,* "Resolution of the Legislature of Rhode Island in favor of the prohibition of corporal punishment and the use of ardent spirits in the Navy," 30th Cong., 2nd sess. (Serial 533), Doc. 63.

_____. *United States Congressional Debates,* 1834–56.

_____. *United States Statutes At Large,* "An Act for the Better Government of the Navy of the United States," 10, Chapter 36, pp. 627–628.

D. Newspapers and Periodicals

Army and Navy Chronicle, January–June 1836, July 1836–April 1842, 8 February 1844.

Military and Naval Magazine of the United States, March 1833–January 1836.

National Era, 1841–1853.

Naval Magazine, 1836–37.

New York Times, 1850–1853.

New York Tribune, 1850.

Niles National Register, December 1842–February 1844.

Niles Weekly Register, 21 September 1839 and August 1840.

Sailor's Magazine and Naval Journal, 1829–52

E. Books, Pamphlets, and Articles

Adams, Charles Francis. *Richard Henry Dana: A Biography.* 2 vols. 1890. Reprint. Detroit: Gail Research Co., Book Tower, 1968.

Aegyptus, Tiphys. *The Navy's Friend; or, Reminiscences of the Navy; Containing Memoirs of a Cruise in the U.S. Schooner Enterprise.* Baltimore: Printed by the Author, 1843.

Almy, John J. [Lieutenant of the Navy]. *Naval Discipline and Corporal Punishment.* Boston: Charles C. P. Moody, 1850.

Ames, Nathaniel. *Nautical Reminiscences.* Providence, R.I.: Wm. Marshall & Co., 1832.

Annual Reports of the American Seamen's Friend Society. New York: Pub. for the Society, 1829, 1832–60, 1865–66.

Barrows, Edward M. *The Great Commodore: The Exploits of Matthew Calbraith Perry.* New York: Bobbs-Merrill Co., 1935.

Bell, Frederick J., Lieut., U. S. Navy. *Room to Swing a Cat: Being Some Tales of the Old Navy.* New York: Longmans, Green & Co., 1938.

Clark, Joseph G. *Lights and Shadows of Sailor Life. As Exemplified in Fifteen Years' Experience, Including the More Thrilling Events of the United States Exploring Expedition.* Boston: B. B. Mussey, 1848.

Colton, Walter. *Deck and Port; or, Incidents of a Cruise in the United States Frigate Congress to California, with Sketches of Rio Janeiro, Valparaiso, Lima, Honolulu, and San Francisco.* New York: A. S. Barnes & Co., 1850.

Cooper, James Fenimore. *The Cruise of the Somers: Illustrative of the Despotism of the Quarter Deck; and of the Unmanly Conduct of Commander Mackenzie.* New York: J. Winchester, New World Press, 1844.

Cutbush, Edward. *Observations on the Means of Preserving the Health of Soldiers and Sailors; and on the Duties of the Medical Department of the Army and Navy, with Remarks on Hospitals and Their Internal Arrangements.* Philadelphia: Fry & Kammerer, Printers, 1808.

Dana, Richard Henry. *Cruelty to Seamen: Being the Case of Nichols and Couch.* Berkeley: Privately Printed, 1937.

_____. *Two Years before the Mast: A Personal Narrative of Life at Sea.* Cleveland: The Fine Editions Press, 1946.

Drury, Clifford M. *United States Naval Chaplains 1778–1945.* Vol. 1. Washington, D.C.: Government Printing Office, 1949.

Durand, James. *James Durand, an Able Seaman of 1812: His Adventures on "Old Ironsides" and as an Impressed Sailor in the British Navy.* Edited by George S. Brooks. New Haven: Yale University Press, 1926.

Dutton, Charles. *Oliver Hazard Perry.* New York: Longmans, Green & Co., 1935.

Edel, William W. "The Golden Age of the Navy Chaplaincy, 1830–55," *United States Naval Institute Proceedings* (June 1924): 875–885.

Fitzpatrick, Donovan and Saphire, Saul. *Navy Maverick: Uriah Phillips Levy.* New York: Doubleday & Co., 1963.

Garrison, James Holly. *Behold Me Once More: The Confessions of James Holly Garrison.* Edited by Walter McIntosh Merrill. Boston: Houghton Mifflin Co., 1954.

Gilbert, Arthur N. "Buggery and the British Navy, 1700–1861," *Journal of Social History* 10 (Fall 1976): 72–98.

Griffis, William Elliot. *Matthew Calbraith Perry: A Typical American Naval Officer.* New York: Houghton Mifflin Co., 1890.

Gould, Roland Freeman. *The Life of Gould, an Ex-Man-of-War's Man ... Including the Three Year's Cruise of the Line of Battle Ship Ohio, on the Mediterranean Station, under ... Commodore Hull.* Claremont, N.H.: Claremont Manufacturing Co., 1867.

Hayford, Harrison, ed. *The Somers Mutiny Affair.* Englewood Cliffs, N.J.: Prentice-Hall, 1959.

Hazen, Jacob A. *Five Years before the Mast; or, Life in the Forecastle Aboard of a Whaler and Man-of-War.* Chicago: Belford, Clarke & Co., 1888.

Horan, Leo F. S. "Flogging in the United States Navy; Unfamiliar Facts Regarding Its Origins and Abolition," *United States Naval Institute Proceedings* 76 (1950):969–975.

Jones, George [Civilian]. *Sketches of Naval Life, with Notices of Men, Manners and Scenery, on the Shores of the Mediterranean, in a Series of Letters*

from the Brandywine and Constitution Frigates. 2 vols. New Haven: He-
zekiah Howe, 1829.

Kanof, Abram. "Uriah Phillips Levy: The Story of a Pugnacious Commander,"
Publications of the American Historical Jewish Society, Part I, 39 (September 1849):1–66.

Karsten, Peter. *The Naval Aristocracy: The Golden Age of Annapolis and the
Emergence of Modern American Navalism.* New York: The Free Press,
1972.

Lane, Horace. *The Wandering Boy, Careless Sailor, and Result of Inconsideration.
A True Narrative.* Skaneateles, N.Y.: Luther A. Pratt, 1839.

Langley, Harold. *Social Reform in the United States Navy, 1798–1862.* Urbana,
Chicago: University of Illinois Press, 1967.

Leech, Samuel. *Thirty Years from Home . . . The Experiences of Samuel Leech,
Who Was for Six Years in the British and American Navies.* Boston:
Tappan, Whittimore & Mason, ca. 1843.

Lockwood, John P. [Anonymous]. *An Essay on Flogging in the Navy; Containing
Strictures upon Existing Naval Laws, and Suggesting Substitutes for the
Discipline of the Lash.* New York: Pudney & Russell, Printers, 1849.

Maury, Matthew E. [Harry Bluff]. "Of Reorganizing the Navy," *Southern Literary
Messenger* 7 (1841):3–25.

———. "Our Navy," *Southern Literary Messenger* 7 (1841):345–379.

———. "Scraps from the Lucky Bag," *Southern Literary Messenger* 6 (1840):306–
320, 786–800.

McKee, Christopher. "Fantasies of Mutiny and Murder: A Suggested Psychohistory of the Seamen in the United States Navy, 1758–1815." *Armed
Forces and Society* 4 (February 1978): 293–304.

McNally, William. *Evils and Abuses in the Naval and Merchant Service Exposed;
with Proposals for Their Remedy and Redress.* Boston: Cassady & March,
1839.

Melville, Herman. *White-Jacket; or, the World in a Man-of-War.* Chicago: Northwestern University Press & The Newberry Library, 1970.

Murphy, John [An Observer]. *An Inquiry into the Necessity and General Principles of Reorganization in the United States Navy; with an Examination
of the True Sources of Subordination.* Baltimore: John Murphy, 1842.

Murrell, William Meacham. *Cruise of the Frigate Columbia Around the World,
under the Command of Commodore George Read in 1838, 1839, and
1840.* Boston: Benjamin B. Mussey, 1840.

Nordhoff, Charles. *Man-of-War Life: A Boy's Experience in the United States
Navy, During a Voyage Around the World, in a Ship of the Line.* New York:
Dodd, Mead & Co., 1895.

Paullin, Charles Oscar. *Paullin's History of Naval Administration, 1775–1911. A
Collection of Articles from the United States Naval Institute Proceedings.*
Annapolis, Maryland: United States Naval Institute, 1968.

*Proceedings of the Naval Court Martial in the Case of Alexander Slidell Mac-
kenzie, a Commander in the Navy of the United States . . . Including the*

Charges and Specifications of Charges, Preferred against Him by the Secretary of the Navy, To Which Is Annexed an Elaborate Review by James F. Cooper. New York: Henry G. Langley, 1844.

Rasor, Eugene L. *Reform in the Royal Navy: A Social History of the Lower Deck, 1850 to 1880.* Hamden, Conn.: Archon Books, 1976.

"Report of the Secretary of the Navy to the President of the United States," *North American Review* 30 (1830):360–389.

Sanborn, Solomon Hewes. *An Exposition of Official Tyranny in the United States Navy.* New York: n.p., 1841.

Sewell, Richard H. *John Parker Hale and the Politics of Abolition.* Cambridge, Mass.: Harvard University Press, 1965.

Sprout, Harold, and Sprout, Margaret. *The Rise of American Naval Power, 1776–1918.* Princeton: Princeton University Press, 1966.

Stewart, Charles S. *A Visit to the South Seas in the United States Ship Vincennes, During the Years 1829 and 1830; with Scenes in Brazil, Peru, Manila, the Cape of Good Hope, and St. Helena.* 2 vols. New York: Sleight & Robinson, Printers, 1831.

Taylor, Fitch W. *A Voyage Round the World, and Visits to Various Foreign Countries in the United States Frigate Columbia; Attended by Her Consort the Sloop of War John Adams and Commanded by Commodore George C. Read.* 2 vols. New York: H. Mansfield, 1845 & 1847.

Toga Civilis. "Rules and Regulations for the Government of the Navy of the United States," *Southern Literary Messenger* 9 (June 1843):371–380.

Valle, James E. *Rocks & Shoals: Order and Discipline in the Old Navy 1800–1861.* Annapolis: Naval Institute Press, 1980.

Van De Water, Frederic F. *The Captain Called It Mutiny.* New York: Ives Washburn, Inc., 1954.

Webster, George Sidney. *The Seaman's Friend. A Sketch of the American Seaman's Friend Society.* New York: The American Seaman's Friend Society, 1932.

Weigley, Russell F. *History of the United States Army.* New York: Macmillan Co., 1967.

Prisoners

A. Manuscript Collections

Houghton Library, Harvard University, Cambridge, Massachusetts
Dorothea Lynde Dix Papers
Samuel Gridley Howe Papers
New York Public Library, New York City
John Bigelow Papers
Diary of Isaac T. Hopper
New York Prison Association Records, 1845–1852

B. Public Documents

New York State Legislature, Assembly Documents (1833–1870).

————. *Senate Documents* (1831–1860).

C. Newspapers, Periodicals, Annual Reports

Annual Reports of the Board of Inspectors of the Massachusetts State Prison (1828–1860).

Annual Reports of the Board of Inspectors of the Eastern State Penitentiary of Pennsylvania (1829–1837).

Journal of Prison Discipline and Philanthropy (1845–1862).

Moral Advocate: A Monthly Publication on War, Duelling, Capital Punishment, and Prison Discipline (1821–1824).

New York Daily Tribune (1844–1847).

Prison Association of New York, *Annual Reports* (1844–1862).

Prison Discipline Society of Boston, *Annual Reports* (1826–1854).

Prisoner's Friend: A Monthly Magazine Devoted to Criminal Reform, Philosophy, Literature, Science, and Art (1848–1861).

United States Magazine and Democratic Review (1845–1848).

D. Books, Articles, Pamphlets

Adshead, Joseph. *Prisons and Prisoners.* London: Longman, Brown, Green & Longman, 1845.

Allen, Stephen. *Observations on Penitentiary Discipline, Addressed to William Roscoe, Esquire, of Liverpool, England.* New York: John C. Totten, 1827.

Beaumont, Gustave de, and Tocqueville, Alexis de. *On the Penitentiary System in the United States and Its Application in France.* Translated by Francis Lieber. Philadelphia: Carey, Lee, & Blanchard, 1833.

Bradford, Gamaliel. *Description and Historical Sketches of the Massachusetts State Prison. With the Statutes, Rules and Orders, for the Government Thereof.* Charlestown, Mass.: S. Etheridge, Jr., 1816.

Brice, James R. *Secrets of the Mount-Pleasant State Prison, Revealed and Exposed ... an Account of the Inhumane Treatment of Prisoners ... with Other Curious Matters before Unknown to the Public.* Albany: The Author, 1839.

Burr, Levi S. *A Voice from Sing Sing; Giving a General Description of the State Prison ... a Synopsis of the Horrid Treatment of the Convicts in That Prison.* Albany: n.p., 1833.

Coffey, W. A. *Inside Out; or, an Interior View of the New York State Prison; Together with Biographical Sketches of the Lives of Several of the Convicts.* New York: James Costigan, 1823.

Crawford, William. *Report on the Penitentiaries of the United States.* 1835. Reprint. Montclair, N.J.: Patterson Smith, 1969.

Dix, Dorothea Lynde. *Remarks on Prisons and Prison Discipline in the United States.* 1845. Reprint. Montclair, N.J.: Patterson Smith, 1967.

Eddy, Thomas. *An Account of the State Prison or Penitentiary House.* New York: Collins & Son, 1801.

Edmonds, John W. *A Letter from John W. Edmonds, one of the Inspectors of the State Prison at Sing Sing to General Aaron Ward in Regard to the Removal of Captain Elam Lynds as Principal Keeper of that Prison.* New York: W. G. Boggs, 1844.

Farnham, Eliza Wood. *My Early Years.* New York: Thatcher & Hutchinson, 1859.

Finley, James B. *Memorials of Prison Life.* Edited by B. F. Tefft. 1855. Reprint. New York: Arno Press, 1974.

Freedman, Estelle B. *Their Sisters' Keepers: Women's Prison Reform in America, 1830–1930.* Ann Arbor: University of Michigan Press, 1981.

Gray, Francis C. *Prison Discipline in America.* 1847. Reprint. Montclair, N.J.: Patterson Smith, 1973.

Haynes, Gideon. *Pictures from Prison Life. An Historical Sketch of the Massachusetts State Prison with . . . Suggestions on Discipline.* Boston: Lee & Shepard, 1869.

Heale, M. J. "The Formative Years of the New York Prison Association, 1844–1862." *New York Historical Society Quarterly* 59 (1975):320–347.

————. "Humanitarianism in the Early Republic: The Moral Reformers of New York, 1776–1825." *Journal of American Studies* 2 (1968):161–175.

Hindus, Michael Stephen. *Prison and Plantation: Crime, Justice, and Authority in Massachusetts and South Carolina, 1767–1878.* Chapel Hill: University of North Carolina Press, 1980.

Howe, Samuel Gridley, *An Essay on Separate and Congregate Systems of Prison Discipline.* 1846. Reprint. New York: Arno Press, 1974.

Ignatieff, Michael. *A Just Measure of Pain: The Penitentiary in the Industrial Revolution, 1750–1850.* New York: Columbia University Press, 1978.

Lane, Horace. *Five Years in State's Prison; or, Interesting·Truths, Showing the Manner of Discipline in the State Prisons at Sing Sing and Auburn, Exhibiting the Great Contrast between the Two Institutions . . . Represented in a Dialogue between Sing Sing and Auburn.* 3rd ed. New York: Luther Pratt & Son, 1835.

Letter of Gershom Powers, Esquire, in Answer to a Letter of the Honorable Edward Livingston, in Relation to the Auburn State Prison. Albany: Croswell & Van Benthuysen, 1829.

Lewis, Orlando F. *The Development of American Prisons and Prison Customs, 1776–1845. With Special Reference to Early Institutions in the State of New York.* Albany: J. B. Lyon Co., 1922.

Lewis, W. David. *From Newgate to Dannemora: The Rise of the Penitentiary in New York, 1796–1848.* Ithaca: Cornell University Press, 1965.

Luckey, John. *Life in Sing Sing State Prison, as Seen in a Twelve Years' Chaplaincy.* New York: N. Tibbels, 1866.

Marshall, Helen. *Dorothea Dix: Forgotten Samaritan.* Chapel Hill: University of
    North Carolina Press, 1937.
McKelvey, Blake. *American Prisons: A Study in American Social History Prior
    to 1915.* Chicago: University of Chicago Press, 1936.
O'Brien, Patricia. *The Promise of Punishment: Prisons in Nineteenth Century
    France.* Princeton: Princeton University Press, 1982.
Powers, Edwin. *Crime and Punishment in Early Massachusetts, 1620–1692. A
    Documentary History.* Boston: Beacon Press, 1966.
Powers, Gershom. *Brief Account of the Construction, Management and Disci-
    pline of the New York State Prison at Auburn.* Auburn, N.Y.: A. F. Dou-
    bleday, 1826.
Remarks on Prisons and Prison Discipline from the Christian Examiner. Boston:
    Isaac R. Butts & Co., 1826.
Reynolds, John. *Recollections of Windsor Prison; Containing Sketches of Its
    History and Discipline with Appropriate Strictures, and Moral and Re-
    ligious Reflections.* 3rd ed. Boston: A. Wright, 1839.
Richards, Laura E., ed. *Letters and Journals of Samuel Gridley Howe.* 2 vols.
    Boston: Dana Estes & Co., 1909.
Schwartz, Harold. *Samuel Gridley Howe: Social Reformer, 1801–1876.* Cam-
    bridge, Mass.: Harvard University Press, 1956.
Sellin, Thorsten J. *Slavery and the Penal System.* New York: Elsevier Scientific
    Pub. Co., 1976.
Smith, Eleazer. *Nine Years among the Convicts; or, Prison Reminiscences.* 2d
    ed. Boston: J. P. Magee, 1856.
Society for the Prevention of Pauperism. *Report on the Penitentiary System in
    the United States.* 1822. Reprint. New York: Arno Press, 1974.
Tobias, J. J. *Nineteenth-Century Crime in England: Prevention and Punishment.*
    New York: Barnes & Noble, 1972.
"Torture and Homicide in American State Prison." *Harper's Weekly* 2 (December
    18, 1856):808–810.
Wayland, Francis. "Prison Discipline," *North American Review* 49 (1839):1–43.
Wines, Enoch Cobb, and Dwight, Theodore W. *Report on the Prisons and
    Reformatories of the United States and Canada.* Albany: Van Benthuysen
    & Sons, 1867.

Index